Fahim Speaks

*A Warrior-Actor's Odyssey
from Afghanistan to Hollywood and Back*

By
Fahim Fazli

With
Michael Moffett

WARRIORS PUBLISHING GROUP
NORTH HILLS, CALIFORNIA

FAHIM SPEAKS

A Warriors Publishing Group Book/published by arrangement with the authors

PRINTING HISTORY
Warriors Publishing Group edition/March 2012

All rights reserved.
Copyright © 2012 by FF&MM Enterprises, LLC
Cover art copyright © 2012 by Gerry Kissell, (gerrykissell.com)
This book may not be reproduced in whole
or in part, by mimeograph or any other means,
without permission. For information address:
Warriors Publishing Group
16129 Tupper Street
North Hills, California 91343

All photographs and images courtesy of FF&MM Enterprises, LLC, which vouches for
all rights and permissions. Warriors Publishing Group accepts no liability for the use
of these images. If you believe an image has been published in error, please contact
FF&MM Enterprises, LLC at www.fahimspeaks.com for correction in future editions.

ISBN 978-0-9821670-7-6

The name "Warriors Publishing Group" and the logo
are trademarks belonging to Warriors Publishing Group

PRINTED IN THE UNITED STATES OF AMERICA

10 9 8 7 6 5 4 3 2 1

To my mother, Fahima Fazli (1945-2011),
and to all the women of the world

Preface

> *"The problem in Afghanistan is that everybody there*
> *holds a piece of a mirror, and they all look at it*
> *and claim that they see the entire truth."*
> *- Mohsen Makhmalbaf, President of Asian Film Academy*

Afghanistan.

Before 1980, most Americans knew or cared little about this impoverished, land-locked, Central Asian nation. After the Soviet Union invaded, though, Afghanistan became a flash point—one that threatened to ignite a Cold War into the flames of a World War. Throughout the 1980s, American foreign policy sought to counter the Soviet presence there. The Carter and Reagan Administrations secretly supported a Mujahedeen resistance movement that eventually led to Soviet defeat and a 1989 withdrawal from Afghanistan. The Union of the Soviet Socialist Republics imploded two years later. The dissolution of the Soviet Union ended the Cold War, beckoning a period of unprecedented world peace. Or at least many Americans believed so at the time—not understanding the unintended consequences and true legacy of our Central Asian policies.

"What is most important to the history of the world? The Taliban or the collapse of the Soviet empire?" asked Zbigniew Brzezinski who served as National Security Advisor to President Jimmy Carter, in a 1998 interview with *Le Nouvel Observateur*. "Some stirred-up Moslems or the liberation of Central Europe and the end of the Cold War?"

Understandably proud of America's Cold War triumph, Brzezinski rationalized and tolerated the emergence of Islamic extremists in post-Soviet Afghanistan, even in 1998. However, in retrospect, he significantly underestimated the Taliban's impact on world history. We collectively washed our hands of Afghanistan after the fall of the USSR—and paid dearly for it.

While the Communist-Mujahedeen conflict in Afghanistan displaced millions of people and destabilized the region, Western leaders largely ignored the chaos in favor of their more pressing national concerns, like trade policy or common currency. Almost every country, including the U.S., slashed defense spending.

In 1992, Francis Fukuyama argued in *The End of History and the Last Man* that with the fall of the Soviet empire, Western liberal democracy had arrived as the ultimate form of government, in a world of diminishing conflict. Fukuyama, like other intellectuals who predicted a period of international tranquility, didn't anticipate the rapid rise of Islamofascism, or what that rise would mean to our national security.

In an August 1996 CBS News/New York Times poll, voters listed the top problems in America to be crime, the budget deficit, the economy, welfare, and jobs—all domestic issues. Foreign policy came in 25th, after illegal immigration and racism. Domestic policy issues dominated the 1996 U.S. presidential campaign, which ended with Bill Clinton's reelection victory over Republican Bob Dole. Their debates focused on taxes, ethics, and even tobacco use. Foreign affairs received scant attention.

That neglectful mindset changed on September 11, 2001, when Al Qaeda terrorists hijacked four airliners and killed almost 3,000 people in New York, Pennsylvania, and Washington D.C. Suddenly, the attention of America—and the world—was focused on Afghanistan, home to the Al Qaeda plotters.

My attention was also focused on Afghanistan. Before the end of October, I was back in a Marine Corps lieutenant colonel's uniform, working on the Operations Staff at United States Central Command in Tampa, Florida. That's where General Tommy Franks took charge of *Operation Enduring Freedom*'s mission to overthrow the Taliban regime in Afghanistan and remove the safe haven it provided to the Al Qaeda leadership.

That mission was accomplished by Christmas. By the time I left Central Command in May, its focus was already shifting from Afghanistan to other theaters, as America's leaders sought to maintain the initiative in what came to be known as the Global War on Terror.

However, almost nine years later, Americans were still fighting in Afghanistan, with a casualty rate that increased five-fold after President Barack Obama doubled U.S. troop levels there, following his 2009 inauguration. I returned to active duty in 2010 to again support *Operation Enduring Freedom*, this time as a field historian for Marine Corps University. My mission was to document Marine Corps efforts in Afghanistan. Accomplishing this mission required me to travel throughout the Marine Corps Areas of Operation in Helmand Province to interview Marines at Combat Outposts and Forward Operating Bases. Connecting with these forward-deployed Marines meant several helicopter flights, usually at night, as aircraft seldom flew without escorts during the dangerous daylight hours.

I also joined ground convoys imperiled by mines and Improvised Explosive Devices (IEDs). Before one motorized night movement, the convoy commander gathered all personnel to review signals and immediate action procedures to take should we run into an ambush or hit any IEDs. Then he held an optional prayer session—a poignant reminder about the dangers of road travel in Afghanistan and not part of the standard convoy briefing format as taught stateside. Accustomed to the secular world of American college campuses, I found this unabashed appeal for divine protection to be sobering and humbling. The brief prayer session allowed convoy travelers to honestly and publicly acknowledge both fear and faith before driving off into the perilous Afghan night. Most of the Marines participated, including me.

The convoy got through without incident, and I spent several days interviewing members of the Second Battalion of the Second Marine Regiment (2/2), nicknamed the Warlords. Over 70 Warlords had won Purple Hearts while taking the fight to the Taliban in the Helmand River Valley, including the battalion commander, Lieutenant Colonel John E. McDonough, who was badly injured and evacuated after an IED blew up his vehicle.

The Warlords shared many accounts of life and death in Afghanistan, and the lessons I learned from them served me well as I moved from outpost to outpost.

In March of 2010, I traveled to Delaram, where Helmand, Farah, and Nimroz provinces converged. This crossroads town was strategically important, and the Third Battalion of the Fourth Marine Regiment (3/4) had been conducting combat and civil affairs operations there since the previous October—to great effect. District Governor Asadullah Haqdost recognized 3/4 for its work by presenting an award to its commanding officer, Lieutenant Colonel Martin Wetterauer, at a special ceremony at battalion headquarters. I attended to take photos and conduct interviews.

A long-haired, bearded interpreter in an American uniform capably translated before, during, and following the ceremony. Afterwards, everyone headed towards a humble table in the battalion conference room for a banquet of sorts, honoring Asadullah. A 3/4 staff officer pointed to the interpreter standing in line with a paper plate to get some chow and mentioned that the man was born in Afghanistan, but had made his way to America to become a Hollywood actor.

While "Hollywood actor" could mean almost anything, the term held some caché with me. Wasn't that a glamorous profession? What roles had he played? Why was he now in dangerous Delaram?

The bearded interpreter posed for a photo with another visiting Marine Corps officer and then sat down across the table from me. His dark eyes sparkled and he laughed easily. Everyone in the room seemed to be his brother. I picked up on his charisma and asked if he'd like to record an interview for USMC History Division.

"Of course!" was his immediate answer. The interpreter and actor showed no reticence about going on the record to talk about his experiences. We sat down later on an outside bench in the battalion compound where he spoke at length of his life's journey. Born and raised in Kabul, he'd fought the Communists who took over his country in 1978. He eventually made a harrowing escape to a refugee camp in Pakistan. Approved for asylum in the United States, he reunited with the rest of his family and moved to southern California where he learned English and pursued his dream of an acting career. For 15 years he accepted Hollywood jobs as an extra, while working at whatever full-time positions he could to get by. Despite subsequent success as an actor, he put on a uniform and certified as an interpreter who understood the Afghan languages, Pashto and Dari. He asked for the most dangerous assignment in Afghanistan—interpreting for a Marine Corps infantry battalion in volatile Helmand Province. He was so effective as an interpreter—bringing together Americans and Afghans—that he earned the special enmity of the Taliban, who offered a sizeable reward to whoever could kill him.

As he patiently responded to my litany of questions, I realized that he epitomized what so many Americans yearned to see—an immigrant-refugee from an Islamic culture unafraid to express a deep love for and commitment to his adopted homeland.

Throughout American history countless people have put themselves in harm's way to defend a country that didn't always treat them as equal citizens under the law. Here was another, contemporary example of such a person. He bravely joined a fight that required him to wear his new country's uniform in a cause that put him in conflict with some kinsmen from his old tribe, back in his native land. This naturalized citizen left his family, community, and acting career at the age of 43 to risk everything while serving with a new, adopted tribe—the United States Marines.

Who was this man?

His name was Fahim Fazli.

This is his story.

Michael I. Moffett
Concord, N.H.

Lieutenant Colonel Michael Moffett with Fahim Fazli at Camp Leatherneck, Afghanistan, in May of 2010

Chapter 1: Escape

"Go out from your village: But never let your village go out from you."
– Afghan Proverb

It's a sad and scary thing to have to escape from your native country—to flee from your own homeland. That's what I did in September of 1983. If I'd remained in Afghanistan, I'd have faced a forced relocation to a re-education camp in the Soviet Union. An escape attempt, however perilous, was preferable to living under Communism. There was no turning back.

Afghanistan was all I knew. However, the cheery land of my youth had turned into a totalitarian nightmare—a police state. So my father, Jamil, decided to take me and my 12-year-old brother, Hares, from our hometown of Kabul to Pakistan. From there, we hoped to find a way to America. Although we'd not heard from my mother, Fahima, in four years, we thought she was somewhere in the United States, along with an older brother and two younger sisters. Reuniting our family meant risking our lives and defying the odds, as we'd need to avoid the Communist secret police, land mines, and Soviet attack helicopters. We'd also have to overcome the elements and scale snow-capped 10,000 foot mountains.

My father had once worked for the Afghanistan National Bank in Kabul, and was under suspicion by government authorities because his wife was rumored to be in America. Schoolmates called my brother and me CIA Kids, or Sons of Reagan—the Afghan Communist equivalent of *sons of bitches*, because the Communists really hated U.S. President Ronald Reagan.

Earlier, my mother served as a midwife for the family of Afghan President Hafizullah Amin. Though Amin had Marxist leanings, he was a nationalist who practiced Islam. Soviet leaders in Moscow didn't trust him. They wanted to see new Afghan leadership, but couldn't necessarily control who'd replace Amin if they got rid of him. So in December of 1979, the Russians invaded my country to ensure that pro-Soviet

Communists retained power after the Soviet Secret Police murdered Amin.

My mother fled to Pakistan, with the help of high level contacts she'd acquired through the Amin family. We'd heard from friends that she was on a KGB target list, given her relationship with the President's family. She took with her my younger sisters Almara and Mina, and my older brother Suhail. Hares and I stayed back with my father in Afghanistan, where we spent the next three years watching our country descend into violent chaos, as the secret police became increasingly powerful. Communist goons sometimes murdered people merely because they were related to someone in the West. Did suspicion that my mother was in the West make them think that my father worked for the CIA? He decided not to wait around to be arrested.

I'd made matters worse for my father by shooting at Russian convoys with my slingshot, and by gathering information on Soviet military forces for the Mujahedeen freedom fighters. Communist officials wanted to send Hares and me to the Soviet Union, supposedly to be educated, although we knew that indoctrinated was a better word. This Marxist indoctrination changed people dramatically. Brainwashed in Moscow or Leningrad, they returned to Kabul to spout Communist dogma. They no longer thought for themselves. Those who raised questions about relatives going to the Soviet Union sometimes just disappeared.

My father hated the idea of my brother and me being sent away, so he sold our house in Kabul and for the next year we moved back and forth between my grandfather's house and my aunt's house, to confuse the Communists. Then one night, when we were at my aunt's, he came home and spoke to his sister in low tones. Something was up. My aunt started crying, and my dad turned to Hares and me. "Get ready. We're going to try to find your mother."

We found traditional Afghan garb to wear, rather than the blue jeans and leather jackets that we usually favored. We went to bed early, as we'd be getting up before dawn. My father didn't want to talk. I tried to sleep, but was too anxious. A few hours later, I heard a stern voice say "Get up. We're leaving."

A taxi took us to a bus stop, where my father spoke to a tall, slender man named Abdul who was in his mid-thirties. He was a coyote—a person who'd guide us to Pakistan for money, like the North American coyotes who profited from guiding Mexicans through deserts and mountains on their way to the U.S.

Abdul was quietly assertive. Clean-cut for our culture, he had a trimmed beard and hair that fell neatly behind his head-gear. His *Payraan tumbaan*, the comfortable and traditional Afghan attire, made him look like most of the other male travelers. He spoke Dari in a calm, confident, and reassuring manner. By looking at him, no one would know that he was both a Mujahedeen sympathizer and a risk-taking entrepreneur. Only later did I realize how dangerous his job was.

We bought four tickets to board an old bus about to travel east—towards Jalalabad, near the Pakistan border. Before getting on the bus, my father explained things. We would escape to Pakistan and make our way from there to America. Abdul nodded slightly as my father spoke. My father had sewn money inside the linings of our coats to make it harder for corrupt officials to confiscate our precious funds. I patted my jacket where the money

Fahim, Hares, and Jamil Fazli

made a comforting bulge. After we got on the bus, we all sat apart from each other, so if one of us was detained, the others might not be compromised. Hares sat near the front of the bus, on the left behind the driver. I was in the middle on the right side, three seats in front of my father. Abdul sat at the very rear, watching everything. We nervously waited for the other passengers to come aboard. The bus didn't fill to capacity, and we all got our seats to ourselves. Shortly after 6 a.m., the driver honked his horn and we started to move. The day brightened and I looked intently at everything we passed.

As we moved through the outskirts of the Afghan capital, I glanced back at my old city's downtown buildings and mountainside dwellings. Early morning traffic was already raising dust which began to obscure the more distant hills. Would I ever see Kabul again?

The sun rose over the eastern mountains in front of us. It was a cold, crisp, beautiful day, the sky cloudless and a bright blue. As I was leaving Kabul, perhaps forever, I saw the beauty of my native land in a way I'd never seen it before.

Less beautiful were the dozens of police and military vehicles moving in every direction. They made me nervous, and I remembered being captured four years earlier when I had tried to get to Pakistan with my older brother and a friend to join the anti-Communist fighters there. The heavy-handed Communist control over every aspect of life in Kabul had alienated us, and we'd been fired up by radio propaganda from Pakistan. Unfortunately for our dreams of becoming Freedom Fighters, the Communist authorities caught us near the border and returned us to Kabul, where our parents thoroughly beat us as punishment for running away.

We stopped at an old, dilapidated bridge and the passengers got out, allowing the bus to slowly roll over the rickety structure. The coyote, my father, Hares, and I all stood apart from each other while watching the bus cross. I looked at the other passengers and figured there must be a least one Communist spy among them, checking us all out. Communist eyes were everywhere.

We walked across the span, re-boarded, and took our previous seats. The bus continued eastward. Twenty miles outside of Kabul, we stopped at a checkpoint. A man wearing the dreaded olive green of the Afghan Communist Secret Police boarded the bus and spoke sternly in Dari to the driver. He had one hand on the pistol in a holster on his right hip. Outside the bus, more secret police took positions on either side of the vehicle, holding AK-47 assault rifles. I felt sick to my stomach.

I was shocked to realize the secret policeman was my cousin Wahid, who'd become a Communist several years earlier. My heart pounded. Wahid turned and scanned the passengers. I lowered my gaze and stared at the floor, but when I looked back up, I was horrified to see him staring right at me.

Chapter 2: Charlie Wilson's War

> "You mean to tell me that the U.S. strategy in Afghanistan
> is to have the Afghans keep walking into machine gun fire
> 'til the Russians run out of bullets?"
> – Former Texas Congressman Charlie Wilson

It's just a bit unnerving to be stared at by Julia Roberts—perhaps the most glamorous of American movie actresses. We sat across the table from each other during a Cultural Awareness Meeting at Paramount Studios in Los Angeles, her chocolaty movie-star eyes locked onto mine. I'd taken the job of cultural advisor for the movie *Charlie Wilson's War* in 2006 and was meeting with its top stars in preparation for some overseas filming. Charlie Wilson was a Texas Congressman who'd supported the Mujahedeen Freedom Fighter movement in Afghanistan back in the 1980s, and we were going to bring that story to life.

Also at the meeting were Academy-Award-winning actors Tom Hanks and Philip Seymour Hoffman; film director Mike Nichols; former Congressman Wilson; and Milton Bearden, a former CIA agent who'd been part of Wilson's secret Afghanistan operation during the 1980s.

Roberts had received Academy Award nominations for *Steel Magnolias* in 1990 and *Pretty Woman* in 1991. She later won the Academy Award for Best Actress in 2001 for her performance in *Erin Brockovich*. Hanks won consecutive Academy Awards for best actor in 1993 (*Philadelphia*) and 1994 (*Forrest Gump*). His resume also included several military-genre films such as *Saving Private Ryan*. Hoffman won an Oscar for best actor in 2005 for his role in *Capote*. He'd later be nominated for best supporting actor for his work in *Charlie Wilson's War*. Nichols was one of only 10 people to win each of the major American entertainment awards: an Emmy, a Grammy, an Oscar, and a Tony Award. He'd directed top films like *The Graduate, Working Girl, Silkwood*, and *Catch 22*. Bearden, the CIA agent, had been Station Chief in Pakistan during the tumultuous 1980s, and was a key player in the anti-Soviet drama that had played out in Afghanistan.

Of course, there was also Charlie himself. I'd first heard of Congressman Wilson in the mid-1980s, after I'd moved to California, watching the news at my uncle's place in Hacienda Heights. He was taller than I'd imagined, older, but still good looking, with a full head of dark hair. Wilson was a colorful figure who really cared about my native land. He started the meeting by talking passionately about Afghanistan.

"I was damn horrified when I saw how the Afghan refugees lived at that Parachinar refugee camp," said Wilson, his voice rising in anger. "They were proxies for the West against the Soviets, and they had next-to-nothing. They were shot up and starving but still took the fight to the Russians. It was shameful that we did so little for them. So I tried to do something about that." Everyone stared intently at the former Congressman, who paused briefly. No one moved a muscle.

Wilson was clearly concerned about how the movie would be developed. "It's got to be accurate," he exclaimed. "Otherwise, people will come after me. I know what it's like to have people come after me and we don't want to give anyone a reason to say we didn't tell the truth."

Roberts wore stylish jeans and a classy shawl over a red shirt. She had a chic, pony-tailed look. I was too busy studying Julia to notice what Hanks, Hoffman, Nichols, or the CIA agent were wearing. Roberts said she knew that the status of women in Afghanistan was far inferior to that of women in typical western societies. She wanted to understand how it would feel to be a strong, assertive American woman suddenly showing up in a remote Afghan settlement. She asked me some good questions about how she should portray her character in our version of Afghanistan.

"So when I meet Afghan officials in character, as Joanne Herring, should I shake their hands?" Roberts asked.

"No," I responded. "Put both hands over your heart and then bow slightly."

"Are you *really* from Afghanistan?" she inquired. I think she expected someone a little more barbaric.

"Of course!" I replied, "Born and raised in Kabul."

Roberts, like so many other Americans, seemed to think of my homeland as a strange and distant place with an alien culture. Whether it's strange or alien depends on how much a person knows about Afghanistan. It's certainly distant. Roberts seemed intrigued to learn that Afghans are very generous, despite their poverty, but they could also be ruthless warriors. She remained poised over her notebook, intently scribbling away. She'd done a lot of cultural research herself already and wanted to know more. She impressed me.

"What about my hair, when I get there?" Roberts followed up.

"People shouldn't see your hair," I replied. "Your scarf needs to cover it all, as well as your neck. You can't let the men see your skin. They may go crazy!"

Everyone laughed. Seeing smiles all around the table built my confidence. Roberts wrote into her notebook and then looked up and asked, "What might I say to an actual Afghan?"

"*Salam alikam*," I replied. "That means 'peace be with you.'"

I told her she'd see many poor people and beggars in that part of the world, and that they should be embraced—not shooed away. "Don't be afraid to acknowledge people," I counseled.

"How about men greeting men?" asked Hanks.

"You kiss three times," I said. "But on the cheek, not the lips. Here, I'll show you."

I asked Hanks to stand up and I then demonstrated with him. Hanks laughed and turned to Hoffman. "Phil, you and I can practice later tonight to make sure we get it right!"

We spent the better part of an hour talking about Afghan cultural issues. These major players wanted the film to be credible, and I appreciated the attention they gave to my counsel. Nichols also took notes as I spoke, though not as furiously as Roberts.

Eventually, there were no more questions. "It's been a great pleasure," I said, standing up. "I'll see you all in Morocco."

"Salam alikam," said Roberts, as everyone laughed.

"You'd be right at home in Afghanistan, Julia," said Hanks.

"Absolutely," said Hoffman, smiling broadly. "You were born to wear a burqa!"

Driving home to Dana Point that evening, I was so euphoric about the successful meeting that I was oblivious to the usual traffic snarls on I-5 South. These major players really valued my advice! Instead of focusing on the stalled traffic, I happily looked to beautiful hills to the east. I thought about what a great land I lived in, a place where a poor uneducated immigrant who didn't speak the best English just had the rapt attention of Hollywood's top movie people.

My wife Amy knew how nervous I'd been going in to the meeting. It was such a great opportunity for me to work with some big names in the entertainment industry and to position myself for future possibilities. Naturally, I was keyed up about the whole thing.

"So, how did it go?" she asked as I walked in the door.

"Well, Julia Roberts kept staring at me," I said.

"Why?" asked Amy. "What did you do? You didn't annoy her did you?"

I laughed and said, "She's a pro. She pays attention and asks good questions." I'm sure Amy could tell by my big smile that the meeting went well.

"What did she wear?"

I laughed. I knew Amy would ask that. I described the actress' attire as best I could remember. "And I kissed Tom Hanks!"

"You what?"

"You know how Afghan men greet people," I said. "Three alternate kisses on the cheeks."

"Did he kiss you back?"

"No," I replied. "But he said he'd practice later with Philip Seymour Hoffman."

Amy laughed that beautiful laugh of hers. Her excitement made me even happier. A designer who appreciated the arts, she was naturally interested in this inside information. She'd been supportive of me during the previous ten years of my American journey and I savored this opportunity to make her proud of me.

Our little daughter Sophia was playing in the living room, where I went and sat down in my favorite chair as Amy patted Sophia's head, and then sat on the couch. "What about the Charlie Wilson guy?" she asked.

"He's super," I said. "He's all fired up about making a great film. Of course, his name's on the movie."

"If they did *Fahim Fazli's War* you'd be the same way."

While Amy liked to tease, she really did believe in me. Although she joked about a movie being made about Fahim Fazli, we both dreamed that someday a big film role would come my way.

"Charlie really cares about the Afghan people," I added, as Sophia, somehow sensing the moment was right, climbed onto my lap. "He wants the film to show that. When he found out I'd been at the Parachinar camp in Pakistan he seemed kind of moved. He was there himself. He knows what a sad place it was for so many refugees."

"Why was it a sad place, Daddy?" asked my beautiful, brown-haired daughter, staring at me with inquiring eyes.

I looked at Sophia and immediately pictured her at Parachinar. The image made me cringe.

"It's a sad place because it's where a lot of people had to stay in tents, because it was too dangerous to stay in their regular homes," I explained.

"Were you ever there?" asked Sophia.

"Just for a little while," I said. "A long time ago."

I needed to change the subject.

"Hey girl," I said. "Your daddy had a great day. I'm going to take you and your mom out to dinner, yes?"

"Yes!" said Sophia.

"Yes!" said Amy.

Off we went. I needed to look ahead to Morocco, not backwards to Parachinar.

A few days later, a Paramount Studios limousine arrived to pick me up for the trip to the Orange County airport, beginning a journey to Morocco that would feature star treatment, luxury cars, first-class air travel, five-star hotels, lavish per diem, and a contracted salary.

Amy was happy and proud of me. "You deserve all this, Fahim," she said as she hugged me good-bye. "I wish I was going with you. You know I love Morocco." Eight years earlier, on an unforgettable day, I'd proposed marriage to Amy on a Moroccan ship right after we'd spent two romantic weeks in that desert kingdom. Fortunately for me, she said yes.

From Orange County I flew first-class to Chicago, then to London on British Airways. From there I took a Lufthansa flight to Casablanca. A small plane flew me to a very modern and clean airport in Marrakesh, where I reunited with the *Charlie Wilson* cast and crew at a nearby five-star hotel. Chauffeured vans would shuttle us to the film sites.

Situated at the foot of the Atlas Mountains, the highest in North Africa, Marrakesh intrigued me more than any other place in the country. Also known as the "Red City," Marrakesh is a former imperial capital with an old fortified citadel, the *Médina*, right next to several modern neighborhoods. The second largest city in Morocco, its population of over a million includes many retired Europeans. Marrakesh has a large traditional market and one of the busiest squares in the world, the *Djemaa el Fna.* In the daytime acrobats, fortune-tellers, merchants, dancers and musicians frequent the vast space. In the evening, night food bazaars open around the square, turning it into a busy, extended open-air restaurant.

I was soon hard at work on the movie set, coaching 200 Moroccans to be Afghan refugees. The producers provided some space for me to teach them near the film site, and I turned it into my personal outdoor classroom. For three days, I worked hard to get to know the Moroccan extras. Mostly young men, these Moroccans were cooperative and enthusiastic. As always with movies, the extras had to hang around and wait a lot, but I never heard a complaint.

While I was reasonably fluent in several languages—Pashto, Dari, Urdo, and English—Arabic was not my strong suit. A friendly Moroccan interpreter, Omar, assisted me in coaching the extras. Tall and skinny, Omar had a great sense of humor and tried hard to understand what we needed the extras to do. Working with him helped me develop a real appreciation for effective translators. During my first session with the Moroccans, I explained that I was actually from Afghanistan, so I'd have some credibility.

"You look like you'd be a great helicopter-killer," I'd banter with a Moroccan youngster, who'd always reply "Yes, Sir!"

I explained to the extras that I'd been in the Parachinar refugee camp, which we'd recreated in Morocco for filming. I described a key scene where the refugees had to react enthusiastically to a visit by high profile Americans, including Joanne Herring, the Julia Roberts character, and U.S. Congressman Doc Long, played by Ned Beatty.

"You must understand how passionate the Afghan Mujahedeen were," I explained. "Imagine if some Communist infidels came to your land, to Morocco, and took away your religion. Picture them taking your sons away and sending them to Russia to be indoctrinated. Think of them dropping bombs on villages, and killing women and children. Consider them destroying your farms and killing your livestock. And know how frustrating it is to be unable to respond in kind, until finally some Americans show up to give you food, supplies, and weapons to take out the Soviet planes. Imagine how happy you'd be to meet the people who brought you the tools you need to reclaim your homeland. And now you have to show how happy, how ecstatic you are to actually meet the people who are giving you the gift of hope!"

It was a little crazy, giving this pep talk in broken Arabic, but Omar helped me. It was better when I used my own acting skills. I jumped up on the front of a truck and thrust my fist into the sky. "Allah Akbar!" I cried.

And then, in Pashto: "God Bless America! Damn the Russians!"

Translating can be a tricky thing, though. In one crucial scene, a Mujahedeen fighter successfully test-fires a hand-held Stinger anti-aircraft missile, and the other fighters celebrate its launch. Since the Moroccans spoke Pashto with Arabic accents, it didn't sound right to me. To solve the problem, Omar and I wrote out what they had to say phonetically, in Arabic, so their Pashto would sound more authentic. Millions of people would watch this movie and attention to detail was crucial. While most movie-goers would never pick up on the linguistics, I had an ear for authentic Afghan accents and I wanted to be sure that anyone watching our film back in Kabul would find the scene realistic.

In an important subsequent scene, the Mujahedeen actually take out a Soviet helicopter with a Stinger missile. The scene was crucial to director Mike Nichols, and it needed to convey the elation of the freedom fighters who knew that this meant the beginning of the end for the Russians. Our fighters took to the rooftops of a simulated Afghan town in a small Moroccan village near our set. The Moroccans became zealots, celebrating loudly, and chanting "Allah Akbar!" It gave me goose bumps.

The Moroccan adventure taught me a lot about filmmaking—working with foreign extras, shooting realistic scenes, and bridging cultures. I made new friends, including Charlie Wilson himself. He'd played a key role in helping the Afghans resist the Soviets—arranging the secret funding that channeled so many millions of American dollars to the Mujahedeen cause. He was a real-life hero to me. I told him how important the Stingers were to the effort. Few thought we could ever defeat the mighty Soviets, but with Charlie's help we did.

Congressman Wilson's efforts and his advocacy on behalf of the Mujahedeen changed American foreign policy toward Afghanistan, although few understood it at the time. Funding for the massive military aid was camouflaged in the budget process and the weapons themselves had to get to the Freedom Fighters circuitously, with the help of the CIA. The eventual consequence was a humiliating withdrawal from Afghanistan by the Soviets, followed shortly by the implosion of what President Reagan referred to as the "Evil Empire." That was cause for celebration. An unintended longer-term consequence, however, was the eventual rise of the Taliban, who later turned Afghanistan into a safe haven for Al Qaeda. That was not cause for celebration.

One day after lunch I sat with Wilson in a large tent which served as a makeshift lounge where people relaxed between shoots. Charlie wanted my thoughts about the script, which I appreciated. He wondered how people would react to the end of the movie, where it was acknowledged that Afghanistan did not turn into a wonderful place after the Soviets left. The emergence of the Taliban really troubled Charlie. In some ways, they were worse than the Communists. At least the Communists allowed music and didn't sponsor public executions at the Kabul soccer stadium. Wilson recalled all the young Afghans at Parachinar and wondered how many of them joined the Taliban.

"After the Soviets left, we turned away from Afghanistan," Wilson said. "Now it's easy to look back and say we did things wrong, but how could we know at the time?"

Wilson acknowledged that America should have been more engaged with Afghanistan during the 1990s. Under the Taliban, the country reverted to an oppressive 10th century feudal society, where women had no rights at all. The country that Charlie helped liberate from the Soviets had become a sanctuary for anti-American fanatics of the worst kind.

"I worry about telling the truth in this movie," said Wilson. "People will be mad at me."

"Afghanistan is a complicated place," I responded. "Some say it is cursed. But no one knew that the Taliban would arise when you were helping the Mujahedeen. At least the Taliban aren't running the country anymore. There is hope. Someday things will be better, God willing."

A small-town boy from Texas, Charlie Wilson graduated from the United States Naval Academy and did intelligence work as a naval officer before getting into politics. He was elected to Congress 12 times. People called Wilson "Good Time Charlie" because he liked to drink and to hang around beautiful women—or have beautiful women hang around him. He was a very colorful real-life character. There was no need for a screen-writer to create him.

In 1980, Wilson learned of all the Afghans fleeing Soviet occupa-tion—people like my mother. One refugee account of Soviet helicopter gunships shooting down women and children moved him to tears, and he thereafter became a staunch supporter of the Afghan resistance move-ment. Because his congressional sub-committee controlled some CIA funding, he was able to secretly redirect Department of Defense money to the Mujahedeen—eventually hundreds of millions of dollars worth of military support. The Freedom Fighters put all that to good use and in

1989 the Soviets left Afghanistan in defeat. Who'd have dared dream of such an outcome in 1980?

Congressman Wilson's work was largely secret and possibly extralegal—if not illegal. Like President Reagan, Charlie was an anti-Communist—compelled to do what he could for the anti-Soviet cause. The 1980s found the Reagan Administration at odds with Congress over anti-Communist efforts in Central America, which Charlie also supported. If the public found out about *Operation Cyclone* and our clandestine pro-Mujahedeen efforts in Pakistan and Afghanistan, then there might have been a scandal comparable to Iran-Contra.

The more I learned about Charlie, the more I realized how extraordinary he was—a charismatic cowboy more responsible than anyone else for transforming my homeland from a Soviet satellite to, well, we're still not sure what.

Charlie Wilson's War was based on the book of the same name by George Crile. It was subtitled "The Extraordinary Story of the Largest Covert Operation in History." Former CBS-News anchorman Dan Rather said that "Tom Clancy's fiction pales in comparison with the amazing, mesmerizing story told by George Crile." Prominent radio personality Don Imus called it "the most unbelievable book … it's fabulous … you can't make up how great this book is."

Many wonderful films are based on fictitious stories, and that's fine, but this movie was based on real people—compelling personalities who changed the world. Now I was working with Charlie Wilson himself, as well as players like Bearden, the CIA technical advisor I'd met earlier at the Paramount Studio meeting. The story was personal to me: an Afghan-American.

Other people played real-life roles in this anti-Soviet drama. Julia Roberts' character, Joanne Herring, was one of them. A fascinating person in her own right, Herring greatly influenced Charlie. A thrice-married Texan, Herring at various times was a religious leader, a socialite, a political activist, a businesswoman, a talk show host, and a representative/consul to both Morocco and Pakistan. Like Charlie, she had strong political convictions and wasn't shy about using her connections—and her charms—to advance her causes. Roberts enjoyed portraying Herring, who like Erin Brockovich, was a real-life woman who changed the world.

Our great story line combined with all our star power promised big box office success. I couldn't wait to see the finished product.

Fahim Fazli with Morrocan movie extras

Shortly before leaving Morocco, I was on the set early, as usual. I noticed one of the Moroccan busses transporting the extras looked like a bus I'd traveled on in Afghanistan. As the bus pulled into base camp, I watched all the extras in the seats, dressed as Afghans, staring out the small windows. The driver honked his horn. It sounded exactly like a horn I'd heard 23 years earlier.

I flashed back to that bus ride out of Kabul in 1983, when we were stopped by the Communist secret police.

Chapter 3: To Pakistan

"Pakistan is the most virulently
anti-American state on the planet."
— Ted Rall, Syndicated American Editorialist

I braced for arrest in my seat as Wahid, the Communist secret policeman, stared at me from the front of the bus. I prayed silently that my father and brother might still get away and somehow continue on and complete the plan of escape to Pakistan.

The visor on Wahid's cap shielded his eyebrows. His tight-fitting, green uniform defined his upper body as well as his big belly. A moustache covered his lip, but typical of Afghan Communists, he was beardless. After he'd first boarded the bus and yelled at the driver, our eyes had locked. I looked down to the floor and prepared for the worst.

To my surprise and relief, he turned and exited. I glanced back to where my father sat but he wouldn't look at me. I offered a silent prayer of thanks.

Soon our ramshackle bus was again rolling east—toward Pakistan.

The bus was typical for our region. Multi-colored. Small windows. Beat up seats. Mostly male passengers. Mostly Pakistani. Photos of Indian actors and actresses were plastered everywhere, inside and out. The radio blared loud Indian and Pashto music and the driver punctuated the music at regular intervals by sounding the vehicles' horn, which made that unique, two-note honking sound.

As we slowly rolled ever-closer to Jalalabad, I closed my eyes and thought back to my early years in Kabul.

I remembered when we still had a King, Zahir Shah—a happy time when our country was not at war. Youngsters freely played in the streets.

We exuberantly flew colorful kites over a peaceful Kabul and people of all ages and tribes moved about unafraid.

Except that there *was* fear in my house. Not of the secret police, but of my father, Jamil. He had a good job with the Afghan National Bank, but he was a domineering tyrant. We grew up afraid of his beatings, his power, and his control. He often bullied and tried to intimidate my mother, Fahima, who was otherwise strong and assertive. In my family, it was always the same. My father sought control; my mother craved autonomy. Afghanistan was not a fair place for wives with grievances. Since males dominated the culture, successful relationships in Afghanistan required female subservience.

Divorce was not an option for my unhappy mother, as women had little legal recourse in Afghan society. My father never showed any regret about the inequality. Nominally a Muslim, he decided which Islamic tenets to observe and which to ignore. He was in alignment with Islam regarding female subservience, for example, but disregarded religious prohibitions on alcohol consumption. He drank regularly, at home and with friends, and alcohol made him stubborn and mean.

My father didn't want my mother to work. He thought it diminished him as head of the household. He felt justified in encouraging his children to give their mother a hard time over her decision to work as a midwife. By putting us in the middle of their disagreements, he made us uncomfortable and bitter. I was too young to be a parental arbiter. I just wanted them to get along.

My mother focused her frustration on me. She always told me I was a bad-luck child. I remember my mother lashing out at me after she argued with my father. "We never had difficulties when Suhail was a baby," she frequently ranted. "But ever since I had you, there's only been trouble and then more trouble."

I cried and cried. I wanted to make things better for my mother, but I just didn't know how. Afghans believe that good pregnancies are indicators of future luck. Many people, including my mother, were superstitious. Conflicts with family members during her pregnancy with me made her think that I would be bad luck after I was born. It became a self-fulfilling prophecy, given the trouble in our house.

Once, after my father gave my mother a black eye for contradicting him, she hid from him at her father's house. Regardless of her bruises, my mother's family considered it a disgrace that she couldn't get along with her spouse. Despite Fahima's great unhappiness, the family forced her to go back to Jamil after two days. So my mother returned to her husband's house to again contend with his threats and violent behavior.

Afghan culture has always been male-dominated. My parents' marriage had been arranged by their fathers. My grandfathers were both Pashtuns, Lieutenant Colonels in the Afghan army and long-time friends from the Durrani tribe. Pashtuns are divided into two large tribal groups: the Durrani and the Ghaljay. My father's family was of the Barikzoy tribe and my mother's the Popalzoy, both of which were Durrani. My mom's father was very kind and loved his kids and grandkids. He always bought us toys, books, and even cash. He encouraged me to become a military man. My dad's father was very serious. We were always careful around him. He was a disciplinarian who wouldn't hesitate to punish us. He wouldn't allow us to fly kites or play soccer. He wanted us to study.

My father was 25 years old and my mother was 16 when they married. They first moved into my dad's father's home to start their lives together. But my father had seven sisters and two brothers, none of whom got along with my mother.

My mother was smart and ambitious. She dreamed of being a doctor, not just a maid or a housewife. My father's many sisters resented her presence in their house and bullied her. She made things worse by resisting their abuse, rather than accepting it. Eventually, she convinced my father to move out. Otherwise, he'd probably have stayed with his parents indefinitely, as he didn't have to pay rent. Extended families often lived together in the same dwellings in old Kabul, and my father was frugal in most areas.

My parents' first new home was a rental apartment in Kabul. While living there my mother gave birth to her first child, who was stillborn— not uncommon in Afghanistan. Losing this child inspired my mother's passion for women's medicine.

Afghanistan is the worst place in the world to be a mother. Women have the lowest life expectancy on the planet—only 45 years. One in ten die in childbirth and about 20 percent of newborns don't live five years. Midwives stand on the battleground between nearly nonexistent obstetrics and the next generation of Afghans.

My mother's next birth experience went better, resulting in my brother Suhail. After losing their first baby, my parents joyously celebrated the arrival of a healthy son and saw Suhail as a harbinger of future good fortune. I was born two years later—a new imposition into a comfortable little family situation.

In Afghanistan, grandfathers receive such special respect that they are often invited to name newborns. My father's father had chosen Suhail's name earlier and in a magnanimous gesture my father allowed his father-in-law to honor Fahima, my mother, by naming me Fahim. In Arabic both our names mean "understanding." Ironically, many years passed before we began to understand each other.

We eventually moved to a new home that my father had built in Kabul's Kartay Parwan complex. This modern neighborhood was classy by Kabul's standards, with grocery and department stores, two mosques, several small parks, and even a movie theater. It was an attractive place for new couples to raise their families.

Four years later my brother Hares was born. Then came my two sisters, Almara and Mina, five years apart.

Around the time Mina was born, I noticed the difference between my right and my left, which meant I was growing up. Afghans use that expression to describe a maturing sense of self-awareness and understanding. In my case, this new capability helped me recognize my parents' volatile and deteriorating marriage. I felt a lot of tension around my own folks that was absent when I was around my friends' parents. Other mothers were more docile than mine. My mom challenged my father—a man bound by conservative Afghan cultural traditions. No wonder they fought.

The screaming and yelling never ceased. Neighbors saw my mother flee, time and again. When my mother's family forced her to return home, my father punished her by refusing to pay for groceries and utilities. Then he'd disappear with his friends for over a week. We had no electricity, and when the food ran out, my mother was forced to beg for money from her relatives. When my father returned, he'd split up the children, sending us to his sisters' and brothers' houses so my mother couldn't see us. My mother's family boxed her in from one direction while my father's family boxed her in from the opposite direction. She had few prospects, but she persevered and four years of part-time studies at a medical school in Kabul yielded her a coveted nursing certification that opened some doors for her—much to my father's chagrin.

Afghanistan modernized during the 1970s. Men dressed, worshiped, and lived as they pleased. Devout people prayed. Others drank alcohol and partied in select resorts and hot spots around Jalalabad, Karga, Korez E Amir, Pakman, and Solang Pass. Afghans with money could find music, drink, and parties. People could safely go out on the town and enjoy a measure of freedom under the peaceful rule of King Zahir Shah, a member of the Mohammadzai tribe. My parents' tribes were related to the Mohammadzais and so my family especially revered the king.

In Kabul, the better-off Afghan families hired maids to do their housework. These maids worked hard, like maids everywhere, doing the cooking, cleaning, shopping, as well as taking care of the children. Our maids' families often lived in our spare room, and occasionally their husbands did chores as well. But we were often without a maid, because frequently my father's demanding attitude drove them away. I often ended up in the kitchen, the quintessential "Cinder-fella." I took care of my younger brother and two younger sisters while my parents worked. My older brother never helped. Suhail was busy being a kid—flying kites and playing soccer. Because Suhail was the first-born son, he had privileges. The Number One Son is the favorite in Afghanistan. Suhail didn't do laundry or change diapers. I did. He didn't scrub the floors. I did. My father also expected me to take care of the yard and property. The Number Two Son is the "Miserable Son" in Afghanistan. I recruited maids so I didn't have to do housekeeping all the time. But the hard work made me stronger.

My siblings and I were not perfect. We skipped school and often went to the cinema—without permission. I loved to act even as a child and played roles for my school's drama department. In Afghanistan, acting, dancing and performing of any kind was thought to be very low-class. So I kept my dream of being an actor a secret from my family.

When we skipped school we flew kites, played marbles, and stole apples. Sometimes we jumped from roof to roof among the houses in the neighborhood, harassing kite-flyers. Most roofs were adobe, so if they were wet we'd mess them up pretty badly. Suhail, Hares, and I were troublemakers, but we weren't that different from other boys our age.

I didn't do well in school. I didn't know it at the time, but I had dyslexia and struggled in class because of it. My classroom discomfort caused me to skip school a lot, and I sometimes got caught. My father punished me with harsh beatings. In Afghanistan, thrashings were routine punishments for wayward youngsters.

In 1973, we heard over the radio that King Zahir Shah had fled Afghanistan for Italy after a 40-year reign. The King's cousin, Sardar Mohammad Daoud Khan, took control of the country—a bloodless regime change. This turn of events initially pleased my father, as Daoud Khan previously worked with my paternal grandfather and both were of the Mohammadzai tribe. So this new regime meant possible favors for our family. However, when Daoud Khan took control, he pressured my grandfather to resign from his government position in order to grant the job to another patron. This humiliated my grandfather—being fired by a fellow tribesman—and it caused my father to hate Daoud Khan.

Daoud Khan later issued a presidential directive eliminating tribal surnames, supposedly to make the country more modern. My father reluctantly changed our last name from the tribal Barikzoy to Fazli—my paternal grandfather's first name.

To secure his position, Daoud Khan accepted an invitation to visit Soviet President Leonid Brezhnev. The omnipresent Russian bear permanently lurked to our north, and Afghans were always wary of provoking it. However, instead of confirming Daoud Khan's authority, Brezhnev lectured him about supporting Soviet policies. Daoud Khan stood up, pointed his finger at Breshnev, and claimed to be the president of a *sovereign* Afghanistan. He left Moscow and came right back to Kabul. He soon made a *Hajj* (pilgrimage) to Saudi Arabia, flaunting his Islamic faith. The KGB didn't like this at all, as the Communists discouraged religion. The Afghan president further angered the Soviets when he sought closer ties with the West.

In 1978, Daoud Khan's presidency crumbled, due in large measure to Soviet intrigues. His administration was sabotaged internally by Communist sympathizers and secret agents. This began an era of constant conflict which has yet to end.

I was 12 years old when revolution came to Afghanistan. Sitting in class one day, I heard bombing, buzzing planes, and machine guns. My school was only ten minutes away from the presidential residence where Daoud Khan lived. Our teacher told us to go home. Communist sympathizers were shelling and bombing his castle. On my way home I saw tanks parked on many street corners. When I finally arrived at our house, I saw my parents sitting at the kitchen table.

"What's happening?" I fearfully asked.

My mother said nothing. We all looked to my father, who just sat there, brooding. When he finally spoke his words were measured.

"The Communists are taking over Afghanistan," he said slowly, his tone chilling. "These new leaders don't believe in God and they want to change everything. And they're happy to kill anyone who stands in their way."

He stared sullenly out a window. "Afghanistan is finished," my father lamented. "Things will never be the same."

He added that Daoud Khan should have killed the five Communists who worked for him. They'd been arrested the week before, but the president released them, not expecting them to start a revolt.

My father said he expected the Communists to arrest or kill Daoud Khan's family as well as those of our Mohammadzai tribe whom they considered untrustworthy. As the sky darkened, we still could hear the planes and tanks. Radio Afghanistan was silent, except for the playing of the Afghan national anthem. The next day radio programming returned, celebrating the ascendant Communist Party as the Khaqi (Peoples) Party, led by Noor Mohammad Taraki, our new President. Taraki named Haffizula Amin as Vice-President.

We soon heard on the radio that Daoud Khan and his closest kin were dead. He'd killed his own family at the besieged presidential palace rather than have the Communists imprison and torture them. He then killed himself—or the Communists murdered him. It was never clear which.

My parents continued working. But our world soon changed forever.

One day, Vice President Amin and his wife visited my mother's hospital, one of the biggest in Kabul, where most babies were born. They asked her boss to recommend a good female medical specialist for their daughters. The supervisor selected my mother out of all the resident midwives to serve as personal nurse for the Amin family.

Afterwards, for security reasons, Amin's people took my mother to the Amin home to assist with the births of the vice president's grandchildren and with subsequent infant care. My father didn't approve of my mother working for the Communists, but he saw no alternative.

Two military vehicles and four body guards escorted my mother to the Amin home every other day, where she helped with babies and did basic nursing. They paid her well. Sometimes my father or I accompanied her to ensure her safety.

Through her proximity to the Amins, my mother picked up on developing governmental intrigues. President Taraki and Vice President Amin were close allies at first, but as the months passed an estrangement developed and they plotted against each other.

In September of 1979, Amin ordered Taraki killed. The chief of the palace guards and two of his lieutenants tied Taraki up on a bed and smothered him with a pillow. Later an announcement was made that the president had "died in bed."

Amin became the new president and while still a Communist, he couldn't bear the thought of Afghanistan becoming a Soviet satellite/republic like our northern neighbors Kazakhstan, Kyrgyzstan, Tajikistan, Turkmenistan, and Uzbekistan. Amin was also younger than Taraki, and friendlier to western interests. He'd previously lived in America and studied at Georgetown University.

The violent political upheavals brutalized my country. Under the new Amin regime, the secret police killed hundreds of people, though usually without the president's knowledge or consent. Kabul became increasingly dangerous and chaotic.

Eventually, President Amin told my parents to leave Afghanistan with their children. He explained that the Soviets and the KGB wanted to take over the country, and since he respected us and appreciated how we'd helped his family, he offered to help to arrange our departure.

"Bad times are coming, Jamil," the President told my father. "The killing is only going to increase. I know people who can help you get Fahima and your children away from here."

My father thought Amin was a good man and a patriot—not a true Communist.

"Thank you so very much," my father replied. "But Afghanistan is all we know. It's our home, as it was for our fathers and grandfathers. We can't just run away from the land we love."

My mother, however, was terrified and wanted to leave Afghanistan immediately. "Jamil, we've got to get out of here!" she later said to my father in a panic. "Amin's daughters tell me that the KGB and the Russians want to take over, and they'll kill the people who helped the old regime!"

"Where are we supposed to go, Fahima?" replied my father. "You have to calm down. Where are we supposed to go?"

"Somewhere where we won't be killed!" she shrieked.

My mother had left home before, from fear of my father. Now she wanted to flee because she was terrified of the Communists. These twin threats to her survival would soon cause her to go somewhere else for good. When that happened, I wanted to go with her—wherever somewhere else turned out to be.

Days later Kha Kha Jan radio in Pakistan reported that Jihad was starting against the Communists and called for Afghans to become *Mujahedeen*—freedom fighters.

Then, during late December of 1979, the Soviet army invaded Kabul. A dread feeling of foreboding afflicted everyone we knew. On December 27, elements of the KGB Alpha Group along with Spetsnaz Special Forces stormed the Presidential Palace and a Spetsnaz officer shot and killed Amin. Babrak Karmal, a true Soviet puppet, became the new Communist president.

Everything changed, including school. One of my new classes was about "Communist Ideals." Supposedly, everyone would be equal under Communism, and the government would take from those who had too much and give to those who had too little. We had to trust science, not God. The government encouraged youngsters to squeal on those who resisted the new ways. I hated all of it.

Kha Kha Jan radio reported daily that the Mujahedeen were killing Russians. These broadcasts proclaimed that the U.S. would help Afghanistan to defeat the Communists. I decided to become a freedom fighter.

I was 13 years old when the Soviets occupied Kabul, and I fought constantly with local Communist kids my age on the neighborhood streets. I actually sought out the Marxists to harass them. I got into fistfight after fistfight and became adept at pummeling the young Communist propagandists entering my neighborhood proclaiming their messages. I was angry and looking for trouble.

And I found it.

One day, I saw three skinny teenaged boys walking down a street passing out Communist leaflets. They wore boots, jeans and military-style jackets. They didn't look too tough, although they had an aggressive, cocky way about them which really annoyed me. After sizing them up, I walked up from behind and taunted these pamphleteers, calling them traitors.

"Hey! Sons of Lenin! Are you Russians or Afghans?"

The tallest of the three immediately turned and responded.

"Things are different now," he sneered. "People like you need to learn the new ways immediately or you'll be sorry. You may need to attend a special school in Moscow. What's your name? Where do you live?"

I approached the smallest of the three and quickly threw the first punch, nailing the kid in the gut. As a budding street-fighter, I knew the importance of striking first, especially if outnumbered. The little guy doubled over and went down hard. I turned to take on the next one, but he'd already pulled out a knife. Then the tall guy pulled out a pistol. This had never happened before. I was suddenly in a knife fight and a gun fight—without a knife or gun!

I quickly decided to make a tactical withdrawal, but the guy with the knife lunged, stabbing me in the back. I screamed and turned to face my attacker. I kicked the knife-wielder in the groin and took off, leaving two of the intruders down on the ground. The tall guy raised his weapon.

"Shoot him in the leg!" the knifer yelled from his knees, as he clutched his damaged goods.

I raced down the street, zig-zagging to avoid the expected bullet, but the kid with the pistol never fired.

He yelled for me to stop. "*Estardasho! Estardasho!*"

I was fast down an alley and over a wall in no time. When you're running for your life you can really move.

I hid in a neighbor's attic. Peeking out of a small opening, I saw Communist authorities and police searching the area. They didn't linger long, but I waited in my hiding space until well after dark before returning home. These Communists were new to the neighborhood and almost certainly didn't know my name. Still, they had my description. My father didn't say a word after I got home. He had no idea what happened.

My stab wound wasn't bad, although I still have the scar to this day.

That incident cemented my hatred of the Communists. I lost all interest in school. My buddies who kept going to classes became Communists and I lost them as friends. Others drifted away from school and became Mujahedeen Freedom Fighters.

I didn't know who to trust. What was happening to my country?

After Amin's death and the Soviet occupation, my mother feared that Karmal's people would come after her. Some of Amin's surviving inner circle understood the dangers she faced. Those like her who'd been close to the previous government leaders were compromised and suspect in the view of the new regime. A well-placed Amin sympathizer told my mother that plans were in the works to get her and people like her to Pakistan and away from grave danger.

One evening, I noticed my mother packing a travel bag.

"Are you leaving, Mother?" I asked. "Where are you going?"

"We'll talk about this later, Fahim," she replied.

Then I saw her putting my sisters' clothes in another bag. Suhail was also packing. Something was going on, but no one was talking. And Hares wasn't packing anything.

"Fahim, are we supposed to be getting ready to go somewhere?" Hares whispered to me.

"Nobody's told me anything," I replied. "Dad's not packing anything."

A little later a taxi came to our house and my mother quickly picked up her travel bag, carried it out the door, and got in the cab, followed closely by Almara, Mina and Suhail. Her face was a mass of pain. She wouldn't even look at Hares or me. Nor did my brother or sisters ever look back or say goodbye. My father just looked very nervous. He hurried to get the taxi on its way, blocking the doorway so Hares and I couldn't see.

My little brother and I yelled after the taxi as we watched it go down the street and disappear around a corner. It happened so fast. My mother and siblings had vanished and I never even had a chance to say goodbye.

Why couldn't we go, too? Would we ever see them again? Hares and I kept crying. My father had nothing to say. He was like a movie director ending a scene. But instead of saying "Cut" he simply shut the door.

A new and scary darkness suddenly came over our house. What next?

"When are they coming back?" Hares asked, the tears streaming down his nine-year-old face.

My father said nothing, as he walked into the kitchen and sat in his favorite chair.

"Father!" I implored. "Where did they go? When are they coming back?"

"They're *never* coming back!" my father finally barked. "We'll talk about this later. For now, you just need to go to bed."

I soon realized that my own father was holding Hares and me hostage. He'd said he'd never leave his beloved Afghanistan. If he let us go, then he'd never see his wife again. If he kept us in Afghanistan, then she'd have to keep in touch with him.

Or so he thought. Four years passed without any word from my mother. We imagined that they all somehow ended up living in America.

The bus hit a bump and I opened my eyes. I looked back to the seat where my father sat next to a window, staring out impassively at the barren landscape. I couldn't remember the last time I'd seen him smile.

We came to a bazaar next to a Soviet checkpoint near the village of Sorobi, not far from Jalalabad. The driver announced he needed a bathroom break before we proceeded through the checkpoint, and the bus screeched to a hard stop. After the driver stepped out, Abdul signaled to my father, Hares, and me to get off the bus. We followed the coyote out the open bus door into a dirt parking lot. The bazaar smelled of roasting kabobs, aromatic tea, and coffee. A small radio played Indian music in a bazaar stall. Other riders followed us off the bus to use the restrooms. Security people and Soviet vehicles filled the bazaar, but no one paid us any particular attention.

While the bus driver talked to an official at the checkpoint, my father, brother and I self-consciously avoided each other. Abdul soon said something discretely to my father, who hesitated briefly, and then approached Hares and me. He whispered that we were to follow the coyote, walking at intervals of 100 feet.

Abdul went first, followed by my father, me, and Hares. We walked to the west, away from Pakistan and back towards Kabul. That would fool the Russians, who'd be less likely to harass us if we were heading *away* from the border. A riverbed flanked with trees ran parallel to the highway. The coyote angled off the road to the left and into the trees. We followed him for about a mile. Then we turned back towards the southeast and continued walking uphill on the narrow, rocky trail. We passed some small farm areas and tiny villages, all the while maintaining that 100 foot separation.

We walked slowly and steadily for around three hours. Abdul had a container of water, and we passed it around and drank it dry when we came together to rest in a grove of evergreen trees. The sun set, but we didn't feel the evening chill, as we continued our uphill walk. We finally came to the village of Jikdalak and approached a house on the edge of the little settlement that had a man standing on its roof, holding a rifle. Abdul warned us that there were mines all around, and to step where he stepped as we closed in on the building. It was a typical Afghan house, an adobe or mud-hut structure with three rooms. Another fighter with a rifle slung over his shoulder stood outside the entrance and motioned to us to enter. A dozen Mujahedeen freedom fighters were crowded inside the house, which was dark and smelly. Each man carried an AK-47 rifle. They all wore turbans, and most had full beards. They stared at us and said nothing, though one of them showed Abdul where he could get us some water. I sensed that they'd ruthlessly shoot us without hesitation if they felt threatened.

The Mujahedeen movement featured seven groups, including factions associated with the likes of Gulbuddin Hekmatyar, Osama Bin Laden, Ahmad Shah Massoud, among others. Some of the factions included fanatical Wahhabis who swore by an ancient Saudi Arabian fundamentalism. I didn't know which faction the fighters in the house belonged to, but they projected a scary, malign energy and I knew they'd give no quarter to any Soviets they might encounter—including those we'd seen earlier just a short distance away.

The coyote explained to the head fighter who my father Jamil was and the Mujahedeen warmed to us when they learned that my mother and siblings were in America.

"You need to rest here tonight," a fighter told us. "You have a difficult journey ahead of you."

They found places for us to lie down in a crowded dark room with one window, but no other light source.

"We need to rest while we can," my father whispered. "Try to go to sleep."

Hares lay down beside my father, closest to the wall, screened by my father's prostrate form. Fighters intermittently slept, worked on their weapons, or spoke very quietly to each other, so softly I could not tell what they were saying—which made me nervous.

I found a bit of space in a corner and stretched out on a dirty blanket. A weather-beaten fighter sat cross-legged on the floor about six feet away, staring at me, but saying nothing. I couldn't relax. This Mujahedeen had yellow eyes and a long black beard, with bits of grey here and there. He wore a black turban and he cradled an AK-47 over his filthy clothes. I noticed that he was lacking two fingers. Our eyes met and he slowly smiled. I saw he was missing most of his teeth.

Unsettled, I quickly rolled over and faced the wall. I was exhausted, but sleep would not come. Was this all a nightmare? Would I soon wake up and find myself back in old Kabul, once again hearing my mother's voice and my father's laugh? But it was not a bad dream. It was all too real. We'd left Kabul and couldn't go back. If we did, we'd probably be killed. My father would be executed for sure. Would we ever get to Pakistan? Could we trust our coyote? And could we trust these scary fighters in this smelly house, surrounded by mines? I prayed fervently that things would be OK. I kept staring at the wall, shivering and fighting off a terror I couldn't comprehend.

I finally rolled back over and saw the fighter still sat there as before. He stared at me eerily and smiled another toothless smile.

The Hindu Kush

Chapter 4: Stranded

"Hope is like a path in the country—where there was never a road. When many people walk a path, a road comes into existence."
- Lin Yutang, Chinese Author

I lay awake on the floor in that Mujahedeen safe house, looking at the ceiling, avoiding the stare of the yellow-eyed fighter cradling the AK-47. I thought back to those days in Kabul after my mother vanished, listening to the Kha Kha Jan Radio broadcasts from Pakistan inciting Afghan freedom fighters to oppose the Communists. Kha Kha Jan also broadcast reports from the outside world, including sports news. We rejoiced when Mohammed Ali won a big fight. And the USA ice hockey team defeated the mighty Soviets during the 1980 Olympics, even though the Americans were just college students. I'm sure the American athletes had no idea how much their victory inspired us. The Kha Kha Jan broadcasts were in Dari and Pashto, both of which I spoke well. The radio reports detailing Soviet atrocities against our people inflamed our emotions.

Even before the Soviets came to Kabul in force, I hated the Afghan Communists, who sought to control so much of our country's life. When I was 12 years old, I ran away from home with Suhail, who was then 14, and another boy, Safie, 15, to go to Pakistan. Kha Kha Jan inspired us so much that we sought to join the anti-Communist forces across the border. We had no contacts there. We just figured, as boys will, that our passion would guide us; we'd ask people to point us to the Freedom Fighters. Simple as that. We boarded a bus and got all the way past Jalalabad to the border settlement of Torkham. Then the Afghan Communist border police caught us at a bus stop. We wore western clothes—school attire. Big mistake. My father reported us missing and the authorities came after us. The Communists brought us back to Kabul on another bus.

Angry parents awaited us at the Kabul bus station. Safie's father grabbed Safie's arm and led him away. My father glared at Suhail and me and pointed to his waiting car.

"Get in and don't speak," he snapped.

I hardly dared to breathe as my father drove home and marched us into the living room. He locked the room's one door while a maid and my mother held Suhail down. My father picked up an electrical cord and slashed at Suhail's backside. This was new. My mother had never previously helped my father to beat us. I was petrified. I wanted to help Suhail but could only stand there and listen to his screams as my father lashed away. I knew Suhail to be the favored son—the fortunate son. I figured they'd beat me even worse. When my father finally let up, Suhail lay wailing on the floor. The angry trio turned to me. I stepped back into a corner as the three of them approached. I pushed the maid out of the way and made a break to the door, but it was locked. Then I felt my father grip my upper left arm as he flung me to the floor, almost tearing my arm out of its socket. His first blow slashed my back, ripping my shirt open wide. He then whacked me so hard that the skin came off of my left upper arm, where I still have a scar. I curled into a ball and pleaded for mercy, covering my head with my arms. The blows continued. I begged my mother for help, but none came. My father lashed away—my back, my buttocks, and my legs. Then in a *coup de grace* he kicked me, threw the cord at me, and screamed, "Learn from this! Don't ever disappear and embarrass us again!"

Our parents beat bloody and unforgettable lessons into us—not just into our bodies, but into our hearts, minds, and souls. We were too young to make big life decisions. We were not to challenge the status quo, either in the family or in greater Afghan society. Asserting our independence meant dire consequences, which my father was happy to deliver.

I told myself, even in the moment of my worst pain and fear, that my father was violent, but not evil. He was a product of a conservative, patriarchal Afghan society threatened by those who challenged authority or the status quo. Perhaps some of his anger stemmed from his worry about our safety. Still, that reasoning only went so far. My home no longer provided sanctuary, and my country no longer felt like home.

After beating us, my parents and the maid left the living room. On her way out, my mother spoke for the first time.

"Think about what happened," she said. "Learn from this." Her voice cracked in anguish as she spoke. I knew my father coerced her participation in our beatings.

Tears streamed down my cheeks, prompted by the physical pain, and also by the emotional hurt of being beaten by the two people who should love me most.

Suhail and I sobbed together, broken and demoralized. Eventually, we stopped crying and silence prevailed. Finally, my brother spoke. "I hate them," he muttered. "I hate them so much. Someday I'll make them know how it feels to be beaten like a dog."

I stared at Suhail, and the cold harshness of his face suddenly made him look much older to me. I suddenly recognized our father. It was a moment of profound insight, for I saw Suhail being caught in the same violent trap that had ensnared our father—the Afghan cycle of retribution. When he took on my father's angry look, I could picture him doing violence—to his own children. I swallowed hard. Suhail stared straight ahead, not at me, but I wondered if he would see our father when he looked at *me*. I couldn't bear that. I vowed, then and there, never to be like my father.

I wanted to love my father, but it was hard. He was mean and cruel. Stubborn. Violent. Domineering. Materialistic. He drank and chased women. He hit my mother. He never showed affection for anyone, unless they had money or things he wanted—then he could be charming. I wondered how he had become who he was.

Jamil Barikzoy was the oldest son of ten children. His father was often absent because of a military career, so my father learned to be an assertive head of the household at a young age. He emulated his own father's authoritarianism. Perhaps his harshness was his way of showing that he cared. However, as I saw Suhail becoming like our father, I understood the need to break this cycle of brutal Afghan paternal violence.

My stinging back stopped hurting so much when a ray of sunshine shone bravely through the room's lone window. It was a spiritual moment, brought on by the intense pain from my beating, the emotional hurt I'd suffered, and the inspired revelation that I'd just experienced. I sensed the presence and lightness of some sort of higher power. I didn't understand it, but that was OK. I felt it. It was real and it gave me new-found comfort and hope.

I was 13 years old when the Soviets arrived the next year—when President Amin was killed. Cries of *Allah Akbar* resounded around the city that very first night. Our resistance movement began with the next morning's light.

Two years later I identified some Soviet convoy routes and occasionally I'd position myself high on a steep hill behind some rocks, take aim at Soviet vehicles passing far below, and fire my long-range sling shot. I had a handy escape route, known only to me, and after launching my missiles, I'd take off.

One day, my young friend Hobid joined Hares and me at my ambush site with their own slingshots. As the convoy approached, we readied our launchers, and positioned ourselves where we could fire.

We saw our targets approaching and prepared to launch a volley. I jabbed Hobid in the ribs and I pointed to the lead vehicle, claiming it. I fired down at a soldier exposed on top of the slowly moving tank. Bullseye! Emboldened by my marksmanship, Hobid and Hares fired at their targets. Moments later, Russian voices resounded from the convoy radios and the vehicles braked and halted, metal tracks screeching and seizing on the gravelly road. Dozens of infantrymen dismounted from armored personnel carriers as tank guns slowly turned and elevated in our direction. We took off, running all out toward a grove of trees on top of the hill, where my escape route began. We heard the snap sound of bullets—small arms fire—whizzing past our heads, while other bullets kicked up dust near our feet before we got into the trees and just kept running.

In that moment I felt marvelously alive. Years later I heard of an apt quote by Winston Churchill. "There is nothing so exhilarating as to be shot at without effect."

We scrambled through the trees and down the other side of a hill and kept running until we reached a residential street in a destitute neighborhood. Hobid and I left Hares far behind and eventually I heard him yell, "Fahim! Wait for me!" I ducked inside an abandoned house with an open doorway, followed closely by Hobid. We both fell to the floor, our chests heaving. Then we heard the sound of Hares' footsteps. He joined us inside and bent over, with his hands on his knees, trying to breathe. He sat down against a wall, and for a while we just looked at each other, gasping for breath.

"That's the last time I ever listen to you, Fahim!" Hobid finally said. He was still panting away, his eyes open wide, sweat dripping off his chin. Poor Hobid. He loved flying kites, and wasn't that interested in shooting sling shots. I'd talked him into coming to my ambush site, where the Russians almost killed him. He looked so frightened that I couldn't help but laugh.

"What if Father finds out?" Hares finally asked.

I stopped laughing.

"We don't need to talk about that," I said. "We'll be fine." Of course, I was bluffing. My father terrified me as much or more than the Soviet tanks did.

From that day on, we watched our occupiers closely. I was curious about them so I tried to ingratiate myself to soldiers on bases around Kabul. I'd trade stuff the soldiers wanted—like Afghan blankets or fresh food—for parts of weapons. Then I'd turn those parts over to store owners, who eventually put together intact weapons for the resistance. Later, I delivered propaganda leaflets to areas where the soldiers could find them. The leaflets, written in Pashto and Dari, stated, "We will get you! Allah is Great, not Lenin! Afghan Collaborator-Traitors Will Die!"

I feigned affection for our enemies and found that I enjoyed acting. I learned to speak Russian. It just came easily to me, as did learning other languages. I thought then that if I was forced to live in China for three weeks, I could probably return fluent in Mandarin!

The stare of the toothless fighter, the snoring of Mujahedeen in other corners of the safe house, and the excitement of the day combined to keep me awake, but eventually my eyes closed and I fell asleep in my corner. No sooner did the dreams begin than the coyote shook me awake. Abdul wanted to move on. He feared a spy among the Mujahedeen would turn us in. My father quietly stood up and helped Hares put on his coat. He whispered to me to give him the money he'd sewn inside my jacket. He gave some of the money to Abdul and some to the local Mujahedeen leader, who stood watching us from just inside the doorway.

Our coyote led us outside where three Mujahedeen fighters waited to escort us. They led us up an old road to the southeast. We passed through a gruesome area filled with destroyed vehicles and blown-up animals. The now-silent battlefield hid active mines. One Mujahedeen guide pointed them out, saying, "These are anti-tank mines. Fortunately, you are too small to set them off." Not at all comforted, I let him go first and I stepped only in his footprints. We moved like ghosts past the moonlit carcasses and battlefield debris.

We walked briskly throughout the freezing night. The next morning we reached a small settlement, where a nervous villager provided us with a place to sleep. He smiled with relief when we moved on after a few hours.

I thought about my mother. Would this wretched journey somehow reunite us with the rest of our splintered family? My father moved ahead of me in our little column. Now I followed him instead of the Mujahedeen. As always, he remained cold, stoic, and emotionless. I yearned for a measure of reassurance, which he never provided. As I literally walked in his footsteps, I pondered who he was. While this journey was essentially a search for my mother, in a different way it was also a search for my father. He often scared and angered me, but he sometimes showed glimpses of the humanity that I wanted—that I *needed*—to see in my father. He'd shielded Hares with his own body at the Mujahedeen safe house. That imagery moved me, but it also made me jealous. Had he ever shielded me from any dangers? Had he ever done anything special for me besides beat me? I was still angry that he didn't allow Hares and me to leave Afghanistan with my mother. He'd held us hostage instead. Maybe by risking his life and fortune to reunite us with our mother he was seeking to make amends for past transgressions. Or was he just trying to save his own life? My search for my father would continue—even as he walked just 20 feet ahead of me.

Thirst became an issue since we traveled light and didn't carry much water. The coyote seemed to know the location of streams or water sources, though, and we were never thirsty for long.

At night we stopped again at a pre-determined safe-house to sleep and eat. It helped our cause that Afghans are famously hospitable to trav-

elers. It was like the underground railway system that had helped southern slaves in the U.S. escape to Canada before the American Civil War.

On the third day of our trek, the three Mujahedeen left us, but our
trustworthy coyote kept guiding us through the remote trails and passes
of the Hindu Kush. Hares' shoes wore out, but Abdul found some replace-
ments in a tiny village and we kept going. Sometimes we rested off to the
side of the trail if we could find cover. Sometimes we'd stop at a safe house
and sleep in a dwelling owned by someone who seemed to know our coyote.

One villager gave us some old blankets in which we wrapped up
small amounts of bread and dried meat. We never got too cold while
moving, but if we stopped for long, the shivering began. I was so glad we
had our blankets—our Afghan quilts.

We stayed dispersed and avoided potential mine fields. Abdul taught
us how to react when we'd hear a plane or a helicopter overhead: step
quickly off the trail, throw a blanket or shawl over ourselves, and be very
still until the danger passed. Then we'd emerge from our camouflaged
positions and continue on.

Hares and I wore down. My little brother kept coughing and we often
had to wait for him. Even my father ran out of energy. Abdul, on the other
hand, seemed impervious to the elements.

Finally, the trail took us to the base of a 10,000 foot mountain. There
was no getting around it if we were to get to Pakistan. My father told the
coyote that we needed help. "We can't last much longer," he said. "I don't
think Hares can make it, and I can't carry him. I can hardly walk much
further myself."

"You have to keep going," Abdul replied, in a soft, patient voice. "You
have no choice. You need to move or die. It will be all right. I've done this
before. There is help ahead."

We soon arrived at a farm, where a man came out of a house and
talked to the coyote and my father, who took out some money and gave
it to the farmer.

The farmer took us to a barn, inside of which were four horses. The
four of us mounted up and the farmer walked in front of us as we moved
single file up a narrow trail, ascending ever higher into the frigid remote-
ness of the Hindu Kush. The horse farmer was an elder, with grey hair and

a grey beard, but he moved with the vigor of a much younger man. I had
the feeling he'd traveled this route many times before.

"Don't try to guide the horses," the horse-farmer said. "They know
how to get to Pakistan."

My horse was all brown, except for a little white near his nose. He
looked at me before the farmer helped me mount him, and I swear this
horse smiled at me, showing his square white teeth. It was comforting.
Compared to trudging uphill, riding on horseback was effortless. The
farmer and Abdul switched off riding the lead horse, the biggest of the
four. My father was next, with me right behind. Hares rode the smallest
horse, at the end of our little column.

The horses indeed knew the way as we continued climbing.
Sometimes they'd move underneath a tree and just stop. Then we'd hear
Soviet aircraft in the distance. The horses sensed danger before we did
and they knew how to hide. There were more trees at the higher eleva-
tions, where the views were magnificent. As we looked back to the north,
we could see for 100 miles in places. Brown valley floors gave way to green
tree-covered mountainsides, which were often capped by white snowfields. Some of the more distant mountains were light blue, rather than
green. The skies were usually dark blue during the day, and sprinkled with
bright stars at night.

Eventually, we traveled on steep switchback trails, wide enough for
only one person or one horse to walk at a time. In some places, a misstep
meant a plunge of hundreds of feet, almost straight down to certain
death. I told myself that the horses knew what they were doing, that they
didn't want to fall either, and to trust them.

I adjusted to my horse's rhythm and we became as one. We eventually came to a natural resting area that evening, where a small spring provided water, and trees concealed our bivouac. Hares' horse carried food
for all the horses and people. My new equine friend quickly devoured all
the oats the farmer poured into a small basket, and then drank thirstily
from the spring.

No longer exhausted, I was in a talkative mood and asked Abdul and
the farmer about previous trips they'd made over this ground.
Unfortunately, they only wanted to sleep. They'd alternated walking and
riding and were beat. I devoured yet another cold meal, while longing for

something warm. We couldn't have a fire. On this cold, clear night even a small blaze could be seen from 20 miles away, inviting Soviet attention. Our trek gave me a new appreciation for many things, especially hot food.

Snowfields loomed above our bivouac. Everyone wrapped up in his own blanket and tried to sleep. I turned my blanket into a cocoon, but then I couldn't breathe. When I'd stick my head out to breathe, I became too cold to sleep. I lay awake most of the night. My father and Abdul took turns staying up, and when the farmer started snoring, one of them poked him until he stopped. It was a quiet, starry night, and sound traveled well—a Soviet patrol might hear him. I fidgeted and froze all night, and was happy to see the dawn.

The next day, we ascended into the snow and soon arrived at Jogjee Mangel near the Pakistan border. From over 10,000 feet, we looked back down into a valley and saw dreaded Soviet aircraft taking off from a small airfield.

By this time I was tired, dizzy, and sick. Even though I'd been riding, I was short of breath at the high altitude. I shivered from the cold while my stomach growled in hunger. Clouds rolled in, accompanied by snow flurries, and a cold wind buffeted us. Still, the dream of escape kept us going. Our difficulties made me more determined than ever to see my mother's face again.

Eventually, the coyote said to stop, rest, and wait for darkness. We found shelter from the wind in a space between several large rock formations. The farmer spoke briefly to Abdul, and then tied the horses together with a small rope that connected their bridles. He mounted the lead horse, waved, and shouted, "Good luck!" He slowly rode back to the northwest, beginning the long descent down toward his farm, the three other horses trailing behind him in a single file.

Despite the cold we slept for a while. Then Abdul shook the three of us awake. "It's time to finish our journey," he said softly, with a hint of a smile. Our lives were in his hands, as they had been for almost a week. I'd developed real admiration for our coyote, and trusted him with my life.

We started a six-hour hike down the mountain while it was still dark. Abdul led the way, and I followed closely. Hares limped along behind me, with my father taking up the rear. He usually walked closest to Abdul, but now he chose to go last to keep an eye on us. I liked that.

We bottomed out in a valley and then made a brief ascent as a new day dawned.

Suddenly, we saw figures in dark uniforms on the trail ahead of us. We froze, but Abdul went up ahead. He spoke with the figures in Pashto for a few moments. Then he waved us forward and told us we were now in Parachinar, Pakistan.

It was the happiest day of my young life.

I looked at my father and saw a smile bloom on his face for the first time in five years.

My first look at the vast Parachinar refugee camp showed a makeshift city of green, grey and brown tents stretching on forever, sheltering tens of thousands of Afghan refugees displaced by the bloody violence in my homeland.

Western powers, including the U.S., provided material aid for refugee camps like this one. Charlie Wilson had visited Parachinar in the 1980s and was so moved by its desperate condition that he swore to do whatever he could as a U. S. Congressman to help the Afghan people. Little did I know then that 23 years later Wilson and I would be comparing notes on the camp when I served as cultural advisor for *Charlie Wilson's War*.

The mass of displaced humanity reminded me of Jews, of all things. My favorite school subject was history and I knew a bit about the Jewish Diaspora, the scattering of the Hebrew people throughout the world when hostile forces dominated their homeland. Also, the Soviets often showed World War II-era propaganda films in Kabul theaters which demonized anti-Communists—like Hitler and the Nazis. Some of these films showed Jews crowded into large concentration camps. The Parachinar refugee camp made me think of those World War II film images. It may seem curious that someone from an Islamic country would liken his people's plight to that of the Jews, but as I looked at all the displaced Afghans and the countless tents, I just kept thinking of Jews.

My father didn't want to take up residence in Parachinar. He wanted to search for relatives in Islamabad, the Pakistani capital, so our coyote led us to where we could board a bus for Peshawar, which was on the way to

Islamabad. Abdul said that we might be able to bribe some Peshawar people to forge us valuable travel documents, so our father decided to investigate there before heading on to the capital. We hugged our coyote and thanked him. My father gave him some more money and Abdul smiled and wished us luck. He turned and headed back to the northwest, walking with the slow but purposeful stride we'd come to know so well. I understood that Abdul was a kind of mercenary. He made a lot of money getting people out of Afghanistan. Still, many other coyotes took payments from would-be refugees and turned them in later. Abdul was true to the bargain he'd struck with my father. As I watched him walking back towards Afghanistan, I wondered if he was an angel, sent to help us escape the terrors of my native land. I still wonder what became of him.

My father, Hares, and I got on the bus. This time, we sat together. Our eyes darted back and forth as we slowly rolled through the vast refugee camp. There were animals all around in the camp—goats, sheep, and cows, just wandering around. Sort of a giant barnyard. Kids kicked soccer balls. Tents and temporary shelters were set up haphazardly. No one wanted to stay permanently in a refugee camp, even though it provided some security. Leaving the squalid tent city required money, which most refugees didn't have—Afghans being among the poorest people in the world. Many just stood and stared at our bus, probably yearning to be on it with us. We speeded up slightly as we pulled away from the camp. Eight hours later, we arrived in Peshawar.

In Peshawar, we could buy official documents necessary for transit to India. From there, we could position ourselves to travel to America. Intrigue abounded in this lawless and scary place. Kidnappings and disappearances occurred routinely. Gulbuddin Hekmatyar's ruthless Mujahedeen fighters dominated Peshawar. They'd hang anyone from Afghanistan with ties to the Communist regime. My father was visibly nervous.

"Stay close to me," he ordered. "If we get separated, we'll never find each other again."

We got off the bus and walked toward the business district—my father in the middle, with Hares and I each clutching one of his hands.

Peshawar was not pretty. The city had electricity, though many of the utility poles angled one way or the other. Boys flew kites. Birds squawked.

Dogs barked. Trash piles emitted an acidic, humid stench that reminded me of Kabul's poorest neighborhoods. Rows of crumbling, dilapidated two-story buildings stretched on for miles on both sides of busy, dusty streets. I wondered why people couldn't build newer, nicer places and put paint on them. And why couldn't someone pick up the garbage?

Downtown traffic snarled and horns honked constantly. White Range Rovers traveled alongside colorfully painted jingle trucks moving produce or other goods. Horses pulled wagons and young men pulled rickshaws. Indian and Pashto music blared from stalls along a street-side bazaar, amid the pervasive smell of roasting kabobs. Vendors and buyers argued over prices as they had since antiquity. We watched a man show off some gems, including what appeared to be rubies and emeralds, to a vendor who displayed weapons on a table. Eventually the vendor merchant accepted several jewels and handed the man an AK-47 Soviet assault rifle.

A few women moved around partially covered, like Arabs, as opposed to Afghan women who wore the traditional burquas covering everything but the eyes. Turbaned men—presumably Mujahedeen fighters—walked about bristling with weapons of all kinds.

The unsettling eyes of these bearded fighters haunted me as we moved through the city. They could probably tell we were transients. They scrutinized Hares in particular. I worried for my 12-year-old brother and stayed close to him.

Finally, an elder approached my father, gestured toward Hares and me, and, asked "Are those your sons?"

"Of course," my father replied. "Why do you ask?"

"You need to take those pretty boys away from here quickly or they'll soon end up in the soldiers' camp."

Hares and I anxiously looked to my father.

"We're going to Islamabad as soon as we can," he replied. "Thank you."

An unfortunate aspect of the fighter culture there involved young boys being exploited sexually. The practice is known as *Bacha Bazi*, literally "playing with boys." The practice of selling adolescent boys to wealthy or powerful men for entertainment and sex sadly thrives in both Afghanistan and Pakistan. Abdul had told us earlier that Afghan culture precluded visits to military camps by women or prostitutes and so boys filled a sexual void of sorts for the fighters. I understood the implications of ending up in the soldiers' camp. My father must have had second thoughts as well, because he decided to pursue the documents we needed in the Pakistani capital of Islamabad instead of Peshawar. The capital was a much more cosmopolitan place, with its atmosphere tempered by the presence of foreigners and embassies. Security was also better there. So we spent the night outside a Peshawar hotel near a mosque, where there was street light and people moving around. The next day we boarded a bus yet again, now bound for Islamabad.

This bus trip was not as scary as the one we'd made out of Kabul— the road was paved and presumably there were no Communist secret police looking for us. Still, we had to contend with five or six checkpoint stops, which always made me nervous. When the Pakistani police boarded the bus, the driver seemed to know what to do. He gave money to the police and they let us move on. I wondered if the payments were some combination of bribes, taxes, or tolls.

Upon arriving in Islamabad, we made our way to the large and impoverished residential district G93, where Afghan expatriates predominated. We stopped at an Afghan bakery, where a man named Omar and his brother Mamoud stood in line ahead of us to buy bread. After finishing his purchase, Omar turned and eyed us with interest.

"You're new here, yes?" queried Omar in Pashto.

"Yes," said my father. "But we're going to America."

Omar laughed. "You'll be here for many years," he said. "There are so many thousands in line ahead of you. How much money do you have?"

"Enough," said my father.

Omar said we could move in with him and Mamoud for a while, for a small fee. And so we did. Even though we ended up five in a room, we felt much safer than we did in Peshawar. Omar and Mamoud lived on the second floor of a four-story apartment building. Our space actually had two rooms, but a rent collector had one room all to himself. We settled in, organized our meager possessions, and talked about what we would do next. Then we walked around to meet other residents and to get a feel for the neighborhood.

A few days later, Omar took us to the American Embassy, located in an upscale part of Islamabad—nicer than any neighborhood in Kabul. Concertina wire crowned the walls surrounding a modern, multi-level structure. Trees grew throughout the embassy grounds. An American flag flew above a guard station by the main gate, where a sliding door occasionally opened to allow a vehicle through.

Pakistani police stood outside and prevented us from accessing the gate without papers. I looked through the gates and saw armed Americans on the inside. Slim and trim, these men projected a comforting, confident presence.

It was my first look at United States Marines.

A policeman spoke to one of the Marines, who glanced at us and then nodded. That simple gesture filled my heart with hope.

Soon, an embassy worker and a translator appeared at the gate. We explained that my mother, two sisters, and a brother had traveled through Pakistan to India in 1980, and we believed they were somewhere in America. They told us to be patient and to give them time to try to track down my mother.

We went back to Omar's place at G93. Neighborhood expatriates said the embassy people would take years processing our requests and told us to go to India, where we could better expedite international travel. To cross the Indian border required that we first return to Peshawar to procure necessary transit documents. A G93 neighbor told my father of a Peshawar man named Chubby the Forger who might help us with passports and visas. Supposedly Chubby could create almost any type of document—for a fee.

We got on a bus and went back to the scary city. After walking a couple of miles from the bus stop, we finally arrived at an old store. We approached a man standing outside and explained that Omar and Mamoud from G93 had told us to meet Chubby the Forger at this location. The man nodded and said "Follow me." We entered a backroom.

"Greetings," said Chubby, who was indeed a very fat man. "I know why you're here. Do you have money?"

"We have some," said my father. G93 people had coached my dad in advance on negotiating with the forger. He and Chubby dickered a bit and then agreed on a price for three passports.

"I can help you," said Chubby. "But you have to wait a while. I have a big backlog."

"What about the police?" my father asked.

"They're my friends," Chubby said with a smile. "I take good care of them."

Chubby took our photos—and our money—and said he'd eventually work up something that could help us. We had no choice but to be patient.

"I'll contact you through Omar when something is ready," said Chubby. "And tell him not to send anyone else this way unless they can pay more than you."

We took a bus back to Islamabad and G93. We returned to the American Embassy, where an official told us to file as refugees seeking asylum in the U.S. He helped us with paperwork and said to expect at least a three-year wait—and even then there were no guarantees.

Everywhere we went we heard, "Be patient. Be patient."

We resumed our boring routines in Omar's little one-room apartment and at G93. The days went by and we got to know the other Afghans in the area, all of whom, like us, wanted to go to America.

Meanwhile, American personnel continued searching for our family in the U.S.

Three weeks later, we returned to the embassy to check for new information. People like us couldn't get into the embassy unless our names were on a list and we always had to stand outside and use an interpreter to communicate with embassy personnel. I saw how empowering it was for translators—to be able to communicate in two different worlds while connecting two different cultures. On this particular day, the interpreter asked the Marine at the gate for news. This Marine looked at some paperwork and responded differently from previous visits. Even though I couldn't speak English, I could tell there was new information.

Suddenly, the gate opened and we moved for the first time into a small piece of America.

I'll never forget the words the translator then spoke in Dari: "They have found your family!"

It was late November of 1983. A man at the Embassy gave us a number for a telephone in Charlottesville, Virginia, where we might reach my mother.

We went back to Omar's apartment and gathered all the coins we could. Then we walked to a local pay phone and stood in line to make an unforgettable telephone call to America.

My dad dialed the number. Hares and I crowded close to him so we could hear any voices that might come over the receiver. We finally heard a tinny female voice say "Hello" in English.

"Salam alikam, Fahima," said my father as he started to cry.

"Jamil?" the tinny voice asked incredulously. "Jamil?" Hares and I started to cry as well.

"Yes, Fahima, it's me, Jamil—your husband," my father said in Dari.

My mother reverted to Dari. "My God! I can't believe it! Where are you?" she asked.

"Islamabad," replied my father. "We're working with the American Embassy to get to the U.S. and find you."

"Who is 'we'?" responded my mother.

"Me, Fahim and Hares, of course," said Dad.

Then we heard shouting at the other end. "They told me you married someone else and have small children," screamed my mother. "And Fahim and Hares are dead! Why are you calling me now?"

"Not so!" said my father. "Whoever told you that was trying to keep you from communicating with me. Fahim and Hares are right here with me! I'll put Fahim on the line."

My father handed me the phone. "Salam madar Jan," I said. *Hello, dear mother.*

"You are not Fahim," my mother responded.

My voice had deepened during the previous four years and my mother didn't believe it was me. "Remember how I used to go with you to deliver babies," I said. "I carried your medical bag. Almost every delivery was a boy, remember?"

"You *are* Fahim," my mother said, her voice breaking.

"Why did you leave us?" I asked plaintively, my own voice cracking with emotion.

Now it was my mother's turn to cry. She said she tried to send photos and letters, but the Communists must have intercepted them. She asked to speak to my brother and I put Hares on the phone. He started to speak and then the line went dead. We were out of coins. We went and got more coins and returned to stand at the back of the line. When we got back to the telephone we couldn't get through to America, but that was OK. Our family had reconnected.

We soon learned from the Embassy that two men—Dr. Anthony Marino and Mr. Robert Finley—had sponsored my mother and our siblings in America, along with Finley's Christian Aid Mission. *What wonderful people these must be*, I thought. *What would prompt such generosity to aliens from a faraway land?* One reason might have been that Dr. Marino turned out to be my uncle. Twenty years earlier, he'd become a Christian and immigrated to America, changing his name from Azmary to Anthony Marino. We hadn't heard from him in all that time, and were delighted that he remembered us and wanted to help shepherd our journey.

The good news was tempered by the counsel we later received at the Embassy. Even though the presence of our family members in Virginia was confirmed, U.S. State Department people told us it could still take years to get to America. Many people were in line ahead of us.

So 1983 turned into 1984, which turned into 1985.

To pass the time, I took classes that would ease my transition to American society, including English. I found that speaking English was easier than writing it. I looked forward to speaking English in America, but wondered if or when that would ever happen.

I also learned Urdu, the predominant language in Pakistan. As always, languages came easily to me. I have a strongly associative memory that allows me to picture words, phrases, and subjects mentally, connect them and more easily remember them.

I played a lot of soccer in Pakistan and tried to blend into society there, along with so many of my fellow Afghan refugees. I watched Indian movies and dreamed about acting possibilities in America. Hares and I visited bazaars where girls sometimes smiled or flirted with us. We liked that, and eventually we got to know some refugee girls. Invariably they'd talk of finding security and opportunity in the U.S. Everyone dreamed of America.

We survived financially with the help of occasional checks from my uncle who lived in California. The approach of the postman to Omar's apartment was always a suspenseful highlight to our boring routine. Though we seldom received any mail we did occasionally get a letter from our family in Virginia which excited us and kept us looking forward.

All was not rosy in Islamabad. It was there that I first felt the sting of ethnic hatred. One day, a disturbance in the city turned into a riot which took on anti-Afghan overtones. Pakistani police stopped busses to find Afghans to beat up. Hares and I rode a bus that day from G93 to a language school, Joma Bazher G94, in Islamabad. Policemen came onto the bus checking identifications. One of them wondered why we sat so close to the women and asked who we were. We apologized that we didn't have our paperwork with us. Another policeman asked if we were Afghan and I replied that we were from Kabul but were going to America. The policemen then pulled us off the bus and hit us with police sticks. I warded off the blows, which bruised my fingers and hands. Hares and I screamed until they finally backed off and let us back on the bus. I pondered what we'd done wrong to get beat up. And I finally figured out that our only crime was being Afghan.

Time passed slowly and week after week went by. I despaired that we'd ever get out of Pakistan.

Then we heard from our embassy contacts that the President of the United States wanted the American Immigration and Naturalization Service to speed up the immigration process for Afghan refugees fleeing Communist oppression. That rekindled hope in my heart.

Soon afterwards a letter for my father came to Omar's apartment. We learned we'd been officially accepted to come to America as refugees. Our sponsors were Mr. Robert Finley of the Christian Aid Mission and Fahima Fazli, my mother.

God bless Ronald Reagan, I thought. *God bless Ronald Reagan!*

Chapter 5: To America!

"America is the greatest, freest and most decent society in existence. It is an oasis of goodness in a desert of cynicism and barbarism. This country, once an experiment unique in the world, is now the last best hope for the world."
- Dinesh D'Souza, Indian-American Author

February of 1985 marked a significant transition period for the Soviet Union. In Moscow, Soviet leader Konstantin Chernenko lay dying. Mikhail Gorbachev maneuvered behind the scenes to position himself as the next General Secretary of the Communist Party of the USSR. Gorbachev's ascension would have significant consequences for Afghanistan.

In Pakistan, my father, brother, and I remained unaware of Moscow politics—or of other major developments on the international scene. What we did know was that we were finally at the end of our Pakistani odyssey as refugees

We'd soon be in America, a legendary place in the minds of Afghans. Stories abounded about the magnificence and wealth of the United States. Some said it was a sinful place, where women shamelessly tempted men. Others claimed that Americans were allies of the Zionists and enemies of Islam. Still others said that the U.S. was a place of tolerance and generosity. The stories only increased my curiosity about what I would find there.

We packed up to leave Islamabad on a cold, windy day. We said goodbye to Omar and Mamoud, who still waited for *their* good-news letter. Omar had laughed at us when we first met—when we told him about our plans to go to America. Now we were actually on our way. I was afraid he'd show resentment, but he generously wished us well.

As for the old country, it remained difficult to communicate with anyone in Kabul and we'd lost touch with friends and family there. I assumed my old classmates just disappeared into the fog of war. They'd never know what happened to me—that I ended up in America.

We took a taxi from G93 to Rawalpindi International Airport. At first I wasn't as thrilled as I thought I'd be. Change is exciting, but with it comes uncertainty. Did I really belong in America or in Asia? And I'd never even flown in a plane before. Soviet and Afghan aircraft regularly crashed in Afghanistan.

We arrived at the terminal and got out of the taxi. We had no luggage, nothing but the clothes we wore and our identity papers. My father seemed to know where to go and we followed him inside.

Eventually we saw the imposing airplane that would fly us out of Pakistan—alone and exposed, out on a runway. Airport personnel rolled some portable stairs out to allow people to board.

Then it hit me. This aircraft was our mighty chariot to a new world where we'd reunite with my mother, brother, and sisters. Suddenly, I couldn't wait to board the jet. An airline official stood by a terminal door checking names and taking tickets as people filed by. I gave him my ticket and ran toward the plane, my father and brother now forgotten. I shot past the other passengers, who walked along orderly, and I bounded up the stairs into the great airplane.

I must have been grinning like a fool, because the beautiful flight attendant warmly smiled back at me. With a knowing look she directed me down an aisle to my assigned seat.

I was 18, but I felt reborn.

We flew from Rawalpindi Airport to Istanbul, Turkey. I liked everything about air travel—the new sounds, the flight attendants who cared about my comfort, the window views, the movie, and even the food.

From Istanbul we flew to London, where we boarded a TWA flight to New York. I fell into a fitful half-sleep over the Atlantic—we'd been traveling for over 20 hours—but I woke up as we descended toward JFK Airport. I didn't have a window seat but I still strained to get glimpses of my new country. My first image of America was a jigsaw of towering buildings. Unable to see the runway, I feared our jet would fly into one of the skyscrapers and I braced for impact. I shouted, "Whoa!" when we touched down hard and other passengers laughed at me. I didn't care.

We taxied to a gate and eventually we all filed into the terminal. I couldn't read anything and the sights and sounds overloaded my senses. Public address announcements I couldn't understand. People yelling things in strange languages. Signs I couldn't read. Then I saw a guy holding a sign that read, "Fazli." I nudged my father and pointed. Robert Finley's Christian Aid Mission had sent this man to New York to meet us and escort us to Virginia.

My father strode over to the sign-holder, smiled, and shook his hand.

"Hello," he said in English. "I am Jamil Fazli." That was the extent of my father's knowledge of English.

"Welcome to America!" exclaimed the escort, who then looked at my brother and me. "And this must be Fahim and Hares."

He shook our hands as well. "How much luggage do you have?" he asked.

My father shrugged. "Luggage?"

The airport terminal was like a Tower of Babel. I tried to remember my English lessons. What did "luggage" mean?

The escort sensed our confusion and did a pantomime. He pretended to carry a suitcase. Then he put it on an imaginary bed, and clicked the latches, opened the top, and pulled out an imaginary shirt—which he simulated putting on.

We understood and laughed. "Ah, baksaw!" said my father.

I spoke up. "No baksaw," I explained. "We have no luggage. Just papers."

"That makes it easy," said the escort. "Let's get you to the hotel."

We went to a waiting van and drove to a big hotel. Standing outside the lobby, I couldn't believe how many yellow taxis whipped around New York City. Well-dressed people were everywhere—black, white, brown and yellow.

My head spun. I bent backward looking up at the towering buildings. People yelled in strange languages. Horns honked. Music played. Vehicles sped around. People dressed in outrageous clothes that fit them like costumes. Could I ever make it in this awesome, alien land? My earlier excitement turned to shock. So much to learn! I tensed up. I felt stupid. I couldn't read anything and I couldn't understand much of what I heard. Traveling from Afghanistan to Pakistan had not required a huge cultural adjustment. But this was something else. This was another planet.

We spent one night at that luxurious hotel. The scale and scope of the place astonished me. When the three of us went for a short walk, cars kept blowing their horns at us. We didn't understand about jay-walking or traffic lights. One cab driver rolled his window down and called us idiots—in Urdu!

"Akmacks!" he yelled. For a moment I thought I was back in Islamabad. What was a Pakistani taxi driver doing in New York City? That there were Urdu-speaking cabbies made me a bit more comfortable to be in the U.S. But what a shame it would be to get so far, to finally arrive in America, and then get killed by a Pakistani driver just before seeing my mother again.

Inside the hotel were stairs that moved. I rode them up and down a few times, and tried to figure out how they worked. What a magical place this was, this America.

What really got my attention were the pretty girls and gorgeous women everywhere—with *legs*. I'd never seen a woman's legs before. As far as I knew, women had no calves or thighs in Afghanistan or Pakistan. After seeing so many female legs in plain sight I said to Hares, "I think I will like it here."

The music playing in the hotel lobby intrigued me. A song's lyrics mentioned blues melting away and making it in old New York. Later, I learned the singer was Frank Sinatra. I didn't know it at the time, but the message fit our Fazli situation so well. That song became part of the sound track of my American journey. Hearing it always made me think of Old Blue Eyes and my first day in America.

Our opulent hotel room had thick carpets and velvet-like curtains framing a fantastic view of New York City. Multi-colored neon signs threw blazing light on the giant buildings, each capped with its own blinking red lights. The moving lights of airplanes and helicopters pierced the black sky, as did roaming searchlights. I stood transfixed by the sight which was so different from the dim, yellow gloom of Kabul.

I also saw my first microwave oven in that room. We put food in it and seconds later it came out miraculously hot. We slept in high beds with clean sheets and found that the television featured more channels than we could count. Even though we couldn't understand any dialogue, we channel surfed for hours. The first television show I watched was a *Three's Company* rerun with John Ritter. Even though I didn't understand the words, I could tell the Ritter character struggled with women. Right away I was hooked. Sit-com programming never appeared on Afghan or Pakistani television. Afghan women would have loved a program showing an Afghan man being tormented by his two wives!

The next day we flew to Washington-Dulles Airport. Once in the terminal, I recognized Suhail in the waiting crowd right away. He looked so American in his Nike sneakers, jeans, and leather jacket. He stood next to Robert Finley, our benefactor. As we hugged and cried, we kept interrupting each other, anxious to tell our stories.

"I can't believe you're taller than me!" Suhail said in Dari. Remembering his manners, he finally turned and introduced us to Mr. Finley. We thanked him profusely in our broken English. Suhail had flown to the east coast from California for our reunion. Out west he apprenticed as an electrician for an uncle—a successful Pakistani builder.

We got in a van to travel to Charlottesville. My father sat in front with Mr. Finley, who drove. Classical music played softly on the radio. We three brothers sat in back, Hares in the middle. I was very happy, but exhausted—and I still hadn't seen my mother or sisters yet.

Although the traffic was heavy on the three-lane interstate, the vehicles moved right along. Big cars, small cars, buses, and trucks of all sizes. I wondered what the tractor trailers carried and marveled at all the female drivers.

We peppered Suhail with questions.

"Where is the snow?" Hares asked.

"It hardly ever snows here," said Suhail. "And it gets so hot in the summer you won't believe it."

"Omar from G93 said to go to a drive-in restaurant if we ever made it to America," I said. "What is that?"

"OK," replied Suhail. "Just watch."

He spoke to Mr. Finley in English and we took an exit off of I-95 to stop at a McDonald's drive-through. Suhail sat next to the left window behind Mr. Finley, the driver. The two of them took turns speaking into an intercom.

"We're ordering for you," he explained.

We pulled ahead and Mr. Finley gave money to a young woman at a window who gave us three bags of food, mostly chicken sandwiches and French fries, as well as sodas and chocolate shakes. It was delicious.

We were soon back on I-95, enjoying our American food. This was Suhail's moment, and he made the most of it, holding court and lecturing us on life in America. You need to do this. But never do that. I drank it all in.

Eventually the interstate highway took us to some secondary routes. Farms were everywhere. Leafless trees flanked the roads but Suhail told us we were seeing Virginia during a barren time. Virginia was prettier during spring, summer and fall.

Our sponsor drove us directly to my mother's apartment—the second floor of a well-kept residential building. I tried to control my excitement and apprehension. Mr. Finley knocked and then opened the door to the apartment. I went in first and saw my mother standing there. I just went to her and naturally hugged her. Hares did likewise. Then we stepped back as she touched our faces.

"Are you really Fahim? Are you really Hares?" she said in Dari. Then she hugged my father. I'd envisioned our reunion over and over again and always expected that my mother would have a lot to say. However, she seemed stunned and at a loss for words.

My sisters were relatively emotionless, which also surprised me. I expected hugs, kisses, and tears from them as well. Instead, they were standoffish. Almara didn't say anything. Mina just said, "Hey! What's up?"

I'm sure they wondered how our presence would change their world.

After a couple of days, the cultural differences between the two Fazli family factions really showed. Mina and Almara knew little of our Dari language, as they spoke English exclusively. My father, Hares, and I spoke

Fahim and his mother reunited

very little English. The English-speaking Virginia Fazlis understood
American television shows. We were at a complete loss. The girls wore
dresses that showed their legs, when they weren't wearing pants. I know
my father wasn't comfortable with that, but he knew better than to
impose Afghan standards on Americanized girls. He could tell Mina and
Almara were no longer docile and submissive. The Afghan Fazlis asked a
lot of questions in Dari and Suhail showed off his knowledge of American
culture with an answer for everything. I wanted to talk about our escape
from Afghanistan and our experiences in Pakistan, but the American
Fazlis didn't seem interested, which hurt my feelings. We all rode an emotional roller coaster, but still we knew things were much better in Virginia
than in Afghanistan. No one sought to kill us in Charlottesville.

I never understood why our family was so fractured and I never
dared to confront my parents as to why things happened as they did. Still,
the ordeal of our long separation haunted me.

We quickly adjusted to our apartment, which was bigger than most houses in Afghanistan. My mom kept her job as a nurse's assistant while my

father got a feel for life in America. Suhail returned to California. My brother and I shared a room; the girls had one of their own.

Soon, Hares enrolled in a local school, just like his sisters. I wanted to go back to high school but being too old I signed up for some adult education classes.

Two weeks after arriving in Virginia, we attended an event at Mr. Finley's church and thanked everyone there for their support. Reporters interviewed us—a family separated and finally reunited after five years. The next morning, our happy story ran in Charlottesville's newspapers.

The *Daily Progress* ran a front-page photo with the story sharing space above the fold with a feature on American Secretary of State George Schulz meeting with Nicaraguan leader Daniel Ortega. Our family's photo was above a front page action shot from a Duke/North Carolina basketball game. Only later did I realize the profound significance of that.

I liked my first taste of publicity—American style.

Not many Afghans lived in Virginia—a lonely place for my father, Hares, and me. My "American" family spoke English with their friends and participated in school and community activities. I needed to try harder to meet people and assimilate better into American society. I helped where I could on Mr. Finley's farm, talking to farmhands, taking care of animals, and mowing the grass. I loved the riding lawn mower—a contraption unimaginable in Afghanistan.

Sadly, the new, positive energy between my parents dissolved. My father didn't work at assimilating. He wanted to move to California to be closer to his brother and to Suhail. My mother and sisters naturally wanted to stay in Virginia. Arguing ensued. As usual, my father won. So less than two months after arriving in Charlottesville, we packed up and flew to Los Angeles. As our plane descended, I looked out the window to my right and noticed the famous "Hollywood" sign in the hills to the east. Secretly, I was glad my father had won the argument. Hollywood was a Mecca for aspiring actors, and I still dreamed of acting.

My uncle met us at the airport and took us to his nice house with great views in Hacienda Heights. He clearly enjoyed America, speaking

English confidently while driving his big American car and wearing expensive American clothes. I wanted to be like him.

We rented a big house, and spent the next few weeks collecting our green cards, social security cards, and identification cards while learning our way around the city. Immigration officials gave us special attention and extra support due to our war refugee status. The U.S. government even guaranteed us refugee salaries—special stipends—for 16 more months. In turn, we needed to improve our English and learn American culture.

I loved and appreciated my new homeland and it troubled me that my some family members took so much for granted. They were annoyed when the government checks were late, while I wondered what we'd done to earn them.

Hares, Almara, and Mina re-enrolled in American schools. I couldn't go to school because I was then 19. I needed to learn English, so I registered at an adult school. I'd only gone through nine grades in Afghanistan and I'd missed a lot of school time anyway with all my truancy. I worried about what I'd do with my life. My father only had those 16 months to improve his English and get a job. I thought I'd need to support the family. Not surprisingly, my mom quickly found a job as a nurse's aide in an old folks' home. Suhail stayed busy with his electrician work.

My first American job was pumping gas at a service station. I thought working there would help me learn English, but it turned out I learned Spanish first. There seemed to be more Spanish speakers in California than English speakers. I found Spanish easier to learn, and it came naturally to me.

A year passed in California and with my improving English I wanted more rewarding work. Being a good listener with a strong memory served me well in my first American jobs. I connected well with customers at the service station and then cooked and waited on tables at restaurants—but I knew I could do even better. I enjoyed bantering with people, all the while improving my communication skills.

I thought about what excited me. I remembered my grandfather,

Lieutenant Colonel Abdul Aziz Popalzoy—a real soldier. I wanted to be like him, to hone my warrior instincts and impulses. As he'd named me, I sought to honor him by joining the American Armed Forces. So I motored over to Hacienda Heights to find offices representing the U.S. Armed Forces to get military information. I soon drove by a United States Marine Corps recruiting station. My thoughts went back to those Marines I saw at the Islamabad Embassy in Pakistan and I recalled how much they'd impressed me. I wanted to be a Marine.

The recruiters welcomed me into their office. They gave me a four-page test with boxes to check—yes or no. I guessed on all four sheets because the questions were too hard for me to understand. I turned the exam in to the recruiters and they told me I'd failed. They gave me a book to study and said to come back once I learned more English. I nodded and left.

My first failure in America stung. What next?

Cooking was easy for me because I'd cooked so much for my family as a youngster. I found a job as a chef at a fancy restaurant in Clairmont, California—a college town. Everyone spoke Spanish in the kitchen. I fit right in at first, handling ten orders at a time. I got so good that the owner of the restaurant laid off two other cooks.

Then the other chefs teamed up against me. The laid-off cooks were their relatives. Of course the owner of the restaurant loved me because I saved him a lot of money. However, he came to me and explained his dilemma.

"Fahim, they are one team and one family," he said. "What do you want me to do?"

"I guess I need to move on," I replied. "You've been good to me and I don't want your business to suffer."

My second big setback in the U.S. stung as badly as the first.

I didn't give up, though. I wanted to keep learning about America, and someday find a niche in my new country. I watched a lot of television news and recorded anything involving Afghanistan or the Soviet Union on my VCR. One night, a story broke that a Stinger anti-aircraft weapon took out a Soviet plane. I was psyched. The Freedom Fighters had new hope and momentum. I imagined the Mujahedeen finally striking back at those monstrous air ships that previously rained fire down upon them. It was like a bully finally getting a taste of his own medicine: very satisfying. I'll never forget that moment, which I later shared with Charlie Wilson—who appreciated and understood my sentiments.

My father continued abusing my mother. During an automobile trip to San Francisco to see some Afghan friends, he got into an argument with her in front of me and my brothers and sisters. I stood up to him and told him that my mother deserved to live somewhere else where she wouldn't be abused.

"If she leaves, I'll make sure you all pay," my father yelled.

"It will be OK, Fahim," my mother said. "Please don't worry."

When we got to San Francisco I took my mother aside and said we'd support her if she wanted to leave my father.

"I can't leave your father," my mother explained. "Divorce is wrong. But I am afraid Jamil will kill me someday."

I just hugged her. I didn't know what else to do.

I continued to split time between my father's and my uncle's. After my 20th birthday I wanted to follow the American way and leave our dysfunctional family nest. So I moved to Orange County.

But—*Pero*—my Spanish was not going to cut it in Orange County in 1986.

People asked me about my weird accent. I needed to speak better English.

It seemed like everyone in beautiful Orange County wanted to be an actor, a singer, or a model. The beach drew beautiful people: the rich, thin, tan, athletic and carefree. People swam, sun-bathed, water-skied, and played volleyball. I wanted to fit in to this new wonderland. Of course, I also needed to succeed financially so I could help my family.

I got a construction job. The money poured in. Since the age of 13 I'd always made money. I used it to help my family, friends, and even strangers. I never asked for money from anyone. I liked the feeling of independence.

"Fahim, I like the way you carry yourself," my mother once told me. "It's hard to tell if you have money or not. When your brothers and sisters don't have money, they have sour looks on their faces. You always look happy."

"Good things happen if you believe in the future," I replied.

While not very religious, I believed in one God and always tried to understand that God better. I also believed in free-will—the power of individuals to make choices in their lives. It shouldn't matter where anyone came from or what religion they followed, because we all descended from Adam and Eve. Didn't Christians, Jews and Muslims all believe in Abraham? I saw how tolerant people were in America, as compared to Afghanistan or Pakistan. If your religious beliefs changed or evolved here no one killed you.

While seeking to understand God better, I also sought to understand myself better. What was I meant to do? The exciting and dangerous escape from Afghanistan, the Pakistani purgatory, the reuniting of our family in Virginia, and our relocation to California must be part of some consequential plan I didn't understand yet.

Down in Orange County, my friend Mark gave me advice about fun places to go, girls, and the best jobs to help pay for them. Although I was doing well in construction, the real money in Southern California came from the entertainment industry. With my outgoing personality and unique Afghan looks, Mark thought acting would be a natural fit for me, which reinforced my own ambitions. People said I looked like Andy Garcia. I liked that comment, especially when girls said it to me— although I didn't know who Andy Garcia was. I finally saw him in the movie *The Godfather.* I did look like Andy Garcia! Mark had a friend from Venice Beach who could help me get into Hollywood. I jumped at the opportunity.

He pointed me to an agency in Hollywood where I signed up for acting classes. I also registered with other agencies as an extra, which meant low-paying non-speaking parts—if I could get them. One of these agencies asked me for $1,500 for a beginning actor package, to include head-shots and more acting classes. So I got my first American credit card, charged the $1,500 to it, and began my acting studies.

Later, I drove my parents to Hollywood. They each reacted different-ly. My father wasn't happy that I wanted to be an actor. He considered entertainers very low class—a typical Afghan attitude. I politely ignored him, though I still respected his values. Afghans considered acting to be frivolous, especially when there was more important work to be done—like farming, goat-herding, or fighting! I knew that I'd be good at acting, and fortunately my mother supported my dream. The sights and sounds of Tinsel Town excited her.

Once a week, I traveled from Orange County to the L.A. acting class. People there asked me where I came from and about my weird accent. Eventually the acting school director gave me a script to read in front of all the other students. Sadly, I just couldn't read it because of my poor English, which really embarrassed me.

I didn't give up, though. I finished the program. For my $1,500 I received a certificate and 50 copies of my 8-by-10 head shot. The school took my phone number, supposedly to share with agencies and contact people. Would anyone ever call me? I figured I'd wasted my money but blamed myself for not knowing enough English.

I continued working—at a department store, at a jewelry store, at a shoe store, and at a finance company. While at these jobs, I waited for that first phone call from Hollywood about an acting opportunity.

Months passed. No call came.

I moved into a house in Orange County with three Afghan brothers: Abdullah, Massoud, and Mustapha. They ran a very successful business—M & M Construction. I made a lot more money working for them. Their Americanized names were Alex, Max, and Marco, respectively. Alex was outgoing, funny, and loved to read. The youngest brother, he was a bit spoiled but was kind and loveable. Max was a businessman but was also kind and generous to people in need. The oldest brother, he was the Man of the House. The middle brother, Marco was quieter—very private. He pushed for people to eat healthy foods, which put him ahead of his time. They learned of my acting aspirations because in that pre-cell phone era I'd come home every day and ask if Hollywood had called.

The answer was always, "No. Sorry."

Though months passed without a call from Hollywood, I kept visualizing my future success as a great actor. Until that dream came true, I'd be a great construction worker, cook, or salesman.

Despite the weird accent.

Fahim Fazli outside the Reagan White House - 1985

Chapter 6: Love and Marriage(s)

"As a general thing, people marry most happily with their own kind. The trouble lies in the fact that people usually marry at an age when they do not really know what their own kind is."
– William Robertson Davies, Canadian author and critic

In Afghanistan, elders say, "Get married before you get too old." On May 30, 1995, I turned 29—definitely "old" to be an unmarried Afghan. However, wedding bells weren't ringing for me.

I'd had plenty of dates during the eight years I lived in Orange County. Life was good with the Three Amigos—Alex, Max, and Marco. I made decent money and could afford to have fun with pretty girls. The fun never led to any long-term commitments, however. This troubled my mother, who kept asking, "Are you ever going to get married?"

"Yes, Mother," I'd reply. "I'll marry when the time is right."

"Both your brothers are married with children. What's wrong with you?"

"Nothing's wrong with me, Mother. I just want to make sure you have the best daughter-in-law ever."

My father also wondered why I remained single. Suhail and Hares had both assimilated enough to take wives and start American family lives.

Because my parents really wanted *all* their children married, in 1995 they persuaded an Afghan woman in northern California to agree to a wedding between her daughter and me, without my knowledge or consent. In other words, they arranged my marriage.

Marrying the woman I'll call Nargus meant leaving my roommates of eight years—the Three Amigos—as well as my job in Orange County. My hopes for a Hollywood career went on permanent hold. I moved closer to Nargus's family near San Francisco, five hours away from my friends and family.

Nargus impressed me the first time I saw her—a statuesque, 5-foot-10, 23-year-old, with long, reddish hair and a cute, crooked smile. A dental hygienist, Nargus was articulate and bright. Unfortunately, the more we talked, the more I realized that we weren't meant for each other. She allowed herself to be pushed around too easily, especially by her mother. I wanted to be challenged by a lively, clever partner. I was concerned that the timid Nargus and I had little in common, besides the fact that we'd both been beaten by our fathers. I asked her about that one evening in San Francisco, as we walked around Fisherman's Wharf.

"Do you hate your father?" I asked.

"I stopped being upset with him after we kicked him out of the house and got a restraining order," Nargus said. "He seemed more human and vulnerable after that. I wanted to love him but I still feared him, probably because he hit me so often when I was young."

"That sounds like my father," I said. "When I was small, he'd pin me down, sit on me, and whack me while he smoked a cigarette."

"I hope he wasn't punishing you for smoking," Nargus said, which made me laugh.

"No," I replied. "It was usually for being disrespectful."

"Are you much like your father?" Nargus asked.

I stopped and looked at her. She was framed by San Francisco Bay and the distant hills of Tiburon. Over her shoulder was the infamous Alcatraz Prison Island. Both us had been prisoners of violence during much of our lives. I understood what prompted the question. She wondered if *I* would someday beat *her*, as some Afghan men beat their women. I took her hand.

"Look at me Nargus," I said. "Listen carefully. I have plenty of faults and will make plenty of mistakes. But I will *never* lay a hand on you. Contrary to what some people may think, most Afghan men are not abusers."

My fiancée silently stared back at me and then squeezed my hand.

Arranged marriages were an Afghan tradition, and I decided to remain true to my culture—but I would do it *my* way. I would not be like my father was to my mother. I'd be respectful to my spouse. Someone as non-assertive as Nargus could never stand up for herself. My generous, protective side felt obliged to advocate for this nice young woman being forced into a marriage she hadn't asked for.

The night before the wedding, a huge fight broke out between Nargus's mother and sister and me. For the first time, I became painfully aware of the elaborate wedding arrangements, special seating accommodations, expensive food and great entertainment that had been in the works for weeks without my input. The guest list was formidable: it included people neither Nargus nor I knew. The band cost a fortune. I was a pawn in a family competition to out-do all previous family wedding celebrations.

"You're part of our family now," Nargus' sister told me. "You need to cooperate and support our wishes."

I needed to assert myself with these women, but I'd sworn never to be tyrannical toward females, like some Afghan men were—including my father. For the moment, I remained silent.

Nargus' mother was a very strong-willed woman. Unlike my mother, she'd actually kicked out her abusive husband. Nargus' sister inherited her mother's fiery spirit and bossy ways. Nargus was used to acquiescing to these strong personalities, as was her sister's husband.

My future brother-in-law was sympathetic. "Look at me," he said. "I've been suffering with these women for ten years. But Nargus' mother knows what she wants. When you marry a daughter you also marry the whole family. You just need to go along."

I didn't *want* to marry her whole family, and finally I decided to cancel everything before it was too late. I called my family and some of the guests to tell them the wedding was off. My parents said they'd disown me if I backed out—even though I'd invested tens of thousands of dollars on the pending wedding. The expenses meant new debt for me. "This wedding was agreed upon long ago and everyone is planning on it happening," my father said to me, impatiently. "Our family honor is at stake. You need to provide Nargus' family with whatever they need."

"If this wedding happens then it needs to be my wedding, not yours—and not Nargus's family's either," I replied. "And if Nargus becomes my wife, then I want her to be my partner, not my slave."

My father rolled his eyes and said, "Good luck with *that*." He was still old school.

Then I got on the telephone to Nargus. "We know what our families

want," I said. "Everyone wants the marriage to happen. But I need to
know how you feel. What do you want?"

"I just don't want any trouble, Fahim," she replied.

"You're telling me what you don't want," I responded. "I asked you
what you wanted."

"Why can't we continue with our plans?" she said.

Nargus' attitude didn't surprise me. Bullied by her father and then
dominated by her mother, she did whatever minimized conflict or confrontation. That meant she wanted the wedding to happen. But I needed
to know more.

"Do you want to proceed because you're afraid of your mother, or
because you care about *me*?" I asked.

"I care about you," she said, after an uncomfortably long pause.

"What I know for sure is that I don't want to be like my father or your
father," I said. "If we get married I want to be a partner. I want a wife, not
a servant."

"I understand," she said. "And I agree with you. Of course."

The next day we went ahead with the marriage ceremony at an
Afghan Center in San Francisco. After a mullah pronounced us married,
we staged a three-day celebration. The celebration was an opportunity for
families to bond. I was pleased to see Fazlis interacting with Nargus' family, and I laughed when I saw my siblings dancing with people from her
side. I loved watching my mother laugh and dance and seeing my father
smile.

Our marriage was not legally binding in America. We'd never registered with the state nor sought a marriage license. That didn't prevent us
from enjoying our honeymoon in Hawaii. We flew to Honolulu, frolicked
on the beach at Waikiki, and sailed to Maui to fish and scuba dive. But
when I tried to talk about our future, Nargus always wanted to confer
with her sister and mother, which really annoyed me.

When we returned to California, we moved into our own place in
Fremont. My in-laws still found ways to drive me crazy. They wanted to
be a party to everything we did. They made plans for us without ever
checking with me. I once tried to surprise Nargus with dinner reserva-
tions at a popular San Francisco restaurant, but when I told her the good
news she said we couldn't go because her mother had already planned on

hosting us for a meal at her house. That type of thing just kept happening. I couldn't seem to get any traction on an intimate independence and it made me feel resentful and weak.

"Nargus, I married *you*," I finally told her one day. "I didn't marry your mother. I didn't marry your sister. Why are they controlling our lives so much?"

My problems with her family put Nargus in an uncomfortable position. But we had to talk about it sooner or later. She tensed up but said nothing.

"Well?" I pressed.

"I love my mother," she finally said. "I love my sister. They are part of me."

I lost patience. "Will I ever be part of you?"

"You know I want that," she replied. "Of course."

We had to get away from Nargus' family if our relationship was going to have a chance.

After a month in Fremont, I talked Nargus into moving to Utah with me. We hitched a U-Haul trailer behind my Nissan 300 ZX and drove east to the Beehive State. We found an apartment in Salt Lake City and I got a job at a pizza place owned by an older Afghan couple. They paid me well to cook, clean, and deliver pizza. We tried to blend in with the community by socializing with the restaurant owners' circle of friends. We skied, hiked, and got to know our neighbors.

Not only did I assume the new role of husband in Utah, but I also became an American citizen, finally passing the citizenship test. I'd first tried to become a citizen in 1991, after the required five years of residence, but I'd failed the test. So I studied up and learned about American history and government and gained an appreciation of our American heritage. Given my tumultuous journey from Kabul to Salt Lake City, I was especially proud to finally call myself an American.

I'd chosen Utah as our new home in large part because it looked a lot like Afghanistan. I thought it might be good karma. Unfortunately, Nargus remained homesick for her family in San Francisco. It didn't help that her mother called continuously to ask her to come back. These phone calls created more and more tension. Nargus denied spending much time on the phone, but when the bills came, I saw the hours she'd logged to San Francisco.

One day, Nargus' brother-in-law called me at work. He'd driven to Salt Lake City with Nargus' sister and mother to take my wife back to California.

"Nargus isn't happy here," he told me. "She wants to be in San Francisco with us."

"Can you please wait for me to get out of work so we can talk?" I asked.

"Then you better hurry," he responded.

It was a Saturday night—the busiest time of the week at the restaurant, and I couldn't just walk out. Two hours passed before I could finally rush home. By the time I got to the apartment they were gone. All her stuff—and some of mine—was gone as well. Part of me was relieved that she'd left, but the precipitous way it happened hurt my heart. I finally accepted the reality that she didn't want to be with me in Utah. This was America, not Afghanistan, and in the U.S. women mostly did what they wanted. I couldn't compete with her family's strong pull on her.

I called San Francisco the next day, and Nargus' mother answered the phone. I asked if I could speak with my wife.

"Nargus is too emotional and too embarrassed to talk on the phone right now," she said. "It would be best if you were here in person."

"I can't just drive over right now," I explained.

My mother-in-law was never at a loss for words. "If you care about Nargus you'll come right back to California."

San Francisco was the last place I wanted to be. "I can't do that right now."

"OK. Call back when you feel ready to commit to Nargus *and* her family. Goodbye!"

"Wait!" I said, but only heard a click and then a dial tone—the two sounds that marked the end of my relationship with Nargus and her family. I never saw them again.

Divorce is considered shameful and inexcusable in Afghanistan. Still, Nargus and I needed to go our separate ways. We didn't require a legal divorce because we'd never legally married. An Afghan elder in San Francisco signed some paperwork nullifying our ceremony. I now had to reorganize my life, pay my off my debt, and chart a future course. I knew

I wasn't destined to remain in Utah. I dealt with my increasing loneliness by dreaming of that elusive acting career.

Fortunately, I could still count on my roommates. The Three Amigos invited me back to our old place in Orange County. Because they'd had their own experiences with difficult females, they were sympathetic.

"I never thought my marriage would end like this," I embarrassedly told my old roommates.

"God must love crazy women because he created so many of them," said Max, the most philosophical of the trio. I moved back in to Alex's apartment and returned to my old job working for Max's construction company.

Utah may have looked like Afghanistan, but Orange County felt like home.

Reuniting with the Three Amigos brought back a sense of normalcy—for a while—though the continuing negative reaction to my short-lived marriage from my family and the lack of understanding in the California Afghan community haunted me. My parents especially frustrated me.

"No one is going to marry you now," my mother exclaimed more than once. "You have a bad name with Afghans." I was sorry to disappoint them, but I still believed that somewhere the right woman waited for me.

I had no desire in those days to return to the land of my youth. In America, I didn't have to worry about Communist secret police trying to trap me. However, I'd been back from Utah for less than a month when my friend Wali called and suggested that I travel with him back to Pakistan. Wali owned a successful carpet business in Orange County, but his wife was still in Pakistan. "Fahim, I'm going back to get my bride and bring her here to America," Wali told me. "And there are many beautiful Afghan refugee girls who'd also love to get away from Pakistan, the way you did. My cousin Shima is one. You should meet her!"

I reacted impulsively. "Why not? I need a change of scenery."

"Great," said Wali. "Pakistan, here we come. I'll tell Shima about you."

I had second thoughts the next day. What was I getting into? I hadn't spoken to Shima in advance. I had only Wali's word to go by, along with an old photo of Shima. However, I also had third thoughts. I wanted to believe in my concept of marriage, as opposed to the arranged weddings of our parents' tradition. But maybe I was supposed to connect with a wonderful person from the old culture, someone—like me—who was meant to escape from Central Asia.

Wali and I first traveled to London to visit some of his relatives. It was liberating to get away from my family and for a few days I relaxed and socialized with the sizeable Afghan community there and enjoyed some sight-seeing. From London we flew to Pakistan.

When we landed in Islamabad, my mind flashed back 12 years. Omar and Mamoud. Our crowded room in G93. Waiting for news from America. Being beaten by Pakistani police. Visiting the embassy. What was I doing back in this forlorn country?

I braced for a four-hour drive to Peshawar, where Wali's wife lived with her extended family, but Wali said we were in luck. He got us on a flight to that city on a beat-up cargo plane so we wouldn't have to travel overland in a taxi or rented car.

The plane was indeed old—an ancient Russian transport full of flour sacks and seed boxes. As I boarded the aircraft, my back tightened up and my stomach started fluttering. I could feel the sweat on the palms of my hands. A bouncy flight marked by strong turbulence made me fire off all sorts of prayers in the hope that we'd survive the buffeting. My pleas to God worked and we landed safely.

Wali's cousin met us at the airport and drove us to their house. Peshawar hadn't changed. It was still hot and smoky. Loud music blared from everywhere. The traffic was even more chaotic than I remembered, with horns constantly honking away.

When we finally arrived at Wali's in-laws, Wali's wife was the first person to greet us. She stood in the doorway flashing a big smile before giving Wali a sustained hug. Her father followed her out of the house and shook our hands. After introducing me to other family members, he took me to a guest room where I finally unpacked and crawled into a bed. I couldn't sleep, despite my exhaustion. The continued blowback from my failed marriage, the two days of international travel, and the uncertainty of this Peshawar adventure left me too keyed up to sleep.

I'd agreed to go to Pakistan to meet Shima—sight unseen. I was taking a chance, but why not? I was almost 30 years old and I felt incomplete. I had to take action to create possibilities for myself.

The next day, Wali took me to meet Shima at her uncle's. A sizeable group had gathered in the living room for the occasion. I looked around expectantly but couldn't tell which woman was Shima.

"Don't you recognize your future wife?" an older woman said to me in Dari. It was Shima's mother, who obviously recognized me. A younger woman stepped forward from behind the older woman.

"Fahim, please meet Shima."

Shima didn't look like her photo. Tall, thin, and dark haired, she wore lots of make-up. I didn't fall in love at first sight. *Definitely not my cup of tea*, I thought. She was nervous, shy, plain, and lacked sparkle. We went up on the roof and tried to talk. I learned that she was 25—relatively old to be an unmarried Afghan woman.

"How could a beautiful Afghan woman like you be 25 years old and still unmarried?" I asked her, trying to be generous.

She smiled sweetly. "It's been difficult for Afghan refugees," she said.

"You mean there haven't been any good looking guys with money asking your father if they could marry you so you could live in their new tent with them?" I said.

Shima laughed. "Yes, I've always dreamed of living in a nice tent," she said playfully. "With many rooms and many windows."

Now I laughed. I think she liked me. It was a warm night. Bright stars shined directly above us, while other stars closer to the horizon were obscured by the lights and haze of Peshawar. I surprised myself by envisioning Shima as Mrs. Fahim Fazli.

"You'll like California," I said. "It's a good place to be a woman."

"I can't wait to see it," Shima responded.

We returned to the house, and everyone turned to stare. I imagined what they were thinking. *The dashing and debonair bachelor from America actually made shy Shima laugh.*

"God bless Wali," Shima's uncle said. "He found a husband for poor Shima."

The next morning after breakfast, I sat in the living room making small talk with Shima's parents and other relatives. A Call to Prayer sounded from a nearby minaret. All eyes went to me, questioningly. I did what I thought any prospective bridegroom would do in that situation. I faced to the west and dropped to my knees.

Shockingly, they laughed at me. No one else knelt. I burned with humiliation and quickly stood up and excused myself. I went outside and stood in front of the house, utterly embarrassed.

Moments later Wali came outside.

"What was that all about?" I asked.

"Shima's family is Communist," Wali explained. "They don't do religion."

"Shit!" I exclaimed. I hated Communists! Suddenly, a wedding seemed like the wrong idea. I decided to return to the U.S. as soon as possible, as I didn't need another shaky marriage—especially into a Communist family! I walked to a transit center to check on bus schedules back to Islamabad, as well as airplane flight times. Since corruption complicates international travel in Central Asia, I paid a bribe to an official to speed things up.

While waiting for travel approvals, I decided to seek out some of my own relatives stuck in Peshawar as refugees—starting with my Aunt Rona. Ten minutes into the cab ride to her neighborhood, Pakistani police stopped the taxi.

"Damn it," said the taxi driver. "I hope you have your papers."

One cop stayed in the police car while another came to the cab driver's window and examined the cabby's documents. The policeman looked at the paperwork for a long time and wordlessly handed everything back to the driver. He leaned down and peered into the back seat where I sat.

"You," he said. "What's your business here?"

I'm sure he was curious about my western clothes. I tried to respond in Urdo. "I'm from America," I explained. "I'm visiting friends and family. We're on my way to my aunt's house."

"Get out of the car," the policeman growled. "I need to see your passport."

I tensed up and hesitated. The policeman glowered at me. He was overweight in an ill-fitting uniform with a mustache that needed trimming. The armpits on his uniform shirt were drenched in sweat.

"Move!" he yelled. Then he called to his partner who got out of the police car and stood ready, night-stick in hand.

I handed my passport to the policeman, who stared at it for a long time.

"This is fake," he said.

I struggled to find the right words in Urdo to explain my situation.

"The consulate can confirm things, I'm sure."

"Get in the police car," he said.

Panicking, I gave some money to the cab driver and implored him to follow us to the police station, which he did. There the cops escorted me inside and sat me down while they conferred with their superiors. The taxi driver followed me in and took a chair beside me in the booking area.

"You can't let them put you in jail," he whispered.

"I know," I said. "I know." Pakistani jails are horrible, dangerous, dirty places.

"Give them money," the cabbie said, as the arresting policeman came to us with a superior officer.

I spoke to the higher ranking policeman in English instead of Urdo.

"I'm Fahim Fazli, an American citizen," I said. "The consulate can vouch for me. I'm sorry about the confusion." I held out two American hundred dollar bills. The senior officer took them.

"Make sure you keep your paperwork in order," he admonished. "Now go where you need to go."

The cabbie and I returned outside to his vehicle. "You should have spoken English at first," said the driver. "It's harder to shake someone down if they can't speak the language well."

"Got it," I said. "Now just bring me back where we started. I'll get to my aunt's another time."

Lesson learned. Back to Wali's in-laws we went.

The next day I sat in on a family discussion there concerning recent political developments in the region. The Afghan refugee enclaves in Pakistan were increasingly dangerous due to a fanatical new group called the *Taliban*—a name which translates to *students*. These Muslim fundamentalists wanted to rule Afghanistan using a corrupted and intolerant version of Islam. They sought to ban music and movies, and ruthlessly imposed their dogma. Some of Wali's relatives spoke of their concerns, but a neighbor named Mohammed made the case for the Taliban way. Tall, slim, and in his mid-twenties, he wore a black turban. His chin hidden by a long black beard, Mohammed stood against a wall, confidently—no, arrogantly—lecturing about the future.

"The Taliban will purify Afghanistan," said Mohammed. "Sharia Law must be imposed to eliminate corruption and thwart the infidels. Women will finally follow the true way of the Holy Quran. We'll create a model for the world. And Pakistan will be the first to follow our example."

A woman in the room countered Mohammed. "I don't have to wear a burqa here in Peshawar," she noted. "When I finally return to Kandahar, will I have to cover myself forever? If so, I'd rather stay here."

Mohammed's eyes flashed with rage at being challenged by a female.

"You've been corrupted by western influences," he snapped. "By people like him." He gestured to me. "Fahim represents all that was wrong with the old Afghanistan. He betrayed his country and ran off to America."

Now *my* eyes flashed. I'm normally easy-going. But I have a warrior spirit that flames forth when provoked. Mohammed's words ignited that spirit.

"Who are *you* to judge *me*?" I exclaimed from my chair at the table. "What do you know? Have you ever been to America? All you know is what ignorant mullahs beat in to your stupid brain."

Shima's Communist uncle didn't sympathize with Mohammed either, and he sensed my anger. "Let's all calm down," he said, from his chair at the head of the table.

Mohammed stared at me. "Traitor!" he hissed. "Spy!" Then, he spit on the floor near my chair.

I jumped up, put both hands on his chest, and shoved him backward. He hit the wall and staggered, but stayed on his feet. Recovering, he took a swing at me, but I ducked and punched him in the mouth. Others quickly moved between us. Wali pushed me out the door into the tiny courtyard next to the street.

My heart pounded as I fought a desire to get back at Mohammed. Once I'm in a fight, it takes me a while to calm down. The altercation with Mohammed gave me a massive adrenaline rush and I had to do something.

"Don't waste your time on him, Fahim," Wali said. "He's just a fanatic."

"Give me some space," I replied. "I'll be back later." I had to channel my energy somewhere so I headed down the street. I needed to walk until I calmed down.

The house was in an ugly neighborhood in an ugly town. *What was I doing in Peshawar? Why had I left beautiful southern California? What made me think that I had to get married again? What was going to happen?* Even though I was Afghan, I felt no kinship with Mohammed—and little more with Wali's family. I felt intensely American. Indeed, I was now an American citizen. Why was I back in Pakistan? Was I crazy?

It had felt so good to whack Mohammed. His ideas were wrong, if not actually evil. Perhaps he thought I was soft because I was polite around Wali's family. Well, he'd found out differently. But who was I? Was I just a kind, good-natured person who tried to be nice to everyone, lest I end up like my father? Or was I a fighter who relished confrontation—the warrior who'd harassed Communist pamphleteers as a youngster in Kabul? That night, while walking a dark street in a strange neighborhood in an alien land, I discovered that I was both the nice guy *and* the warrior. And that was OK. I just needed to find the right combination of qualities. I was neither a violent jerk nor a passive push-over. I was Fahim Fazli—a decent guy capable of standing up for himself. I liked that guy, whose identity had suddenly emerged. I could assert myself, protect and support a family, and still not be like my father. Ironically, after the violent clash with Mohammed, I knew in my heart I would never strike my wife or kids. Force may be needed, occasionally, but those times are rare and should never involve family. Compassion and understanding attracted true respect. So I needed to balance a little force with a lot of compassion. This proper ratio would make my new marriage work while allowing me to be true to my new American self.

When I got back to the house, Mohammed was gone. I ignored the people still there, went straight to bed, and finally fell into a deep, restful, much-needed sleep.

I awoke the next morning to find Wali missing. His cousin said he'd be back soon and that I shouldn't leave the house again. This only added to my confusion and discomfort—but I stayed put. Wali returned that afternoon with a grave look on his face. He said that his relatives and in-laws were angry because I didn't want to marry Shima. The family had already taken the money I'd given Wali and spent most of it on elaborate wedding arrangements. I thought back to my former in-laws' actions three months earlier. Déjà vu.

I despaired over all the money I'd wasted and wondered if I'd ever get back to America, much less make my mother happy about me taking a wife. I still wanted to see Aunt Rona. Perhaps she could offer some helpful perspectives on my situation. This time the police didn't stop my taxi and I enjoyed a happy reunion with Rona, her husband Akbar, and my cousins Nadia and Mustapha. They explained that both Pakistan and Afghanistan had become chaotic places to live. The struggle against the Soviets had turned into a brutal civil war in 1989 after the Russians left, with the seven factions of Freedom Fighters/Mujahedeen vying for power and influence in Kabul. Militias split the Afghan capital into warring enclaves. My relatives witnessed the constant rocketing that killed and maimed people all over the city—most of them non-combatants. Rona repeated what I'd heard about the Taliban and their fanatically strict rules. They were especially harsh with women, who couldn't show their faces and were required by Sharia Law to cover their whole bodies with burqas. Females could no longer work or even go to school. My aunt said that marrying an Afghan woman and getting her to America meant saving her life. Nadia said she worried about surviving in Pakistan. The conversation reminded me of my own time as a refugee in 1984, and I felt sorry for these Pakistan refugees and those still trapped in Afghanistan. The generous part of me wanted to help Shima get away because my own escape had liberated me to pursue real dreams in America. Still, a different part of me worried that this marriage could be another mistake. I explained all this to my relatives, and added that her parents were Communists.

"We should have spoken earlier," said Nadia. "You've gotten yourself into a terrible mess here."

"Yes," I said. "I'm stuck."

"Is Shima a Communist?" asked Rona.

"She's clueless about politics," I replied. "That's not an issue for me."

After dinner, I left Rona's place and returned to Wali's in-laws' house. Family members there said that the wedding was scheduled and paid for and that I couldn't leave. They'd spent most of my money on the wedding arrangements and on a reception for 1,000 people.

I went for a long walk with my prospective bride and we talked candidly about possibilities. I emphasized that I wanted an equal partner to complement me, not a servant to take care of me. My new assertiveness felt natural and comfortable—and tempered by patience and compassion. Feeling very good about myself, I now wanted to make a difference in Shima's life.

"I've heard so many stories about America," Shima said. "Do you think it is a place for me? Could it be a place for *us*?"

"I'm an American," I said. "I'm proud of that. Be careful of what you hear about the U.S. from people like Mohammed. It is a beautiful place where people from different cultures live together. It's a place of dreams. Many poor immigrants, like me, make their way there and succeed."

I paused, took her hand, and looked her in the eye. "And we can, too."

Shima had no passport and so I faced a disturbing refugee scenario again, staying in a crowded Peshawar apartment with Shima's family for a year or more waiting for immigration clearances, as Wali had done. I had to come to terms with that possibility. So I spent the next few days getting to know Shima and her family better.

On March 10, 1996, I put on a suit I'd brought from the U.S., and Wali drove us to the Continental Hotel in Peshawar, where I married Shima in a traditional Afghan wedding ceremony. A mullah presided—and then told me he needed more money.

"I'll get back to you," I said, knowing that he'd get nothing more from me.

Only four of the 1,000 people at the reception were my invitees—Rona, Akbar, Mustapha, and Nadia. The rest were Shima's family and friends. A ten-person band played traditional music, while hundreds of guests danced and ate lots of great food. I saw where my money went.

The reception area took up much of the hotel's second floor. The bride and groom sat in two over-sized wicker chairs resembling thrones. Guests mingled and laughed but few paid much attention to me. Shima looked pretty in her bright wedding dress and some guests took her picture without me, which gave me a bit of an attitude. I went downstairs to find a place to check out the look of my suit and ran into two drunken British guys—one fat and one thin—on their way to the bathroom. We went into the john together, where I found a mirror.

"Why are you all dressed up?" asked the fat one, eying me from a urinal, as I adjusted my outfit.

"I just got married," I explained. "That's my party upstairs."

"Too bad for you!" he laughed. They cracked up when I told them I had a throne upstairs worthy of Queen Elizabeth. I invited both to my wedding reception.

"We'll brighten up your bloody party," said the skinny Brit, taking a swig from a small bottle that he pulled from an inner coat pocket. They followed me upstairs and pulled me out on the floor where we danced to the Afghan music—western style. The mullah glared at me. Out of the corner of my eye I saw him speak with someone who soon approached me.

"Fahim," he said. "The drunken infidels must leave. You're defiling the ceremony by dancing with men."

"Who are you?" I responded. "I invited them. This is *my* wedding reception. How about some respect for me and my guests?"

I returned to my throne and sat next to Shima, but my bride didn't speak to me. Both Brits were talking and having fun with female guests. I looked around the room and sensed that most of the women were intrigued by the Brits, and they looked at the Englishmen with smiles. Most of the male guests seemed annoyed or threatened by the Brits, and just glared at them. Their intolerance annoyed me. The Brits weren't wedding crashers—they were guests of the groom.

Unfortunately, someone told the band to wrap things up and the reception soon ended. Before they left, the Brits shook my hand and thanked me. They tried to acknowledge Shima, but she turned away in a sulk, still sitting beside me on *her* throne.

"Have fun tonight, old chap!" said the skinny one, waving good-bye while walking toward the exit. I can still picture the fat one laughing heartily as he walked out the door. Unlike me, they'd enjoyed the reception. When Shima's uncle came over and chastised me for my behavior, I'd had enough.

"How dare you dance with western men at my niece's wedding?"

I didn't respond. I just sat there reflecting about what an unhappy wedding and reception I'd endured.

Perhaps cued by the negative energy her relatives directed towards me, my bride became imperious. "We need to talk but not tonight," she said as she left her throne and stalked out of the room, escorted by her uncle. I watched her go, with a sinking feeling that this wedding was another horrible mistake.

Rona and Nadia wished me well before they left, and I really appreciated their words, as I felt like a ship moored in a hostile harbor. Then I just sat there alone, watching the guests file out of the big room. Shima went home with her mother for our wedding night. Her uncle returned to tell me they might bring Shima back to me the next day. I stood and walked out of the great hall and went up the stairs to my expensive and expansive room—the honeymoon suite. I took off my dress coat and shoes, sat in a chair, put my feet up, and watched it get dark outside, listening to the chaotic traffic sounds of downtown Peshawar. I turned the television on, but the crappy government program reminded me of what I was missing in America, and I soon turned it off. I lay on the middle of the big bed, on my back, staring at the ceiling fan above. Alone on my wedding night, I made my decision: *I'm out of here.*

I never saw Shima again. Wali never came by my room—which really disappointed me and effectively ended our friendship. In just three months I'd married and separated twice, and now I was flat broke. I'd bottomed out. Yet I also had a new sense of pride. I had no money but I was rich in the knowledge that I'd discovered my authentic identity, and that I finally liked who I was.

The ceiling fan whirred round and round and round as I drifted off to sleep.

The next day I called my mother and told her I'd gotten married and separated on the same day. Naturally, that news upset her. But *her* reaction upset me, too. I hoped for some words of support and encouragement from my mother, especially since part of my motivation to come to Pakistan was to find a suitable bride to please her. Of course, that was precisely why she judged me. I'd failed her again. The new Fahim quickly asserted himself.

"Stop it, Mother," I said. "Listen to me. I want you to love me for who I am, not for who you want me to be. This is a hard time for me, but I've learned a lot and I'm going to take these lessons and do very well someday. Right now I just need and want a little patience and understanding from my mother, whom I love."

My mother was taken aback. Her son had never asserted himself with her that way before. The line remained silent for several moments.

"Fahim, you've never spoken to me like that before," she finally said.

"You are a very wise and good woman," I responded. "Do you understand what I'm trying to say?"

"I understand," she said softly. "Please get home safely."

After I hung up I thought maybe, for the first time, I'd given her an insight and perhaps helped her to get to a better place. I realized that not only men, but also women—like my mother—were trapped by aspects of their cultures. I'd given her too much credit for being able to escape what no one could run from.

I checked out of the hotel and took a three-hour taxi ride to Islamabad and Rawalpindi Airport. I spent the last of my money on plane tickets. I got on a British Airways flight to London and then flew back to America from there. While in transit to California I did a lot of thinking. What was my dream? *To act.* I was an actor and my gifts in that area had already served me well—from bartering with Russian soldiers to succeeding in various jobs in Orange County. Someday my acting would somehow make a difference in the world.

What was my passion? *To help people.* To give them hope. To make them understand that dreams can come true, and that when we stop dreaming we start dying. I wanted to show that men can be strong without being abusive. I wanted to inspire as well as entertain, to demonstrate that people need not be cultural prisoners, that they can choose their own paths.

I'd learned from my experiences and vowed go on with my life. *Be optimistic and forward-looking,* I told myself. *What's done is done. Things happen for reasons which will make sense later, if we have faith and hope. Don't dwell on the past. Think about possibilities.*

One of the first things I did when I got back to California was to meet with some Afghan elders to nullify my Peshawar wedding. I then returned to Orange County and my loyal friends: Alex, Max, and Marco. Once again, the Three Amigos took me back with open arms.

A month later, in a Laguna Beach restaurant called Las Brisas where I went to celebrate my new freedom and my new outlook, I met two beautiful young American women named Amy and Maryann. We bantered for a while and they laughed and laughed—as I am quite a funny guy. Maryann asked me for my phone number. I looked at her, hesitated, and changed the subject. I actually wanted *Amy's* phone number—and before I left Las Brisas I had it.

I couldn't wait to call Amy when I got home. We spoke at length and made plans to get together, the next night at a small, intimate restaurant in Orange County. During an evening of wining, dining, and talking I shared everything. I'd married and separated twice in three months and was broke. In fact, I'd declared bankruptcy due to the credit card debt from the two marriages. The honest disclosures did liberate my soul, but I braced for Amy to excuse herself and say goodbye.

God was on my side that night. Amy remained in the chair across from me. Instead of running away, she asked me about my dreams. I said I wanted to be an actor. She talked about the importance of having a positive outlook—putting out good thoughts. Goodness, she said, attracted goodness and evil attracted evil. Her words acted like a powerful balm on my spirit. I tried to remain a bit nonchalant, but it was hard not to jump impulsively at this new sensation. I savored Amy's message and felt myself falling in love with her. We went out again and again.

I explained everything about me, from A to Z. She impressed me as a sincere and attentive listener. She said she thought that I'd had a hard life—although I'd never thought that myself. She added that arranged marriages were terrible ideas. She thought she knew healthy from unhealthy. "You need to balance your Afghan self with your American self," she advised.

Amy worked for an interior designer, and I appreciated her artistic mindset. She used her talents to help me with my portfolio, my photos, and my agency contacts. Her enthusiasm and zest energized me. She made me happy.

A year later, in April of 1997, we moved in to an apartment together in Dana Point. Good things kept happening: I got some movie work as an extra and a steady job at Nordstrom's. I also worked in the office at MVP Mortgage Company.

I again saved a lot of money. So the next year, in July of 1998, I asked Amy a question: "What's your favorite country?"

"Morocco!" was her surprise answer.

"OK. I'm taking you there!"

With money in the bank, I could afford to do something out of the ordinary so Amy and I flew off to Morocco. We landed in Casablanca and spent two days there before we got on a train to Rabat—an ancient, intriguing city.

We rented a car and toured all around the desert kingdom, thoroughly enjoying our adventures. I'd picked up enough Arabic so we could banter a bit with the different people we met—other tourists, waiters, shopkeepers, and so forth. The terrain reminded me of my homeland, which I hadn't seen in over 13 years.

After a week of driving around Morocco, we took a ferry from Tangier to cross the Straits of Gibraltar on our way to Seville. After the boat left the dock Amy and I climbed to the ship's upper deck. It was so clear we could see Spain in the distance. Dolphins swam alongside, and Amy thought they were looking at her.

"Fahim, I think the dolphins are trying to tell me something," she mused. "What could it be?"

"Maybe we'll soon find out," I replied.

While Amy continued her dolphin encounter, I stepped away from the railing and headed for the boat's gift shop, which sold jewelry. I asked the saleswoman about a diamond engagement ring in the jewelry case that had caught my eye.

Two American girls from New York were in the gift shop. We'd spoken with them earlier, before boarding the boat in Tangier. Recent college graduates, one was blonde and the other brunette. They wore shorts, sandals, t-shirts, and sunglasses. They asked what I was doing in the jewelry section. I told them I was going to propose to my girl.

"Will you come with me and provide moral support?" I asked.

They looked at each other and grinned. "How romantic," said the blonde. "We'd love to be there! Thank you for including us in your special moment!"

We went up a deck and found Amy still watching the dolphins. I told her I needed to ask her an important question.

"Sure," Amy said, eying the two young women. "Is everything all right?"

"That depends upon how you answer my question. Will you marry me? I think that's what the dolphins want!"

Amy didn't say anything right away. She stared at me, as a smile slowly grew on her beautifully tanned face. She took off her sunglasses.

"Yes!" she said and she hugged and kissed me. The New York girls cried as they embraced us and took pictures.

It was the happiest moment of my life. I was finally with a wonderful woman the American way—true partners for life. Things happen for reasons. Had it not been for all turmoil associated with my arranged marriages, I'd have never asserted myself and found my true identity and purpose while in Pakistan. My road to happiness with Amy in Dana Point needed to take me through San Francisco, Salt Lake City, and Peshawar. I was better, wiser, and humbler for the journey—and now blessedly in love.

After a pleasant sojourn in Seville, we traveled to Portugal. We celebrated our engagement everywhere we went. Proud and happy, I told every waiter or waitress of our good news. Amy wasn't as outgoing as me, but she enjoyed my excitement and smiled good-naturedly whenever I asked her to show off her ring.

We flew from Lisbon back to America. On our return to California, I told everyone about our engagement, and all shared in our joy—even my parents.

I wanted to sanction our union spiritually before we had any children. Even though Amy had been raised as a Christian Scientist, she agreed to have my friend Taha, an Afghan priest, marry us. Amy was surprised that I suggested a modest, modified Afghan ceremony, given my experiences with Nargus and Shima. But my new confidence allowed me the freedom to honor my parents and my culture. I wasn't superstitious. Having an Afghan ceremony was one way to affirm that part of my identity.

Our wedding was non-pretentious and inexpensive. We held it at my parents' house, of all places. Only immediate family attended, along with one of the Three Amigos—Max and *his* wife.

Max got some laughs when he repeated his bromide about females at the reception. "God must love crazy women, because he created so many of them."

Later my mother gave Amy a long hug. Fahima's dream of seeing her son happily married had at last come true. After a few heartfelt toasts, Amy and I returned to our place at Dana Point.

We hadn't needed a reception with 1,000 people or a honeymoon in Hawaii. We only needed each other.

On June 4, 1999, Amy gave birth to our beautiful daughter Sophia.

Fahim and Amy

Chapter 7: Hollywood

"Hollywood has always been a cage...a cage to catch our dreams."
- John Huston

I've always loved movies. As a youngster in Kabul, I'd skip school about once a week to sneak into the cinema. My favorite theater sat right next to the Continental Hotel, and the ticket-taker would laugh when he saw me. "Shouldn't you be in school?" he'd ask.

"School was canceled today," I'd explain, with a wink.

Once inside the darkened movie house, I'd sit near the front and wait to be transported to other universes—places of danger, drama, and adventure. My head would buzz when I emerged from this magical, fantasy world back into Kabul's harsh sunlight. Then, I'd sneak home and hope my father wouldn't find out about my truancy.

Most of the movies I saw were made in Bollywood. Located in Bombay—now called Mumbai—Bollywood was and is the capital of the Hindi-language movie industry. My favorite actor was the great Amitabh Bachchan, who's appeared in almost 200 movies over the past 40 years. My favorite Bachchan movie was *Don* (1978), where Bachchan played two roles: Don, an underworld gang leader; and Vijay, Don's alter ego. I also loved Bachchan in *Muqaddar Ka Sikandar* (1978), where he portrayed a heroic figure that battled evil and saved beautiful women.

Of course, we also saw Western movies in Kabul. Charles Bronson was my favorite American actor. I enjoyed watching him take on the Mafia as a detective in *The Stone Killer* (1973), playing a boxer in *Hard Times* (1975), or countering Soviet spies in America in *Telefon* (1977). The American movies were voiced over in Farsi, so I ended up learning that Iranian language instead of English. It annoyed me when the actors' words didn't match their lip movements, and I wondered what the English versions sounded like.

This movie fixation left me with twin yearnings. While I wanted to be a heroic actor, like Bachchan and Bronson, I also wanted to be a heroic warrior, like the films' characters. I wondered if someone could be both a real-life actor and a real-life warrior. Some Bollywood actors were military veterans, but I'd never heard of anyone who was first an actor and *then* a warrior.

My all-boy school put on a play every year. My auditions for the lead always ended in futility, but I kept trying. While playing smaller parts, I studied those chosen for the lead roles. They were confident and assertive. I needed to gain and project confidence.

My parents influenced my desire to become an actor in different ways. My father thought acting was a silly profession and a waste of time. My mother thought acting was exciting and that it gave people reasons to dream. So I became doubly determined to succeed as an actor, to prove my father wrong while also proving my mother right.

My father taught me more about acting than he ever suspected. To avoid his abuse, I learned to become the son he wanted, at least some of the time. When I couldn't be that boy, and the beatings began, I became someone strong enough to withstand the violence—and least inside. I could change myself, and I could change my surroundings, too. In my mind, I created elaborate fantasy worlds that transported me away from the pain.

As a teenager, I earned spending money for movie tickets by doing business with Mujahedeen sympathizer and store owner Said Amir. Amir needed weapons, and most of the reliable parts were in Russian hands. I honed my acting skills, making myself known at the local Russian installations, until I was able to convince them to barter with me. Had they known where the parts were headed, my life would have been forfeit. I traded blankets and fresh food from Amir's store to the Soviets, then took the gun parts back for eventual Mujahedeen use. I loved fooling the Russians, and playing the part was crucial to my survival.

Everyone is an actor on occasion, regardless of cameras or audiences. When I talked to a pretty girl, I acted a certain way. When I met with a strict teacher, I acted in a different way. I assumed different personas at different times with my parents. Sometimes, I was especially respectful. Sometimes, I was particularly contrite. Often, I was truly terrified of my father.

As a re
made it to
need som
which w
to supp
W
screer
did (
acti
iti(

(88

Fahim Fazli

for Afghan characters. There was so mu
patron.
Therefore, I'd become an Ameri
I'd hustle and persevere. I'd netw
A week later, I was workir
while day-dreaming about a
poured off me as we wor
Somehow, all the persp
absorption. I realized
me. How could m
Being too s
when I becam
fortune. W
dramatic
realize
opp
O

sipped lem...
goal?"

I thought for a while before a...
I replied. "I have a vivid imagination and I m...
one else while entertaining people."

"Yeah, you're a ham," said Max. "You're good at all that."

"I guess I like the validation," I went on. "Once you've experienced applause, you want it again."

"But what is your goal?" he asked again. "To make money? Win an award? Travel? Meet people?"

Again, I thought a while before answering. "Those are all goals, I guess. I want all those things. But it's more than that." I didn't know how to articulate it at the time, but I also aspired to _create_ something. Max was a builder, and houses were his legacy. I wanted to be an actor with a film legacy.

"OK," I finally said. "My first goal is to get some work as an extra. Then I want to join the Screen Actors Guild. Eventually, I want a lead role in some movie and see a marquee that says: 'Starring Fahim Fazli.'"

"I'll buy a ticket to that movie," Max said. "Hopefully there will be hot women in it."

"Oh, there will be," I said. "Many hot women."

So what stood in my way?

I was an immigrant with limited English skills. There were few roles

ch competition. I didn't have a

can and improve my language skills.
rk and hope for a break.

g with Alex on a roof for several hours,
ting. It was a hot summer day, and the sweat
ed in the sun. I couldn't drink enough water.
ration seemed to purge me of some of my self-
that my thinking was very Fahim-centered. Me, me,
acting serve others?

lf-absorbed meant missing out on true happiness. If or
e a successful actor, I'd do good things with my fame and
en I was a boy, I was most excited about school during the
productions. I never skipped classes during those times, and I
that Afghanistan schools needed to offer more performing arts
rtunities, like many American schools did, especially in California.
ur school plays had only boys in them and Afghan girls needed opportunities, too.

While I was pounding nails that day on that roof in Orange County, I added a more altruistic goal to my "Me-me-me" list. If I ever enjoyed success as an actor, I'd support a school in Kabul that included girls, and pay for a coeducational performing arts department. I'd name it after my mother, Fahima.

I now had a laudable, generous goal to go along with those other personal goals I'd earlier discussed with Max. Good things would happen for Afghan boys and girls if I ever had a successful acting career. I needed to figure out a way.

In the meantime, I'd continue to pound nails.

Now I needed to develop a plan to get a foot in the doorway that led to the acting world. I took acting lessons in Hollywood and sent my head shot and phone number out to many theatrical agencies. I got to know other aspiring actors, and picked their brains about contacts and possible work. I needed to build a resume, I'd know I was on my way when I finally got an agent, but a real signal of success would be when someone asked me for an autograph. I daydreamed about that rite of passage. I'd always treasure my first autograph request, whenever it finally happened, just as military officers always remember returning their first salutes.

Months passed before I finally got the phone call I'd prayed for. It came from a friend, Hamid, who was also trying to break in to the entertainment world. "Fahim, I just heard of a movie project that needs extras," he said. "They might be able to use us. The only thing is we'd have to get ourselves to Arizona."

"When do we leave?" was all I had to say.

My first American movie was *Rambo III*. Moviegoers will remember Sylvester Stallone and me from that 1987 action film. Stallone played John Rambo, the fictional American Vietnam veteran and Medal of Honor recipient, who went to Afghanistan to help the Mujahedeen take on the Soviet war machine. As for me ...

OK. Maybe moviegoers won't remember me. I was an extra who appeared in some scenes filmed at the Fort Yuma Indian Reservation in Arizona. Extras are crucial in movies. A cast of hundreds accompanied Rambo when he impulsively took part in Buzkashi, the Afghan national game. A barbaric version of polo, Buzkashi pits mounted horsemen against one another as they try to throw the carcass of a headless sheep, goat, or calf into a target circle without dismounting. Naturally, Rambo proved to be adept at Buzkashi, picking a fast horse, scooping up a dead sheep, fighting off opposing horsemen, and throwing the carcass into the scoring area—just as Soviet Hind helicopters appeared overhead, scattering the horsemen with their rockets as explosions and fireballs abounded.

The 1990 *Guinness World Records* rated *Rambo III* as the most violent film ever made, with 221 acts of violence, at least 70 explosions, and over 108 characters killed on-screen. I survived the experience, though I may be the only one who could pick me out in the final movie product. Well, me and Amy, as I later showed her a VHS tape of the movie, stopping it at the precise moment I appeared.

I also proudly directed her attention to the rolling quote at the end
of a long line of credits: *This film is dedicated to the brave Mujahedeen
fighters of Afghanistan.* Years later, I rented the video again to watch with
friends and noticed a different dedication. Instead of to *"the brave
Mujahedeen"* the new dedication went to *"the people of Afghanistan."*

After the 9/11 attacks, the Afghan Mujahedeen freedom fighters were
no longer seen as the brave, American allies that we'd embraced so warmly throughout the 1980s.

The *Rambo III* opportunity got my foot in the door. Granted, it was a big
heavy door, and it only opened into a room crowded with hundreds of
other extras—but it was a start. Once I got through that door, I'd make
my way to the next one, and eventually get that to budge as well. I kept
pushing.

I'd have to learn the rules, though. I'd have to become a member of
the Screen Actors Guild for a credited speaking role, and unless I knew
someone, getting a SAG card would be a major challenge. I needed to
learn more about how Hollywood worked, how to network, how the casting process worked, and what assistant producers and directors did and
what they expected.

Hollywood has many rules, norms, and ways of doing business, some
of which are informal and unspoken, while others are flat-out policies. I
learned some of these rules the hard way, over time, including a bitter lesson years later on the set of FOX-TV's *24*. I was playing a terrorist, knock-
ing around Kiefer Sutherland during the show's sixth season. After one
scene where I beat him bloody, I asked if I could get a photo of us together. He agreed, and I handed my digital camera to a nearby production
assistant who snapped a picture. An assistant director saw all this. She
called me over and fired me on the spot. I'd violated a policy. I thought it
was a benign request—just a simple photo—but in this digital age there
are real concerns about set security and photographic image manipula-
tion.

I went straight to Kiefer and confirmed that he'd given permission.
He intervened with the assistant director and kept me working on *24*—

for a short while. I finished the shoot, but soon received a message from Central Casting that they no longer wanted to be involved with Fahim Fazli. They fired me too.

Ironically, when *24* was nominated for an Emmy Award, a special video clip was used from that very scene during the awards show. I laughed when I saw it. Being fired taught me another lesson. Know the rules in Hollywood, and follow them. Failure to do so could end a career. A friend told me that a young Brad Pitt also got fired by Central Casting for a similar situation. I took solace from that as I knew that Pitt eventually found real work in Hollywood—without Central Casting!

Between background roles during the early 1990s, I worked at various jobs to help support my family. During my first ten years in California I worked as a chef, a laborer, a construction worker, a salesman, and a taxi driver. Some days were better than others, but every day I dreamed of acting—regardless of my job at the time.

The years went by and I took what movie or television jobs I could as an extra. I learned the value of networking and the importance of being dependable if I wanted to keep getting calls. I learned to be leery about fake friends, insincerity, and people with agendas. The entertainment industry is a business—often a cut-throat business. I'd tell other aspiring actors about casting calls, but I didn't stew about it if they didn't reciprocate. I'm not someone who acts kindly just to get a favor in return. Expectations like that in any competitive field create a path to disappointment and cynicism. Most aspiring actors in greater Hollywood are decent people—just hoping for that break. However, I tried not to be naïve.

"If you open your heart, watch your back," a veteran extra once told me.

I tried to be nice to everyone—hair dressers, camera operators, sound technicians, wardrobe people and other people on the crew. Work is easier when you can enjoy the people around you, and I needed to network to accomplish my goals.

Movie production involved plenty of down-time and standing around, but I still loved the energy that surrounded the sets. I wanted to be around movie creation, even as an extra. Film locations are fantasy-factories, creating and fulfilling impossible dreams. Actors are immortal, as movie images will last forever—or at least as long as the celluloid holds up. My Arizona experience confirmed my desire to be an actor.

Actors without SAG cards usually don't talk in movies. Typically, only SAG members speak in front of the cameras on union productions. One way to get a SAG card in those days was to collect vouchers proving that you put your time in doing the little things—like showing up early and looking the part. Vouchers came from the assistant directors, who needed to hire a designated minimum of SAG extras each day. If one of the SAG extras didn't show up, they'd give the union voucher to a nonunion extra. That lucky extra was almost always one of those who worked the hardest. Sometimes, you had to hang around a movie set for 12 hours. I did what it took. I was always on time. I performed as expected. Then I'd get out of the way. Little did I know that I faced a 15-year wait for my own SAG card.

By 2003, after all those years of paying my dues as a Hollywood extra, I'd earned enough voucher credits to qualify for the coveted SAG card—the key to speaking parts. When I got the letter from SAG notifying me of my eligibility, I was ecstatic. I shared the momentous news with Amy and called my friends and parents to tell them I was now an official, card-carrying actor. The next day I jumped in my Mitsubishi Montero and sped up to the SAG offices in Los Angeles to fill out the paperwork. The membership cost $1450.

Some of my friends were happy for me; some were jealous. My friend Joe had been trying to get his own SAG card for years, and he didn't seem to be too happy for me. "With all the handsome, good-looking people in Hollywood trying to get SAG cards, how could they pick a dubber like you?" he asked.

I just laughed. So it had taken 15 years. I didn't want to be snarky like him. I thought of the famous headline when Greta Garbo first appeared in a talking movie: "Garbo Speaks!"

Maybe someday I could send a message to my friends.

"Fahim Speaks!"

My SAG card allowed me to audition for roles that were previously beyond my reach, and I was grateful for my new, elevated status. I'd accomplished two of the goals I'd set for myself when I worked for Max at M & M Construction. I'd gotten my foot in the door by getting lots of work as an extra, and then I'd finally earned my SAG card. My next goal was to use my SAG status to get speaking parts and eventually position myself for a featured role, which would gain me the attention and wherewithal I needed to return to Kabul and establish that coeducational performing arts school department in my mother's honor. I kept visualizing that "Fahima Fazli Academy" for Afghan boys *and* girls who dared to dream.

While the September 11 attacks were a horrible blow to our country, part of the aftermath involved a spate of movie productions and television shows that required terrorist types. Consequently, I received more calls for work than ever, especially after getting my SAG card. However, as a proud American citizen it troubled me to be repeatedly cast as a terrorist. Most people wouldn't sympathize with the characters I played on television or in the movies. I certainly didn't. I wanted a crack at playing more appealing roles.

Some friends had earlier compared me to Andy Garcia. Born in Cuba, he was an immigrant, like me. He was typecast for years before breaking free of Latin stereotypes. Garcia finally got some great roles in *The Untouchables* and the third *Godfather* film. Hopefully, my career would follow the same path.

The important thing, though, was getting more acting opportunities. My small role in the movie *Homeland Security* gained me admission to a Wrap Party—the celebration marking the end of work where everyone who'd worked on a movie production could show up and celebrate the project's completion. As time went by I went to more and more of these Wrap Parties and began to feel like a real member of the Hollywood Tribe.

My work with the *Homeland Security* movie underscored the obstacles I faced as I sought more acting opportunities. I was more confident than ever, and eager for speaking roles that had substance and depth. However, decision-makers with *Homeland Security* saw me through an ethnic prism. I had to play Afghan President Hamid Karzai's Pashtun bodyguard. I wanted to play more diverse roles, but how might that happen? I'd continued to network and scramble for opportunities and learned that successful actors without industry connections needed that "big break" to launch them to new professional levels. Luck was part of it, but many breaks happened because people did everything they could, big things and small, to get into position for success. I had to keep believing—and scrapping.

Homeland Security starred Scott Glenn and Tom Skerritt. This project was a made-for-TV film intended as a pilot for a series that never happened. According to DVDtalk.com, *Homeland Security* was "a bland and fairly tasteless bullet-point history lesson on how the 9/11 attacks happened, how a bunch of generic TV characters deal with it, and how many soaring musical strains can be employed while the rah-rah chest-thumping speechifying goes on in front of a flapping American flag."

Not exactly a glowing review.

Though the movie failed to earn critical acclaim, I had a good time playing the bodyguard role. Still, the grind wore me down one December night. At 2 a.m. on a location in Santa Clarita, California, the cast and crew were tense, still trying to coordinate and effectively shoot a night firefight. I'm usually positive and animated, but on that night I got tired and impatient. We shivered outside and stood around for hour after hour. Was it worth it? I wondered, thinking about the low pay and how I was nearing my 40th birthday. Maybe I should consider a different career. *Why am I doing this?*

Because you need to hang in there and keep dreaming, I answered myself. *Tomorrow is another day.*

While wrap parties were fun, I especially loved invitations to premieres, the Hollywood bashes that introduced the finished film products to the media. My first Red Carpet experience was the premiere for *Kite Runner*—another story about Afghanistan for which I did voice-overs.

The *Kite Runner* premiere was at the Egyptian Theater in Hollywood. I escorted a beautiful actress named Nabella. She'd served as a technical advisor for the movie and had become a good friend. I learned a lot from watching her, and later applied those lessons as a cultural advisor for *Charlie Wilson's War*. Movie officials assigned me to be Nabella's escort, and Amy was perfectly content to miss the premiere hoopla that so excited me. Unlike her actor-husband, she didn't seek the limelight.

Theater representatives checked everyone's name at the door, and after they waved Nabella and me through I felt as though we'd entered a new fantasy world. We had seats in the fifth row and as we sat there I thought of old friends in Afghanistan, like Hobid and Safie, and wished they could see me now—not because I wanted to gloat, but because I wanted to share my exciting new world with those who'd understand my life's journey and where it had begun.

Afterwards, I longed for more such experiences. Eventually, that SAG card opened more doors for me. While there were limited potential roles for Afghan immigrants, I had certain qualities that could help me fill ethnic niches. Not only did I talk like an Afghan, but I looked like someone from that part of the world. Consequently, I played numerous Middle Eastern stereotypes: everything from a camel handler in *GI Joe: The Rise of Cobra* to a horse auctioneer in *The Unit* on CBS.

I also did more post-production voice-overs in movies like *Brothers* with Toby Maguire. That 2007 film had featured some frightening and disturbing Afghanistan scenes. Maguire portrayed a Marine captain named Sam Cahill, whose helicopter was shot down by the Taliban. First reports indicated that no one had lived through the crash, but Captain Cahill and Private Joe Willis survived and were captured by the bad guys, who relentlessly tortured the two Marines. Eventually, the bad guys forced Captain Cahill at gunpoint to beat Private Willis to death with a lead pipe. Cahill was later rescued, but the experience ruined his marriage and put him in a mental hospital. While I hadn't played a terrorist on-screen, when I saw *Brothers* I was as horrified as anyone else to watch evil Taliban types torturing Americans. I'd continue to be a pro and do the work that Hollywood offered me, but I dreamt of eventually portraying more sympathetic—if not heroic—characters, instead of shuffling between two personas: villainous terrorist or lowly goat herder.

Battered and bloody during filming of a Pat Tillman documentary

In *Lions for Lambs* I did voice-overs and played a Taliban fighter who killed an American soldier. "More typecasting," I told Amy the evening after shooting that scene. "They have me shooting Americans again."

I added that I'd had a minor run-in with the director when he caught me failing to recycle a soft drink can. "I guess he's one of those environmentalist types," I told Amy.

"Well, you need to know what the boss likes and then keep him happy," Amy said. "You know how fanatical some environmentalists are."

"Yeah, I know," I said.

"Who was the boss?" Amy asked.

"The movie director," I replied. "Robert...um...Redding?"

I had a temporary brain-block regarding the director's last name. Sometimes names and words from six languages bumped into each other in my mind.

"Robert Redding?" Amy responded. "Never heard of him."

"I mean Redford," I corrected. "Robert Redford."

"Robert Redford?" exclaimed Amy. "Robert Redford? I love him! He's my favorite actor. Don't you ever forget to recycle!"

More lessons learned. Know your boss and don't forget to recycle.

In 2008, I got a break by winning a role in *Eagle Eye*—a very rewarding project for me because the role gave me more speaking lines, and after all those years as an extra I wanted my voice to be heard. I played a leader in a tribal village killed early in the movie because of suspected terrorist connections. Hollywood continued to typecast me, as I continued playing stereotypical, ethnic roles, but I appreciated the all the chances for work.

While my dreams centered on the larger silver screen, there were also smaller screen opportunities, in television. In addition to my work on Fox's *24*, I played an Afghan entrepreneur on an episode of *The Unit* on CBS in 2008. I also worked in a number of Spike-TV productions, such as *Deadliest Warrior: IRA vs. Taliban* in 2009. Later, I played Saddam Hussein in *Deadliest Warrior: Saddam Hussein vs. Pol Pot*. As Saddam, I killed a bunch of hapless Iraqi political opponents with a pistol. Amy and Sophia didn't savor the imagery of me portraying Saddam, but they understood that it was part of my job.

"Hey!" I said to the girls when they rolled their eyes about me playing the Iraqi dictator. "Don't you know it's every actor's dream to play Saddam Hussein?"

Fahim Speaks - As Saddam!

A true Hollywood professional does more than just dramatic acting. For example, voice-overs are crucial, and I did a lot of rewarding work providing story narrations, additional dialog, and occasional commentary. Also, because Hollywood is not exactly crawling with Afghans, I eventually became a "go-to guy" when questions came up about Central Asian culture. The respect given to Nabella as cultural advisor for *Kite Runner* inspired me to seek the advisor position for *Charlie Wilson's War*. I was thrilled to get that job. Now, I would be able to directly influence roles available to Afghan actors, and help to educate Americans about reality in Central Asia.

I achieved another benchmark in 2006 when I signed on with an agent, Tulci Ram. He knew a lot of people and helped me expand my contact list and land more auditions.

Charlie Wilson's War was also a crucial networking opportunity. I enjoyed meeting cast members while on location in Morocco in November of 2006. After one long day of shooting, I returned to our hotel lobby, where I ran into Philip Seymour Hoffman. He generously invited me to join him for dinner. After we left for the restaurant, we ran into Tom Hanks.

"Hey, Tom," said Hoffman. "I finally got a call from my girl."

"So how's Mimi doing?" asked Hanks. "It must be almost time for the baby."

"She said her tubes were leaking or something," replied Hoffman.

"Leaking tubes?" said Hanks. "Is something wrong with her car?"

"No," responded Hoffman. "It has to do with the pregnancy."

"You must mean that her water broke!" Hanks exclaimed.

"Yeah, that's it," confirmed Hoffman. "The baby's on the way."

By the time Hoffman invited Hanks to join us for dinner, my head was spinning about sharing a table with two Academy Award winners. Unfortunately, Hanks had another commitment. Hoffman and I still enjoyed a memorable dinner—at least for me—and we talked about having kids, among many other things. His newborn daughter Tallulah and her three-year-old brother Cooper Alexander delighted Hoffman, and I loved telling stories about my own Sophia.

I also got to know Amy Adams in Morocco. She played the character of Bonnie Bach in the movie—Charlie Wilson's administrative assistant.

We also had dinner one evening and Adams talked about her break-through role as Ashley Johnsten in the 2005 independent film *Junebug*, for which she received an Academy Award nomination as Best Supporting Actress. I described my job as our movie's cultural advisor.

"Many Americans might not know the difference between an Arab and an Afghan," I said. "But people will watch this movie in many places around the world, and if it's not authentic, it won't be successful the way it could be. I make sure people wear Afghan clothes the right way, speak like Afghans, move like Afghans, and so forth."

"You're right," Amy replied. "If I had to take a test about how Arabs and Afghans were different, I'm sure I'd fail."

"Charlie Wilson and the producers are keen on the movie being realistic," I explained. "It needs to be accurate about how things were in Afghanistan. A film like this can be more than just entertainment. It could be something that teaches, that raises awareness about how Afghanistan and America became so caught up with each other. Afghanistan is now part of America's story."

"Thanks for all you've done here," she told me. "And don't give up your acting dreams."

We talked about our experiences with auditions and rejections and jointly concluded that while timing and luck meant a lot in Hollywood, hard work was important as well. And then there was that talent thing...

One of my more interesting film projects was *Iron Man*—filmed in 2007 for release in 2008. Starring Robert Downey Jr. as industrialist Tony Stark, the movie grossed well over $300 million world-wide. I was Omar, Terrorist #2, the one who found Iron Man's scattered pieces in the desert after an explosion and who put things back together for use by the forces of evil. I learned a lot from working with Downey. I had to slug him when we did a scene outside a cave and he didn't mince words with me about making the scene work.

"Be in character." Downey told me. "Make me feel the pain."

I learned a lot from Robert, like how important it was to immerse yourself in your role and in your scene. It was also no secret that Downey had had to confront some personal demons. His drug problems ten years earlier had landed him in jail. He talked about incarceration and the lessons he learned. We discussed our shared practice of meditation to control our overactive minds without drugs. He'd meditate in front of his personal trailer, often referred to as a honey wagon, near the set each morning. I visualized someday having a central role in a movie, like Robert had in *Iron Man*, and experiencing some star treatment. I fantasized about having my own trailer and personal assistant—while still remaining generous and accessible, like Downey was.

Fahim/Omar watching Robert Downey Jr./Tony Stark

I liked working for director Jon Favreau. He appreciated that I was the only authentic Afghan in a movie about Afghanistan, and he knew I worked hard.

Some of the *Iron Man* scenes were filmed near Edwards Air Force Base in California. The terrain was reasonably similar to Afghanistan's and working there made me wonder if I'd ever see the old country again. I recalled watching movies as a youngster in Kabul. With the Taliban ousted from my native city, I knew they'd show *Iron Man* there. I wondered if any of my old friends or classmates would watch the movie and see Omar the Terrorist and recognize their old pal Fahim.

I also imagined Taliban types watching the movie and identifying with me as I depicted a terrorist. They'd rejoice with any punch I landed on Robert Downey/Tony Stark. I wasn't entirely comfortable with that, but as a pro, if I had to play a terrorist, then I'd live the part.

I also did a scene with Jeff Bridges, who played Obadiah Stane, Tony Stark's Number Two guy—who eventually turned on him. Unfortunately for my character Omar, Stane's minions killed him—me!—in the movie.

Bridges had been born into a show-biz family. He and his brother Beau appeared as kids on the television show *Sea Hunt*, which starred their dad, Lloyd Bridges. Jeff went on to earn six Academy Award nominations. No 15-year wait for a SAG card for him. Like me, Bridges also played a bad guy in *Iron Man* and he seemed to draw from me when trying to project an evil persona.

"Fahim, you can really put on a scary look when you want to," Bridges told me. "You inspire me to look like a tough bastard, too!"

The next year I worked on the film *Hired Gun*, starring Michael Madsen and Shane Wood. I played a character named Abdul-Aziz—a really evil terrorist type.

Abdul Aziz took no prisoners

Madsen himself often played bad guys—a psychopathic gunman on *Cagney and Lacey*, an arrogant baseball player in *The Natural*, a crazy murderer in *Kill Me Again*, a sadistic convict/thief in *Reservoir Dogs*, and so on. I asked him about being typecast.

"Son, look at me" he replied. "I'm busy. There's plenty of work for bad guys. And it's more fun playing a bad guy. Don't worry about it."

So I concentrated on the role, and like a good actor, I sought to become Abdul-Aziz. The problem was that I stayed in character after the workday ended. I went home to Amy and Sophia as Abdul-Aziz, the scary, evil terrorist. The girls objected. They loved Fahim, not Abdul-Aziz.

When I was too-much in character they'd say "Hey Abdul! Get out of here. Go away and send Fahim back to this house."

I heard that when Jack Nicholson played Jack Torrance in *The Shining* it took him a while to disassociate himself from his insane character. Fortunately for Amy and Sophia, I left Abdul-Aziz behind after we finished filming *Hired Gun*. I learned that I had to lighten up and have fun as my career progressed.

As Jack Torrance might say, "All work and no play make Fahim a dull boy!"

After putting Abdul Aziz behind me, I wondered what villainous character I'd next portray. Despite Michael Madsen's counsel, I did worry about it. Why couldn't an Afghan like me be a heroic figure? I recalled my youthful dreams of playing good guys, inspired by watching Amitabh Bachchan taking out bad guys in the Bollywood movies I'd watched as a youngster in Kabul. I thought about working with a real writer who understood Afghans to develop a story where an actor like me could play a more sympathetic role. Unfortunately, I wasn't confident enough or experienced enough yet for such a partnership. Still, the very idea of me helping to put a story together showed how far I'd come—from an immigrant to an extra to an actor to an established Hollywood professional who also did post-production work, technical consulting, special appearances and more.

I also got involved with special projects, including a documentary on Pat Tillman's life called *The Tillman Story*. Some of the filming took place at Blue Cloud Ranch, not far from Magic Mountain, near Los Angeles. I provided cultural advice and played a multi-lingual Afghan named Khan who interpreted for Tillman's army unit when it was operating near Khan's village in eastern Afghanistan. The project made me increasingly curious about the details of Tillman's death.

Tillman was a premier National Football League defensive back with the Arizona Cardinals who'd earlier played linebacker at Arizona State University. A true maverick, Tillman turned down a five-year, $9 million contract offer from the St. Louis Rams to play for his home state Cardinals. For him, loyalty meant more than money. Playing football after the 9/11 attacks left Tillman unfulfilled, despite a big NFL salary. Something inside him pushed him towards military service, like the many Americans who raced to recruiting offices after the Japanese attacks on Pearl Harbor on December 7, 1941. He joined the Army in 2002 and qualified for an elite Ranger outfit. He served a short stint in Iraq in 2003 and later went into harm's way in Afghanistan, where he was killed by friendly fire in 2004.

John Krakauer's 2009 book *Where Men Win Glory: The Odyssey of Pat Tillman* accused the Army of covering up the circumstances of Tillman's death when it awarded him a Silver Star, citing his heroism in the face of devastating enemy fire. Eventually, the truth came out. Pat's brother Kevin had served in the same unit and he angrily accused the military of trying to exploit Pat's death with phony accounts of heroism during a supposed enemy ambush. Kevin and others, particularly Mary Tillman, Pat's mother, were offended by the notion of Pat's death being used to inspire support for what they felt was a misguided mission in Afghanistan.

The lies about Tillman's death were shameful. Tillman was the ultimate Army poster boy, and apparently the military brass couldn't bear the thought of the public knowing he'd been killed by fellow soldiers. *But was our military mission in my native country a mistake?* That question haunted me. I kept thinking about it. I also kept thinking about how my character Khan's linguistic skills significantly helped Tillman's unit.

Despite the lack of consensus on the Afghanistan mission, Tillman's story inspired me enough that I considered stepping away from the comfort of southern California to do something for my country. But what? I was too old to join the Army, as Tillman had.

At the start of each New Year, I count my blessings. As 2008 turned to 2009, I reflected on my good fortune. I had a beautiful wife and daughter. We lived happily in the sunny California seaside community of Dana Point. I had my SAG card and was earning a comfortable living as a Hollywood actor. I had many good friends. Life was swell.

I was proud of how far I'd come in my life's journey, though I still dreamed of getting that major acting role which would position me to return to Kabul to establish the "Fahima Fazli Academy for the Performing Arts."

Like others in Hollywood, however, I was starkly aware that actors played in a safe, fantasy world. In the real world, real people did real heavy-lifting and faced real dangers. They couldn't reshoot scenes that didn't work out well. My country was at war and Americans were fighting in Afghanistan, while I hung out and had fun near the ocean in Dana Point—when not playing terrorists in Hollywood. I regretted not serving in the military, and that I'd failed that test to join the Marines 22 years earlier. I admired men like Audie Murphy and Lee Marvin, Hollywood actors who'd actually been in a war—instead of wielding an empty weapon and just pretending. Charlie Wilson's words from 2006 kept coming back to me. *You should think about going back and helping out in Afghanistan.* I also kept thinking of Pat Tillman's story. Could I somehow get over to Afghanistan, where the action was? Could I ride to the sounds of the guns?

However, even if I could ride to the sounds of the guns, did that mean that I should?

During those many long drives back and forth between Dana Point and Hollywood, I thought a lot. *How could people from my* original *homeland develop pride in Afghanistan as a place of beauty and hope, as opposed to a place of violence and terror? How could people in my* new *homeland better appreciate the wonders of America, and not take our freedom and security for granted? Could I somehow make a difference? Did some real-life role—as opposed to an acting role—await me somewhere?*

Chapter 8: Into Uniform

"War is an ugly thing, but not the ugliest of things. The decayed and degraded state of moral and patriotic feeling which thinks that nothing is worth war is much worse. The person who has nothing for which he is willing to fight, nothing which is more important than his own personal safety, is a miserable creature who has no chance of being free unless made and kept so by the exertions of better men than himself."
- John Stewart Mill, 1806-1873, British Philosopher and
Moral Theorist

Afghanistan stayed on my mind, and I often thought of somehow returning there someday. I knew first-hand how frightening my old country had become in the late seventies, but it would always be my native land. In some ways I remained a refugee, haunted by so many youthful memories. Although it had turned into a place of terror, I preferred to remember Afghanistan as a country of unsurpassed beauty, populated by the world's most generous people. It was a land where older folks once laughed easily together in public, completely unafraid. Boys yelled and flew kites from Kabul's rooftops while black-haired girls in colorful, round skirts chattered away as they freely moved about the city.

In 1979, the Communists shattered my homeland. After ten long years as a Soviet puppet state, Afghanistan finally freed itself of the Russians, only to descend into the bedlam of civil war. In 1996 the Taliban gained control of Kabul. While these religious extremists eliminated some of the chaos, they continued fighting with the Northern Alliance into the new century. Life for rural farmers and tribesmen didn't change drastically during these years, but people in cities like Kabul or Kandahar saw their worlds turned upside down. Those living in these more cosmopolitan communities had to rearrange their lives around new pronouncements by fanatical mullahs who imposed restrictions on almost everything. Girls could no longer go to school and women could no longer work or appear in public without burquas. Even singing was forbidden.

At least the damned Communists allowed music, I thought.

Morality Police were everywhere in the cities, with their black turbans, long beards, and stern visages, watching people, and informing local Taliban leaders and mullahs about any violations of *fatwas*—pronouncements, or new interpretations of the Quran. While the Communist police state had had its own network of insidious informers, this new theocracy was even worse. If a man raped a woman, then she was to blame for tempting him, and the Taliban leaders sentenced her to death. The old Kabul sports stadium, once the site of spirited soccer competition, became a killing ground. The television accounts and newspaper stories of countless executions horrified me.

In 1999, a woman named Zarmeena, a mother of seven, was executed at the stadium—shot by a young Taliban soldier with a Kalashnikov rifle. Supposedly, she'd disrespected her husband. Thousands of people turned out for the spectacle, including women and children. Women wearing blue *burquas* dragged the body away as people chanted "Allah Akbar" or "God is Great."

This summary justice became routine. The new regime established laws calling for adulterers to be stoned to death and for thieves to suffer amputations. Life in the new Afghanistan wasn't much different from that of ancient Rome, where gladiators brutalized each other and hungry lions devoured hapless Christians—largely to entertain the masses who filled the Coliseum to take in the depraved spectacles.

The Taliban gained power due to a backlash against institutionalized Afghan corruption. The police didn't protect people—they harassed them on behalf of local tribal elders, corrupt government officials, or themselves. Life grew so oppressive that people eventually sacrificed their freedom in exchange for some stability and harsh justice. In village after village, town after town—particularly in Kandahar and Helmand Provinces after 2004—the people acquiesced and tolerated a return of local Taliban rule. Young religious fanatics murdered and displaced corrupt government officials, for whom there was no local support or loyalty. It saddened me to think there wasn't a third way, as opposed to having to choose between a venal ruling hierarchy and the Taliban.

Afghanistan's deterioration made me appreciate the U.S. all the more, despite America's own imperfections. Yes, there were plenty of stories about corruption or crooks in the U.S. Like the one about California Congressman Duke Cunningham, who was hauled off to jail in 2006 for conspiracy and fraud, which especially disappointed me, as he'd been an ace Navy Fighter Pilot during the Vietnam War. Still, it was also easy to find good people—most people—making honest livings and taking care of each other. I saw plenty of that in Hollywood, too. Aspiring actors often lived together, sharing expenses and hardships, often welcoming other dream-seekers into their midst—much as the Three Amigos had taken *me* in.

My first-hand experiences under Afghan Communists and Pakistani authoritarians made me look at America with special wonder. I loved reading immigrant success stories—like that of Vinod Dham. He came to the U.S. from India in 1975 as an engineering student with just $8 in his pocket. He became a chip engineer and later the CEO of Silicon Spice, which he sold for $1.2 billion in 2000. Or actress Catherine Bell, who was born overseas to an Iranian mother, but became a naturalized American citizen. I loved watching her as Major Sarah McKenzie in the television series JAG—especially when the script called for her to speak Farsi!

However, many people in our land of opportunity—including some in my own family—just look around and focus on what's wrong or lacking in their worlds, and become sad. Why not look around and savor what is right and good? Talking to one of my daughter's teachers one day made me realize how much she did for her students—extra efforts she didn't need to make, but that she simply wanted to. In Afghanistan under the Taliban, my daughter wouldn't be allowed to go to school, much less enjoy the attention of a talented female teacher.

For example, Kabir, a fellow aspiring actor, once lamented his bad luck: "Well, I blew that audition," he said during lunch one day at Khyber Pass, our favorite Afghan restaurant. "Damn, I really wanted that role. And my old car needs new tires, new everything. And Cindy and I are through. She's gone."

"Look, nobody gets all the jobs they want," I replied. I didn't want to sound preachy, but Kabir needed a reality check. "Nobody does. Every car needs maintenance. And you can do a lot better than Cindy. But please don't tell her I said that in case you get back together. And we both know she's going to call."

He just stared at his iced tea.

"And you live in America," I added. "There are thousands of young people in Afghanistan with no legs and no future because of all the mines that keep blowing up there. So what are *you* complaining about?"

"Shut up, Fahim," he said. "I'm not in the mood to listen to that crap." He paused and sighed. Then he chuckled and took a sip of his iced tea. "OK, you're right," he admitted. "I don't know if I'll ever get another audition, but I can definitely get a better girlfriend."

I smiled too. "At least you still have your health," I said.

"Damn you, Fahim," he said, laughing.

Deborah Norville, host of *Inside Edition* on CBS, wrote a book called *Thank You Power: Making the Science of Gratitude Work for You*, which focused on *doing*. Don't just count your blessings, she advised, but write them down and take action. A positive mind-set in and of itself doesn't necessarily lead to positive results—you need to follow up those thoughts with actual deeds.

I admire people of action—those who just go after their dreams and don't give up. I try to be like them. That's why I'm always early and that's why I'm always hopeful—and willing to go with my feelings. I also felt an obligation to pay back my adopted country. President John F. Kennedy's famous words always inspired me. *Ask not your country can do for you—ask what you can do for your country.*

Many Americans take so much for granted. And sadly, many fellow immigrants—legal and illegal—somehow seem to think that America owes them. It makes me want to go up to them and ask "Do you have any idea how blessedly lucky you are just to be here in America?" Of course, how could they really know, unless they'd lived in a place like Afghanistan? My own life's journey gave me a special love for my adopted country.

That love has been tested from time to time—like after September 11, 2001.

Amy and I were with baby Sophia on vacation at a Las Vegas hotel. They gave us a smoking room by mistake when we checked in on the tenth, so the next morning when we woke up I called the front desk to ask about changing rooms. Curiously, no one answered for a while, and when someone finally did pick up the phone she said she couldn't help me for a while.

"Well, why not?" I asked, my voice conveying some annoyance.

"Turn on your television and you'll see why," she replied.

Like so many other Americans, we were then transfixed by the horrific images of that day—crumbling skyscrapers in New York, the Pentagon ablaze in Washington, D.C., and a passenger plane crash in Pennsylvania. It soon became clear that the 9/11 attacks were the work of Islamic extremists from the Middle East. Increasing speculation from television commentators focused on Al Qaeda, Osama Bin Laden, and Afghanistan.

I remembered Bin Laden's name from the 1980s when his faction was part of the *Mujahedeen*, fighting the Soviets with American assistance. He later developed the Al Qaeda terrorist network which committed a series of atrocities—including the first bombing at the World Trade Center in New York City in 1993, the U.S. embassy bombings in Kenya and Tanzania in 1998, the attack on the USS *Cole* in Yemen in 2000, and other criminal assaults. The Taliban gave him and his crowd safe haven in Afghanistan.

True to their fundamentalist Wahhabi precepts, Bin Laden and Al Qaeda turned on the West after America helped them drive the Soviets from Afghanistan. *Wahhabism* is a puritanical form of Sunni Islam associated with Saudi Arabia that strongly influenced Bin Laden—who directed its energy against the Soviets. After the Russians left Afghanistan, that energy was redirected against Western interests. American military presence in Saudi Arabia and elsewhere in the region particularly angered the Wahhabis, who were utterly intolerant of those who didn't follow a rigid interpretation of the Quran.

The September 11 attacks were the most spectacular of their terrorist actions. While not a religious scholar, I knew the Quran didn't sanction or encourage the slaughter of innocents. I tried to comprehend such a mindset. How could it be countered?

With airports closed, we remained in Las Vegas for a week. Like everyone else, we tried to cope with the shock of 9/11. But as I moved around, I sensed people staring at me—probably because I looked Afghan. I *was* Afghan! But I was an Afghan who loved the United States—

a proud American citizen. Still, I understood the anxiety and fear that spread through America after 9/11.

We eventually traveled from Las Vegas to Angel Fire, New Mexico, where we spent time with Amy's parents, Richard and Barbara McPeek. They remained loving and protective of me, but were nervous about my prospects—with some reason, as it turned out.

One day, Amy, Sophia, and I took a drive to a local mall. While we were away, there was the proverbial knock-on-the-door at the McPeek home—that harsh knock made by government men looking for someone. The same knock that's reverberated many millions of times in Communist and totalitarian lands, but a knock that's thankfully rare in America.

Barbara opened the door and was taken aback to find a sharply dressed, officious-looking man standing there, with an intense look on his face.

"Hello," said Mrs. McPeek. "How can I help you?"

"I'm looking for Fahim Fazli," said the man.

"Is something wrong?" Barbara nervously asked.

"I'm with the FBI," he explained, displaying badges and credentials. "I'm sure you're aware of recent events in New York City and Washington. We're just following up on some information that was sent to us."

"Please come in," replied Barbara. "Fahim's wife is our daughter, Amy. They took our granddaughter Sophia to the store. My husband Richard is also out in town, but I may be able to answer some of your questions."

"Thank you, Ma'am," said the agent.

The G-Man went inside with Barbara, who seated him on a couch in the living room. As she went to the refrigerator to get him a bottle of water, she wondered if he carried a weapon under his dark suit coat, which he didn't remove. She gave the agent the plastic bottle and then sat in an easy chair as the agent peppered her with numerous questions about me. Where did I come from? How long had the McPeeks known me? Did they know any of my friends or associates? Why had I left California?

The questions naturally left Barbara shaken, but she responded to everything as best she could. The agent occasionally made notes, often looking at his watch.

"When will your son-in-law be back?" he eventually asked.

"I'm not sure," said Barbara. "It may be a couple hours, but I'm planning on everyone for dinner. I'm making something special for Sophia."

Mrs. McPeek pointed to Sophia's toys lying around.

"Could you please confirm Fahim's phone number and address?" the agent asked.

"Certainly," replied my mother-in-law, who gave him all my contact information, and explained that Amy, Sophia and I were getting ready to return to Dana Point. That seemed to reassure the FBI agent.

"We'd received a message that he'd vanished from California," he explained. "We're just following up where we need to. I'm sure you understand. We'll get in touch with Fahim as necessary."

The agent stood, shook Barbara's hand, and left.

When we returned to the house late that afternoon, Mrs. McPeek was still visibly shaken by the visit. She recounted the questioning, which agitated Richard, which in turn further unsettled poor Barbara. I didn't know what to think at first, but then my overactive imagination took over. I braced myself for another knock on the door, either in Angel Fire or back in Dana Point. It unsettled me that a government agent had questions that obviously stemmed from me being an unaccounted-for Afghan-American right after the September 11 attacks.

I had nothing to hide, but memories returned of the Afghan Communists hunting for me in Kabul. I was anxious, and couldn't sleep that night. I tossed and turned and wondered about how I'd answer the FBI's questions. I didn't want to appear nervous if I was interrogated, and resolved to use my acting skills to reassure them as best I could.

I was frazzled about the Feds coming after me—when I'd done nothing wrong. Eventually we found out that a nosy neighbor in Dana Point had reported me and my little family missing after 9/11. Given the tenor of the times, the FBI was obliged to follow up.

Over the next couple of days I struggled to get out of a resentful funk, until I saw something on television about Americans of Japanese ancestry being rounded up in 1942 and interned in detention camps. Their only crime was their Japanese heritage. President Franklin Roosevelt, the U.S. Congress, and even the Supreme Court all supported the "War Relocation Camps," as they feared the Japanese-Americans would collaborate with Imperial Japanese enemies seeking to invade California.

In hindsight, it seems irrational and ridiculous, but given the fear that Americans felt after Pearl Harbor, it was understandable. When people act out of fear, bad things happen. American leaders were reluctant to assign Japanese-Americans to fight in the Pacific, preferring to deploy patriotic Japanese-Americans to the European Theater. The 442nd Regimental Combat Team, made up of Japanese-Americans, fought with distinction in Italy, France, and Germany. This unit became one of the most highly decorated regiments in the history of the U.S. Armed Forces. Twenty-one of its soldiers won the Medal of Honor.

Learning about the Japanese-Americans—the Nisei—helped me get over my funk. Americans in 2001 acted out of fear, just as they did in 1941. So what if some agents asked me a few questions? I got it. I understood the fear. They weren't throwing me, Amy, and Sophia into a relocation camp, as happened to so many in 1942. I wanted to be happy, and I wouldn't be if I dwelled on grievances or assumed a victim status.

My in-laws, however, feared that I'd be profiled or blackballed professionally. I wondered the same thing, given the often unfriendly looks now directed my way. But I told Richard and Barbara not to worry and we stayed in New Mexico for a few more days before heading back to California.

Everyone braced for the next terrorist attack, but 2001 turned to 2002 and we didn't get hit again. Ironically, 2002 actually turned out to be a good year for me. I got some small parts and lots of work doing movie voice-overs. Also, as had occurred during World War II, the Pentagon looked to Hollywood for help with training videos to prepare soldiers and Marines for the rigors of combat—this time in Afghanistan and Iraq. The productions weren't for public release so the general population didn't get to see me playing forgettable village elders or terrorists in these Department of Defense videos.

While working in the film *Homeland Security*, I met Sam Sako, an Iraqi-American. He spoke of a need for more Afghan actors and described his Arab-American casting business.

"If you join our group, we can keep you busy for the rest of your life," said Sako.

"For the rest of my life?" I replied. "Tell me more."

Sako had an intriguing background. Born in northern Iraq, he'd attended high school in Baghdad and then moved with his family to Greece. After coming to America, Sako received a Bachelor of Arts Degree in Motion Picture and Television from California State Northridge in 1987. Sensing a need for better support for Hollywood projects involving Arab countries and the Middle East, he established *Middle East in Hollywood* to fill this niche. The company became a technical and creative consulting leader—for films, television shows, commercials, training projects, multimedia, and live events.

Sako took my phone number and soon I was busy with movies, television series, military productions, and special documentaries—including the one on Pat Tillman, later on. Tillman had served in Iraq before deploying to Afghanistan, and I also followed developments in Iraq closely. Many Hollywood people opposed *Operation Iraqi Freedom* and our 2003 invasion. I listened with interest when politicians said we shouldn't be in Iraq but that we should focus on Afghanistan and pursue Al Qaeda. Did they mean it? Or did they just want to be critical of the Iraq effort? While we then had a relatively small military presence in Afghanistan, 40 other countries had also committed troops and resources there. The international community clearly didn't want the Taliban to return to power—a hopeful sign.

So while my life was good professionally, I kept thinking of other Americans risking their lives in Central Asia to change that part of the world for the better. Over the next few years, Amy and I occasionally talked about the possibility of me going back to Afghanistan in some capacity.

"Fahim, you're 40 years old," Amy said. "You're too old to join the Army. You can find fame and adventure here in California. So many people would love to have a SAG card and a chance to make a living as a Hollywood actor."

"I'm incomplete," I responded. "I'm restless. I think I'm supposed to do something different, but I'm not sure how or what."

"I know," she replied. "I can tell. You're ready for something else, something special. Maybe you'll hear about an audition for a major role.

Or maybe something else is supposed to happen. You know I'm here for you. I know about following your dream. But you need to figure out what that dream is."

Why would I want to put myself in harm's way just as my Hollywood fortunes were improving? After playing the terrorist Omar in *Iron Man* I had more work offers than ever before—like for the Abdul Aziz role in *Hired Gun*. But I still felt less than whole—like a broken ring, or an interrupted circle that needed completion. Something was missing. Should I consider opportunities or possibilities away from the confines of Hollywood?

During 2008, an election year, presidential candidate Barack Obama kept repeating what he and others had said for years: *We need to do more to support Operation Enduring Freedom in Afghanistan.* After the election, it became clear that we'd send more troops to Afghanistan.

In Iraq, an *Awakening* had occurred, where tribesmen turned on Al Qaeda and began working with American forces. This development, combined with an American surge of troops, resulted in a dramatic reduction of violence there. So our national security focus shifted from Iraq to Central Asia.

Watching the Afghan Channel one night at my parents' house in Orange County, I saw a commercial soliciting potential interpreters, linguists, and translators for *Operation Enduring Freedom*. With my gift for languages, might there be something extra I could do for America—beyond just paying taxes? Could I simultaneously help both my new country and my old?

In February of 2009, Amy helped me fill out an application with a company called Mission Essential Personnel (MEP). Within a week, I was on a plane to Baltimore for initial screening. At MEP headquarters, a CIA official interviewed me.

"So, Mr. Fazli, what is your civilian occupation?"

"I am an actor," I replied.

"Really? What types of roles?"

"I am a terrorist," was my unfortunate response.

The CIA guy excused himself.

I should have replied that I *play* terrorists. The interviewer soon returned and we straightened things out. Following the interview they took my fingerprints and gave me a medical examination. After the required background checks were completed, MEP sent me on to Fort Benning, in Georgia, for preliminary military training. There I met Army Sergeant First Class Roberto Chavez, who'd earlier done wonderful work in Iraq training indigenous personnel. An excellent leader, Chavez helped prepare 45 of us for the rigors of military life, as we continued pre-deployment screening and training. We took physical fitness tests, learned how to use basic military gear, studied first aid techniques, and practiced Immediate Action Drills on how to react if attacked while in a convoy. We learned about Improvised Explosive Devices (IEDs) and how to take cover from indirect fire. It wasn't exactly boot camp at Parris Island, but with each passing day I felt more comfortable wearing a uniform and getting into Army routines. Learning the military culture satisfied my desire for a new challenge. I loved the energy, the discipline, the sense of mission, and the growing camaraderie with my fellow trainees and our instructors.

SFC Chavez was a smart, charismatic soldier, and we developed a close relationship during my time at Fort Benning—from February through July. Eventually, he made me an informal assistant and I took on added duties while helping train new translator candidates.

Later, school personnel at Fort Benning needed to make future assignments and they polled our group of potential translators about where we'd want to work in Afghanistan. At a session in the biggest classroom, with all the translator candidates present, a MEP official explained that there were numerous jobs in different places in Afghanistan, with various commands and services.

"Let's start with the USMC," he said. "Who wants to work with the Marines?"

Naturally, we'd talked among ourselves about possible scenarios and the word was that working with the Marines meant tough duty, as opposed to working in the relative safety of various headquarters buildings in Kabul.

One person out of 45 raised his hand—my friend Daoud.

I thought back to my days as a teenager, our regular visits to the American Embassy in Islamabad, Pakistan, and of how much the Marine Security Guards there had impressed me. I remembered unsuccessfully trying to join the Marines after moving to California. Marine imagery had never left my mind. I raised my hand. That simple gesture committed me to the journey of a lifetime.

Before checking out of Fort Benning on July 23, I had one last lunch with SFC Chavez.

"The Marines are different from most Army units," the veteran soldier counseled me. "You'll find a leaner, meaner warrior mentality. It's not better or worse—just different. Marine infantry duty means tough work. Show them that you can hang in there. Learn their culture. Jump in and help where you can. Do extra little things. If you become part of their family, they'll always be there for you. You can count on that."

I thanked SFC Chavez and told him I'd never forget him, or all that he'd taught us. As I packed my gear that night, I had no second thoughts about the new direction my life was taking. The next day, a MEP van brought me, Daoud, and six other interpreters to the Atlanta airport. As we drove along, one of the other men stared at Daoud.

"You must be crazy," he finally said.

"Why?" Daoud stared back and shrugged.

"Nobody wants to go with the Marines." The other translator laughed and shook his head as if the answer should be obvious. "You'll end up getting shot or blown up on the ground in Helmand Province. The Marines are crazy killers and they'll drag you into danger with them."

Daoud said nothing, so I challenged the man's contentions. "Sergeant Chavez congratulated us on our decision. He said it would be very rewarding."

"Try to remember that when you're in a tent or a hole somewhere in Helmand," the translator responded. He looked at me as if he was talking to an idiot, and added "I plan to be in a Kabul hotel."

Daoud and I soon boarded a flight from Atlanta to California. From my window seat, I watched Atlanta disappear as we ascended into white clouds, our plane buffeted by turbulence. Unsettled by both the wind and the earlier conversation, I knew it wouldn't be long before we'd find out first-hand if the Marines were really crazy killers.

I was both excited and apprehensive about working with the Marines. It was a new role for me and I had little idea what was in the script. Daoud sat next to me on the plane.

"Do you think we'll get shot at?" Daoud asked, beginning to show a serious case of jitters.

"That depends on where we go." I did my best to show a confidence I didn't really feel. "Maybe. Time will tell."

As we flew westward, I stared out the window at the land below. The lush greens of Georgia eventually gave way to the harsh, flat browns of the western high desert. Brown was about to become a constant in the palette of my life for at least the next year. I decided the best bet was just to get used to it and worry about the rest of the colors in the spectrum later— if and when I survived what lay ahead at Twentynine Palms and in Afghanistan.

MEP representatives met us at the Palm Springs Airport and took us to a hotel. In the lobby there we linked up with ten other translators also headed to Twentynine Palms, known to Marines as "The Stumps." Apprehension was palpable as we speculated about our futures. We were a mixed bag of nervous people who spoke English with varying skills and accents. As we talked, I occasionally broke in with phrases of Pashto and Dari to see how well this group—all different ages and physical conditions, from different areas of Afghanistan—spoke the predominant languages. Most spoke Pashto better than Dari. My proficiencies placed me somewhat in the middle. My skills were admittedly a little rusty, as I'd been in America for the previous 24 years.

As we waited for someone from the Marine Corps to tell us what came next, we spent time in that hotel lobby feeling each other out and wondering about our specific roles as attached interpreters. One of the translators speculated that we'd spend most of our time at different headquarters, interpreting for senior officers when visitors or dignitaries were in the area. An interpreter named Said—quite heavy for active duty— guessed that we'd mostly help translate during prisoner interrogations. It all seemed a little naïve and short-sighted, given my understanding of what could be expected of us.

"Don't you think they might need us to go out and help *take* some prisoners?" I asked the heavyweight.

"Are you crazy?" Said seemed anxious to convince himself he wouldn't have to face much danger. "That's not our job."

Maybe he had a point, but I wasn't confident that we were headed for some cushy, rear area jobs—not with what I'd heard about the Marines.

The next day some Marines arrived at the hotel in a small bus to get us. The translators and a MEP official piled in for the long drive to The Stumps. My excitement increased when a sharp-looking sentry at the gate waved us on to the base. I felt a bit cocky—probably like countless other Americans who'd earlier answered their country's call and were suddenly surrounded by the sights, sounds, and might of a major military installation. I'd hooked up with the world's finest fighting force. Seeing all the armored personnel carriers, hum-vees, tanks, howitzers, helicopters, and firepower along with so many Marines moving purposefully about in their desert garb made me proud and confident about my new tribe.

Bring on the Taliban! I thought. I took in every detail as we drove through the base. It was dry and hot, but we saw a group of Marines running in formation wearing gear, carrying weapons, and chanting.

The MEP official turned towards us from his seat in the front of the bus. "You all need to be ready to run with these guys," the official said, smiling. "You're committed now."

"Is 'committed' another word for 'screwed'?" a translator asked.

Everyone laughed—even Daoud.

The bus dropped us off at a temporary billeting area. A sergeant directed us into a large conference room where he gave us an orientation to the base. The 12 of us were assigned to the 3rd Battalion of the 4th Marine Regiment, or 3/4. The unit was commanded by Lieutenant Colonel Martin Wetterauer, whose ominous radio call-sign was Darkside 6. The battalion was conducting intense pre-deployment training at Twentynine Palms, in an area where both terrain and weather closely resembled what the Marines would encounter in Afghanistan. Darkside 6 later impressed me when I observed him leading the battalion. Like many Marines, Wetterauer was a southerner, a Louisiana native who exuded an air of confidence and power. Tall and trim, he had a strong, forbidding presence, but his Marines—including the interpreters assigned to 3/4— quickly discovered he was usually approachable, despite his no-nonsense demeanor.

Wetterauer was what the Marines called a Mustang. He'd begun his service as an enlisted man and compiled a long and distinguished record. As a lieutenant in 1995, he'd commanded the platoon that famously rescued Captain Scott O'Grady, the Air Force pilot who'd been shot down in hostile Serbian territory. The movie *Behind Enemy Lines* with Owen Wilson was loosely based on that incident. Darkside 6 also served with distinction in several capacities in Iraq. He had a lot of history with 3/4, which seemed to make everything that happened to the unit and the Marines in it personal to him.

A Marine infantry battalion consists of five line companies supported by special attachments. The 3/4 companies included Headquarters and Service (H & S), Weapons, Kilo, India, and Lima. Interpreters were special attachments that could be assigned to any of those line units. After the sergeant completed his orientation, an earnest young captain followed up with an exhaustive, sometimes confusing briefing. He concluded by telling us to "Stand by" for our individual assignments. That's when I met First Sergeant David Haley of India Company.

"Are you the Hollywood actor?" Haley pointed a finger in my direction as he approached my chair from the side of the briefing room, where he'd been standing with other senior NCOs.

"That would be me." I jumped to my feet and shook his hand.

"Welcome to India Company. Let's go meet Captain Benson, the Company Commander."

"So he'll be my boss?"

"Yep. He's the skipper."

Haley also grabbed Mohammed, the other interpreter assigned to India Company, and the three of us walked to the company office, where Capt Benson was in a meeting. We waited outside, watching a continuous parade of young Marines. One Marine, a young lance corporal, stopped to let me know knowledge of my Hollywood history had preceded me into the battalion. Grinning, he said, "I saw you on Spike TV."

"You have a good eye for talent," I replied. The recruiters at MEP had forwarded profile information on me to 3/4. The battalion discovered not only my Hollywood background, but the fact that I was one of only two—of 150—interpreters who'd specifically asked for duty with the Marines. Some of those Marines, like the friendly lance corporal, had looked me up on the Internet to learn more about my movie and television work.

Finally, the First Sergeant brought us into the office to meet the company commander. "Welcome to our team," Capt Benson said, extending his hand over his desk while eyeballing me and Mohammed. "We looked at your profiles. Very interesting. So you grew up in Afghanistan, Fahim?"

"Yes, Sir," I replied. "Kabul."

"You can speak Dari and Pashto, yes?"

"Absolutely."

"Can you teach Marine Jarheads like the First Sergeant some of that lingo?"

"Yes, Sir"

"If you can teach someone like *me* how to speak Afghan," the First Sergeant interrupted, "then you'd be a damn fine instructor."

Capt Benson was a recent graduate of the Marine Corps' Expeditionary Warfare School. An Illinois native, he was bright and articulate. He'd written several articles for journals like *The Marine Corps Gazette*.

Getting down to business, Capt Benson said, "We're going to the desert for more field training. Have you got all your gear?"

Mohammed and I needed sleeping mats and goggles, among other things, so Capt Benson told the First Sergeant to take us to the Company Gunnery Sergeant, who was in charge of issuing field equipment. I walked out of the office thinking that the man I'd call "Boss" was articulate, thoughtful, and organized.

Haley introduced us to Gunnery Sergeant Luis Romero, India's Company Gunny—a tall, soft-spoken Mexican-American and a workaholic. He was the company's go-to-guy for logistics and supplies—and someone always needed something. Romero once dreamed of being a pilot, but vision problems precluded that. He then sought to become a military policeman, but finally decided that he was meant to be a plain old grunt. Still, he didn't fit the stereotype of the grizzled and growling Company Gunny, always yelling at the troops. He was quiet and conscientious, not afraid to show a gentle, caring side. I learned he'd give people in need the shirt off of his back or the shoes off of his feet—and that he loved being a Marine.

The Gunny got the stuff Mohammed and I needed and then showed us where to rack for the night. As I drifted off to sleep, I again felt that I was right where I was supposed to be.

The next day, Mohammed and I got our gear together and 1stSgt Haley brought us to a convoy staging area, where the company got into trucks and Humvees, heading to a designated training area in the desert. Haley was a tough Texan with a perceptive squint and a laser-like gaze that missed very little. If something was wrong or out of whack, the First Sergeant always noticed, and fixed it in a hurry.

"Where'd you learn to shave, Marine?" Haley settled his gaze on a lance corporal who had razor scrapes showing through his tan. "Your face is all messed up." I scratched at the full beard I'd grown and wondered what the First Sergeant thought of my shaving situation—or lack thereof.

The company assigned me to a truck with some radio operators which followed behind Capt Benson's vehicle. As we rolled out of the company's rear area, I looked ahead, beyond the Boss's vehicle, and saw scrub-covered mountains ahead of us that looked very much like some of the high country I remembered from my homeland, still some 10,000 miles away.

Other Marine tribe members on our truck included an Asian, a Hispanic, an African-American, a white guy, and Mohammed, my fellow translator—who, like me, understood the tribal dynamics we'd soon encounter in Afghanistan.

I'd always heard that Marines were tough. This proved to be true. I'd also heard that they killed first and asked questions later. This proved to be untrue. The 3/4 Marines were strong and fit but also kind, motivated, patient, and professional. They didn't project the ruthlessness I'd imagined.

After we arrived at our bivouac site, I met the India Company Executive Officer, First Lieutenant Scott Riley, another sharp and highly-educated Marine officer. Riley was preparing for his first deployment and wanted me to give a little cultural lecture after the company devoured an evening meal in the field. The XO was a perceptive man who always asked insightful questions. Later, when we got to Afghanistan, he regularly sought my counsel on cultural issues. On this first evening in the field he wanted me to talk in general terms about Afghan language and culture while introducing myself to the India Marines.

I stood nervously as the Marines gathered for my presentation. I told myself to relax. I was the expert on the material and knew I could find the right words in English when I needed them. The XO introduced me, explaining I was from Kabul, but was now an American movie actor who could speak Pashto and Dari.

"Hello Marines," I began. "I'm happy to be here with India Company." And then, because it was easiest I suppose, I began with a few language lessons. "Let me start with the word hello. In Pashto we say *salam alikam.*"

I covered the pleasantries: thank you, peace be with you, and some others, as well as a few specifics I knew they'd need, such as halt, put your hands up, and so on. The Marines took careful notes and I felt a bit like a language professor. I also spoke about Islam and pointed out cultural considerations they should bear in mind—like respecting mosques as holy places and remembering that Fridays for Muslims were like Sundays for Christians. I told them about the habit among Afghan males of kissing upon greeting another man—three times on alternate cheeks. They seemed surprised that sometimes men held hands and women seldom left their homes. When females were outside, they remained covered from head to toe and were not to be touched or spoken to directly by males they didn't know.

The Marines asked plenty of questions and some stayed behind after the lecture to discuss more specific issues. I was euphoric when I finally headed to my sleep spot, near Capt Benson's headquarters area. I'd demonstrated useful knowledge and already seemed to be part of the team. The Marines' many questions made me feel needed, wanted, and welcome. I took off my boots and stretched out on my sleeping mat, staring at the heavens. The intense heat of the desert day dissipated rapidly and it became quite comfortable. The Marines demonstrated impressive noise and light discipline. You wouldn't know there were 200 of them in the area. I looked up at stars that were brighter than any I'd seen since my escape from Afghanistan.

Twenty-two years earlier I'd tried to enlist in the Marine Corps but couldn't pass the tests. Now, at age 43, I proudly wore a desert utility uniform, teaching and training with some of the world's top warriors, as the 3/4 Marines prepared to deploy to Afghanistan to take on the Taliban.

Chapter 9: To War with the Marines

> *"If the Army and the Navy ever look on heaven's scenes,*
> *they will find the streets are guarded by United States Marines."*
> *– The Marines Hymn*

Training with the India Company Marines in the field at Twentynine Palms meant understanding their SOPs—Standard Operating Procedures. I quickly learned where to sit in my assigned vehicle when on the move and where to throw my gear when we stopped. I was part of the company headquarters element, which included the Company Commander, Capt Benson; the Executive Officer, Lt Riley; the First Sergeant, 1stSgt Haley; and the Company Gunnery Sergeant, GySgt Romero, as well as the Weapons Platoon Commander, Lt Patrick Kelly, and various radio operators and navy corpsmen. As part of this group, I needed to stay close to Capt Benson—without getting in the Boss's way.

An important Marine SOP was the daily shave. This created a problem as I'd purposefully grown a full beard to fit in better with locals when we got to Afghanistan. When Capt Benson asked me about it I explained that Afghans think a clean-shaven look is ugly and they consider hairless westerners weird. Islam sanctions facial hair as a sign of manhood, respect, honor, and righteousness. They take their cues from holy sources: Mohammed, Jesus, and the prophets all wore beards. I'd connect better with Afghans if I looked like them. So Capt Benson gave me a waiver.

As the hot summer days went by, I got more and more comfortable with the India team. Early each morning we'd mount our vehicles and head out to yet another training area—bouncing through the desert in our trucks and Hum-Vees. Some of the training was purely tactical—small unit operations on the platoon and squad levels, where there wasn't a role for me. My job focused on the civil affairs training scenarios involving noncombatants. As the platoons rotated through those scenarios, I got to know Marines from throughout the company.

My uniform was the same MARPAT digital camouflage desert utility garb worn by Marines, except for the missing *Eagle, Globe and Anchor* insignia that can only be earned at a Marine Corps boot camp. My name tag read "Hollywood" instead of "Fazli"—a tag the Boss thought would protect me since the Taliban targeted interpreters and their families in Afghanistan. Unlike the local families of Afghan interpreters, or "terps" in Marine Corps shorthand, my wife and child were presumably safe in Dana Point. Still, given that I was fairly well-known in the Afghan-American community and that there were presumably some Taliban sympathizers in southern California, the thinking was "Why invite trouble?"

Fahim in the field

It was beyond hot at Twentynine Palms—around 110 degrees. However, the Marine units in Afghanistan were deployed in the country's southern desert, where temperatures of 120 degrees were common in the summer. We received regular reports from Afghanistan about Marines suffering from heat exhaustion in Helmand Province. The required helmets and body armor just trapped heat around bodies. We needed to drink lots of fluids and plan for access to adequate water supplies. Overheating made people careless and erratic, putting their lives—and missions—at risk.

Southern Afghanistan's intense summer heat often made it too hot to fight, for both coalition and Taliban forces. Heat exhaustion routinely sidelined infantrymen who patrolled during the day, so British and American forces often moved in the dark. aided by night-vision devices.

The Taliban couldn't compete with that technology, so they largely limit-ed their summer activities to placing IEDs and occasional sniping.

Fortunately, 3/4 would be in-country from October through April and would miss the worst of Afghanistan's summer temperatures. We wouldn't have to contend with the infamous "Wind of 100 Days" where the extremely high temperatures so warmed the earth that convection currents created hurricane force winds whipping up sandstorms of bibli-cal proportions, restricting almost all movement or outside activity. While we'd miss the intense summer heat, we *would* arrive just in time for the fighting season.

Operation Mojave Viper was designed to prepare Marine infantry battalions to work in the Afghan desert. Some of the training scenarios required us to engage "native" Afghans in mock villages. That's where I came in. The natives were actors—mostly Pashto speakers—who'd been assigned certain roles. My job was to communicate with them and inter-pret for Capt Benson.

A week into training, in a particularly realistic scenario, two Afghan men from different tribes started screaming at each other. They were actors, but I still thought they might kill each other over some notional dispute in a mock Afghan village street. LtCol Wetterauer—Darkside 6— got involved and approached the scene with a couple of well-armed Marines and a terp. Their presence immediately diffused the situation. It didn't hurt that Darkside 6 himself had a pistol in his holster. He separat-ed the antagonists so they could cool off and then spoke to them individ-ually. He found some common ground and promised to take action. I was impressed. This is what we needed to do to succeed—communicate and bring people together.

Interpreting meant more than just converting Pashto to English, and vice versa. Many of the role-players were native Afghans and we needed to properly interpret cues and cultural signals. A simplistic misconcep-tion on the part of some Marines, for example, was that the Taliban wore black turbans and friendly Afghans wore white ones, like in Hollywood cowboy movies. In reality, anyone might wear a turban of any color. Sometimes body language and demeanor indicated political mindsets. Smiles were good. A failure to look you in the eye was bad. If someone relaxed after talking with me a while—that was good. If they continued to be nervous—that was bad. And just because someone claimed he didn't know anything about the Taliban didn't necessarily make it so.

We spent considerable time discussing how to deal with native Afghanistan women in a culturally conservative region. I began one evening lecture in the desert by stating, "Dealing with women in Afghanistan can be complicated."

A sergeant interrupted me. "Dealing with women in *America* can be complicated."

Everyone laughed.

"You're likely to see very few women," I explained. "And if you do see any, keep a respectful distance. Don't try to talk to them. They'll probably be fully covered by blue burquas. An exception could be poor widows. If you see some older women in black outside begging, then it may be OK to given them money or certain types of food."

"What if we have to clear a building and there are women inside?" asked Lt Riley.

"Good question," I replied. "Keep your distance from them. Hopefully a terp like me will be around to help. If not, then use words and gestures to get them into a room that is not being searched while you're securing other places. Then move them into a cleared space when you need to search their room. Ideally, we'd have female terps, but those are few and far between."

I anticipated playing a significant role when it came to Afghan women. It was hard enough to get male terps to work with Marines, much less female terps. The USMC was frantically trying to get women Marines trained in Pashto, but that would take time.

Bilingual native women would have been ideal interpreters. Unfortunately, they were rare and better suited for all-female engagement teams than to be embedded with infantry battalions.

"Don't the women leave their mud huts to buy groceries or clothes?" asked Staff Sergeant Cooke.

"Not necessarily," I replied. "You'll find men selling women's lingerie to other men in stalls at bazaars."

"I guess we know where Luffy-Lips will be spending his spare time when we get there," said Cooke. The Marines laughed and all heads turned towards an embarrassed lance corporal.

Humor aside, the Marines were now thinking more like Afghans. The training evolutions at Twentynine Palms were well-thought-out and really tested India Company—and me. We returned to base camp much more confident about operating in Afghanistan.

While born of the Barikzoy Tribe, I now felt like I was part of the Marine Warrior-Tribe. Since Afghanistan is a tribal land with an embedded warrior culture, I assumed Marines *could* fit in well there if they did the right things to connect with the native Afghans, and not alienate them, as the Soviets did. Americans tend to appreciate people as individuals. Afghans take mental shortcuts by assigning commonalties to whole groups of people—to whole *tribes*. The Marines were tribal in many ways. They wore the same uniform. They shaved every day. They had their own jargon. They treated their weapons with great care. They were loyal to each other. They projected strength and confidence. Color was of no consequence. You could be in the Marine Tribe whether you were white, black, yellow, or red. Afghans later found this dynamic curious and interesting, especially when they sensed that I, an Afghan, was of the Marine Tribe as well.

It was unfashionable to say that we sought to win Afghan *hearts and minds,* as that brought up uncomfortable memories of Vietnam-era jargon—but that was exactly what we needed to do. When I was a teenager, Soviet soldiers had made little effort to get to know us. Most people came to hate the Russians and ranks of Freedom Fighters swelled into hundreds of thousands of warriors, sworn to defeat these outsiders. It was the beginning of an epic *Jihad* for the Mujahedeen. I talked to the Marines about Jihad, and the Jihadist mentality.

"True believers *want* to die in a Holy War," I explained. "If your enemy wants to become a martyr, he'll do anything."

"Don't they believe that they'll get twenty-two virgins in Paradise if they die for the cause?" asked Luffy-Lips.

"Seventy-two virgins," I corrected him. "Seventy-two!"

"Wow," he responded to laughter. "It's hard enough finding even one around here!"

The India Marines listened to my lectures with discipline and respect. Platoons of around 40 Marines rotated through "school circles" for my classes in Afghanistan 101. Intensely interested in learning as much as they could about this remote and exotic land where they'd soon be risking their lives, they took copious notes and asked salient questions. I emphasized that one reason the Soviets hadn't prevailed in Afghanistan was because they'd totally alienated the native population.

"The Russians didn't make much of an effort to connect with local Afghans," I explained. "I know that first-hand because instead of trying to befriend me, they stabbed me and shot at me when I got out of line in Kabul." That really got the Marines' attention.

"The Soviets relied on brute force," I said. "They had incredible fire-power and air supremacy. They could go where they wanted. But they totally pissed off the native Afghans, many of whom swore to fight to the death. And when Reagan gave the Mujahedeen some Stinger missiles, Soviet pilots were scared shitless. Check out the movie *Charlie Wilson's War*. After the Soviets lost control of the air, and had millions of Afghans on a Jihad against them, they were beaten. They pulled out in disgrace in 1989. Two years later, the Soviet Union collapsed. Who'd have ever thought that the Afghan Mujahedeen would have helped to end the mighty Soviet empire?"

Using Soviet tactics could be fatal to many of us. No world power ever subjugated Afghanistan by force alone. Combining the judicious application of military might with smiles, patient interaction, and respect could help Americans prevail. We had to avoid provoking Jihad and that fast track to heaven for eager martyrs. Committed Communists had fought hard in the 1980s, but they didn't believe in an afterlife and were never fanatical or eager to die. We needed to appreciate Afghan culture, which meant understanding Islam, area history, the role of elders, and the non-public status of women.

In Afghanistan a code called *Pashtunwali* guides many tribes. It's a belief system that emphasizes honor—*Nang*. If an insult—*Benanga*—should occur, then Afghans are obliged to regain honor by any means. "Turning the other cheek" is an alien concept for those who follow Pashtunwali.

Revenge or justice—*Bada*—must be exacted.

For example, the old zoo in Kabul had a famous lion. To show off, a man jumped in a cage with the lion to taunt the animal—who promptly killed him. The man's brother returned to the zoo the next day with a grenade to kill the lion and avenge his brother's death, even though his brother was an idiot and the lion just did what lions do. Revenge must still be exacted.

Pashtunwali accounts for tribal blood feuds that go back generations. If a tribe member is wounded or killed, then that member's relatives swear eternal revenge. Pashtunwali beat the Soviets. When one Afghan was martyred, ten would swear revenge. What seemed a tactical success for the Russians only planted the seeds for more resistance, and every Afghan casualty created exponentially more Freedom Fighters.

The Americans—my Marines—could not make the same mistakes. Yes, we needed to deal with Taliban fanatics by any means necessary. And yes, that meant some family members would swear eternal revenge. Our challenge was to minimize casualties while engaging the population and winning their trust. If we did that, the Taliban could be isolated and eventually countered by the Afghans themselves. So we had a challenging dual mission requiring us to balance combat operations with civil affairs outreach.

The Marines had a history of working closely with indigenous forces. In Vietnam, USMC Combined Action Platoons (CAP) lived with native Vietnamese, won their trust, and eventually became effective partners. Typically, a Marine squad matched up with a Vietnamese platoon to establish a CAP. This approach was based on earlier models used by Marines in Haiti, Nicaragua, and the Dominican Republic. The Marines also utilized a version of CAP to great effect in Iraq. This partnering needed to happen in Afghanistan as well but it wouldn't happen without effective interpreters bridging the linguistic and cultural gaps. The success of the American mission depended heavily upon our terps. It was a major responsibility—difficult and dangerous. I took it all very seriously.

After several weeks of desert training, I'd gotten to know Marines from all the India platoons, as well as radio operators and Navy Corpsmen—usually referred to as docs. From staying close to the Boss, I picked up on some of the challenges he dealt with while running a company of over 200 men. Emergency leave was often required for everything from births to funerals. Some Marines occasionally needed to be disciplined, for which the Boss would hold *office hours*—non-judicial punishment short of a court-martial—to deal with transgressions. With my linguist's ear, I noted that Marines pronounced certain English words differently. Various accents indicated that someone was from Boston, New York, Texas, or Minnesota. So not only did I listen intently to *what* each Marine said, I also listened to *how* they said it. I immersed myself in the Marine Corps culture and also tried to learn as much as I could from every individual Marine.

I had minimal contact with 3/4 Marines from the other four companies, although I'd try to compare notes with other terps when I got the chance. Sadly, I found out that Daoud left 3/4. He had a run-in with the first sergeant in his company and asked out of Twentynine Palms. I later heard he hooked up with the Army in Afghanistan.

I met some Marines from the battalion headquarters staff, people I'd get to know much better in Afghanistan, including the battalion executive officer, Major Dale Highberger—Darkside 6's right hand man. The Battalion XO was another articulate, highly-educated officer with great interpersonal skills. He was especially smooth when dealing with visitors and civilians. He later gave me clearance into some headquarters areas and also encouraged me to write about my experiences. Maj Highberger emphasized how much the Marine Corps needed its interpreters which further reinforced my sense that accomplishing 3/4's Afghan missions would largely depend on linguists like Mohammed and me.

Beyond the role-playing during tactical scenarios, I became well-drilled in Immediate Action procedures so I'd know what to do if we were attacked or ambushed. I hoped to get some weapons training and carry a rifle. I'd done that in front of a camera before, and I wanted to see what it would be like in the real world, but the policy was to keep the terps unarmed. I figured I'd talk the Boss into giving me a weapon once we got to Afghanistan. Intelligence officers brought us up-to-date on the local military and political situations in southern Afghanistan and how developments might affect our dealings with Afghans in our Area of Operations (AO). We also learned more about basic medical care and first aid—lessons I'd later use.

The Marines' sense of purpose impressed me. They took everything seriously, giving attention to every detail. They asked me question after question about Afghanistan. Will there be dust storms? Will there be camels? Can we give candy to the kids? Some were easy to answer but others were harder—like the ones specific to recent developments and key personalities in our AO. The battalion intelligence people, the S-2 staff, tried to answer those questions. I reminded the Marines that I was from Kabul, that I'd never lived in southern Afghanistan, and that I'd also been out of the country for 26 years. In other words, a New Englander wasn't automatically an expert on Texas.

Back from the field—in the rear with the gear—the Marines concentrated on embarkation, logistics, administration, and medical issues as our deployment date drew nearer. Admin people gave me a checklist of things I needed to do in order to deploy with the battalion, such as getting a valid will approved. Some Marines wrote letters to loved ones, to be opened in the event of their deaths. I thought about that, but was afraid it might be bad luck. I wrote no letter, but instead got a voice recorder to keep an audio diary—and for that possible book.

As our departure date approached I looked forward to leaving behind the training at Twentynine Palms to do the real thing in Afghanistan. I still felt no fear, only anticipation. I wondered when the fear would finally come—and what would prompt it.

One early September day, an India Company officer, Lieutenant Troy Gent, invited me to his house on base for dinner. The Gents lived in a modest grey and white two-story dwelling with a perfectly manicured yard that featured a big dog and two kids chasing each other around.

Upon arriving, I immediately felt a welcoming, positive energy. Lt Gent was a Mormon from Utah, and one of the first things I noticed when we went inside was a framed picture of Jesus in the living room.

After dinner we talked about India Company, Afghanistan, living on base, and religion. I told Mrs. Gent that my wife shared her first name and that we had much in common, even though I was from Central Asia.

"So, are you a Muslim?" Amy Gent asked.

"I'm from an Islamic culture," I explained. "My belief system was shaped by a Muslim influence early on. But as I've traveled around and met many different people, I've learned that all religions have something to offer and they all deserve respect."

"Do you believe in Jesus?" Amy asked.

"I do," I responded. "He's in the Quran. And I also believe he's coming back, somehow, someday. And believe it or not, I used to live in Utah myself. That's where I became an American citizen."

"Did you ever make it to the Tabernacle in Salt Lake City?" asked Lt Gent.

"Of course," I replied. "What a beautiful place. I loved the music and architecture."

The Mormons are so giving, going out of their way to help each other. Their volunteer actions like feeding the poor are more than just words. I pointed out similarities to Islam—a belief in prophets, a prohibition on alcohol, and so forth. "There's common ground if you choose to look for it."

The Gents were thoughtful and inquisitive, as well as generous. Their hospitality reminded me of the Afghan tradition of making guests feel welcome. I shared what I could about the spiritual aspects of Afghan life.

"Some people laugh at religious rituals and discipline," I explained. "But strictly following rules can make people thoughtful and spiritual— like when Muslims fast during Ramadan. Catholics, Jews, Mormons and people from other religions use rituals that help them focus."

The Gents were devout and didn't even consume caffeine, much less alcohol. I sensed that their faith gave them structure, definition, and hope, which moved and impressed me. Their serene home reminded me of a chapel, a place of respect.

Our nice evening had an undercurrent of apprehension. In October, the 3/4 Marines would head off to Afghanistan for seven months. We knew that we were going to a dangerous place in a dangerous country, where many other Marines had been killed or maimed. In some ways it's harder for the loved ones left behind, who can only wonder, worry, and pray. My own Amy visited Twentynine Palms several times and the uncertainty took a toll on her as well.

Before I left the lieutenant's house, Amy Gent took me aside. "We're really depending on you, Fahim," she said. "You know the languages. You know Afghanistan. You know what to look for. Please keep my husband safe."

"I promise," I told her.

As I drove away from the Gents' place I turned around and looked back. My evening at their loving home had been more than a social event. It also had a powerful spiritual component. My personal beliefs combine elements of several religions. I know there are powers in the spiritual realm that guide and protect life on earth, according to an unknowable plan. I sensed the presence of angels at that house. Lt Gent and his fellow Marines from 3/4 were risking their lives to give my native land a chance at a better future—and the importance of my role had just been underscored by the lieutenant's wife.

I'd often considered my homeland to be cursed. In my darkest hours, I doubted Afghanistan could overcome the profound challenges of being a war-torn, divided land—among the poorest countries on earth. If there were to be any hope for such a backward, impoverished nation, it lay with the Americans now committed there. I'd seen first-hand how hard the Marines trained and I felt a new sense of hope—*and* responsibility. I thought of my daughter Sophia, and how I'd feel if I had to entrust *her* safety to someone else. Then I really understood Amy Gent's poignant plea.

We had to trust in God, but I had to trust my own linguistic and acting skills as well. Precious lives were at stake. I felt sober and focused.

As the deployment date drew near, the Marines spent extra time with their families. I wanted my parents to meet our 3/4 Marines. My mother liked that the U.S. sought to make Afghanistan a better place. She was proud of me and I appreciated her support—support that hadn't always been there. Earlier, she and my father had made it clear that they didn't want me to go back to Afghanistan. Yes, they worried about me getting hurt or killed, but it was more than that, especially with my father, who thought some in the Afghan community would consider me a traitor. Some Afghans were reflexively anti-American, even after the U.S. had invested so much blood and treasure in Afghanistan. Did these Afghan expatriates want the Taliban to return to power in Kabul?

Afghans in America occupy a broad philosophical spectrum. Many, like me, assimilate and develop a love for their adopted country. Others choose to remain segregated in various cultural enclaves and hang on to the old customs, traditions, and language. Those who don't assimilate continue to identify with elements from the old country—sometimes even the Taliban. I know many of them hated me, and some of them were close to my father, who wasn't much of an assimilator himself.

American Marines wanted to help Afghanistan, not conquer or exploit it. I thought that if my parents visited Twentynine Palms they'd understand things better. So in late September I went over and picked them up in Orange County. As we drove back east on I-10, I explained as much about the Marines as I could, emphasizing their professionalism and proficiency. When we got to the base, the sentry checked my credentials and waved us in with a flourish. My parents nodded to each other, recognizing the respect I'd been given.

We parked the car and walked around. I showed my parents the Base Exchange, library, theater, and finally the 3/4 and India Company areas. My mother talked to some of the troops, who were always polite, confident, and reassuring. She kept saying, "I'm from Afghanistan. Thank you! Thank you!" to every Marine she met.

The Marines appreciated her sentiments. They smiled and replied with various versions of "Thank you ma'am. Happy to help. That's our job. We'll kick their butts."

Even my father softened a little, but he remained conflicted. I wondered if perhaps he and I might get to a better place in our relationship after I returned from the deployment—if I returned. Still, while driving my parents back to Orange County, I decided that their visit to the

Marine base definitely brought us closer together.

"What wonderful young men you work with, Fahim," my mother gushed.

"Yes," I replied. "They're impressive professionals. Don't you think so, Dad?"

"Maybe," said my father.

"They said they can't wait to get the Taliban," my mother added.

"They are so motivated," I said. "Aren't you pleased that I'm working with such people?"

"Maybe," said my father.

With 3/4 back in garrison making final deployment preparations, Capt Benson hosted a barbeque at his off-base residence. He wanted families to mingle and get to know the India Company leadership better. Our team was really coming together.

Amy couldn't make it, so I ended up as one the few there without a wife. Mohammed also arrived stag. I got there early with a 12-pack of Corona for Capt Benson and then I put my culinary skills to good use by helping the Boss's wife, Susan, cut vegetables.

The Bensons had a dog named Gunny, who jumped all over me in the kitchen. When Mohammed walked into the kitchen a few minutes later, Gunny immediately growled at him. Mrs. Benson noticed.

"Susan told me that Gunny liked you," the Boss told me later. "She said she trusts you but not Mohammed, because Gunny doesn't like Mohammed."

"Just call me 'Dog's Best Friend,'" I replied with a smile.

When we were all outside after eating, Mrs. Benson tried to get the dog back in the house. She yelled from the doorway, "Gunny! Get in here right now!"

"Yes, ma'am," replied GySgt Romero, the real Company Gunny. Everyone laughed—even Mohammed.

Then the Boss spoke and—among other things—said that the presence of trained interpreters like Mohammed and me gave him great confidence that India Company would succeed in Afghanistan.

The day after the barbeque, SSgt Cooke saw me in the company area. "Fahim, can we talk?"

"Sure," I said. "What's up?"

"Mohammed says he may not deploy," explained Cooke. "But he wouldn't elaborate. Are you OK? What's going on?"

"I'm good to go," I said. "I'll try to see what's happening."

I found out that some linguists were afraid. They'd learned that 3/4 was headed to northern Helmand Province—one of the most dangerous places in the country. Marine battalions that deployed there earlier suffered terrible casualties, mostly due to IEDs. Besides those who'd been killed, there were many single, double, triple and even quadruple amputees. 3/4 would be responsible for a vast and hostile area.

Our battalion would replace 2/3, the latest in a string of Marine battalions seeking to establish a presence in a region long-dominated by the Taliban. Before the Marines arrived, British troops—including Prince Harry—had fought for years throughout that AO. The Brits and then the Marines suffered heavy casualties and remained over-extended. Coalition forces were spread so thin that the Taliban still controlled most of the area. Our AO included northern Helmand Province as well as parts of Nimruz and Farah Provinces, where the great Hindu Kush Mountains abruptly rose from the flat desert floor. We'd eventually establish a headquarters in the crossroads town of Delaram, where the three provinces converged. It was also only a short distance to Kandahar Province—the birthplace of the Taliban.

The Taliban flourished in greater Helmand Province, since the Helmand River Valley is the center of the world's greatest poppy fields. Poppy farming and opium and heroin production powered the local economy and provided considerable revenue for the Taliban. They'd fight hard to protect their drug enterprise. While most of the people were not members of the Taliban, they distrusted foreigners who might threaten their way of life. Soviet forays into the area 25 years earlier had been disastrous.

The locals also distrusted the central Afghan government. In fact, they hated anything associated with Kabul. District governors or sub-governors were constant assassination targets, and the government officials who survived were thought to be compromised by the Taliban.

Before the Taliban re-emerged in the years following their 2001 overthrow in Kabul, corrupt local police had completely alienated the Helmand population. Official corruption was so bad that nothing happened without bribes. Eventually, the corruption was so bad that people tolerated the Taliban as a less crooked alternative that could bring some stability—but at the terrible cost of what little freedom the people still enjoyed.

When I was young, Afghanistan's many tribes had co-existed with little conflict, but after 1978, the Communists successfully created tribal jealousies to divide the people. The Taliban similarly exploited these rivalries.

Major tribal groups in Afghanistan included the Baluchi, Hazara, Nuristani, Pamiri, Pashtun, Tajik, Turkmen, and Uzbek. Almost all were Sunni Muslims, except for the Shiite Hazara. In northern Helmand, the Durani—a Pashtun tribe—predominated. Sub-tribes like the Barikzoy, the Nourazai, and the Popalzai were often at odds. These tribes fought over precise boundaries between tribal village areas, or about who controlled certain roadways and distribution routes. At one time, elders resolved these problems, but now the Taliban exacerbated these tribal divisions, knowing that subsequent violence could create a cycle of conflict and chaos they could exploit.

In the eastern part of the AO—around Now Zad—the Taliban dug in so deeply that they actually created World War I-style bunkers and trenches behind vast minefields. The continued existence of this pervasive defensive complex was a defiant representation of Taliban power. It seemed to invite attack by signaling that the Marines were too weak to assault or liberate Now Zad and displace the Taliban. The 3/4 Marines would have the mission to take down this symbol of Taliban dominance when they arrived in-country. Now Zad meant a huge fight.

Rumors of this future showdown filtered down to the terps, who knew that Darkside 6 and 3/4 faced a daunting AO. Although the Marines looked forward to the challenge, some linguists thought our mission there to be not only dangerous, but hopeless, and they expressed grave doubts about surviving in Helmand Province. Finally, all the terps got together to talk in a Best Western hotel room just days before our deployment. Most were afraid and wanted to quit and turn in their gear.

"Daoud left and got a better job with the Army," said Abdullah, one of the youngest terps. "I don't want to live in a hole over there in Helmand and help find IEDs. I have a life to live. I heard we can all get reassigned to Army jobs in Kabul if we request that."

I looked around the room and sensed most of the terps felt the same way.

"I don't know about any of you, but I'm going forward," I said. "I want to pay my dues to America. And when I come back, I'll be able to sleep well and live with myself."

The fat terp named Said looked at me with a pained expression. "Fahim!" he exclaimed. "Don't you know what they expect us to do over there? They want us out on patrols! We don't need that. You're a Hollywood actor. You have a family. A home. Money. A future. Are you crazy? Why do you want to go get blown up in Helmand?"

I knew we could make a difference over there. How could we break faith with these Marines—and their families—who so depended on us? I thought of Amy Gent.

"I'm going with the Marines," I said. "I've been here for 24 years and I'm an American. I owe this country."

"Then you're a fool!" exclaimed Said.

Some of the terps were Afghans who'd just come to America with green cards. They'd stayed with the Mission Essential Personnel program long enough to collect a $10,000 bonus. Now they wanted out.

"Yes, you've been safe in America for 24 years," Mohammed shot back. "You have no idea what it's like now in Afghanistan. You don't understand what the Taliban have done to our country."

"That's OK," I replied. "I'll go back and see with my own eyes. It's wrong for you to take the money and walk away. It's stealing. The Marines need us. I'm going to pay my dues to my country."

The situation was a microcosm of what we'd face in Afghanistan. The terps with the green cards were products of a culture of corruption. They were survivors from a land that had been at war for 30 years. They were cold and calculating, with no loyalty to America or the Karzai regime.

They were pragmatists who understood the complexities of life in Afghanistan. Things were not black and white for them—only various shades of grey. I recalled a couple of them laughing at a Marine who'd been hurt training in the desert.

After the meeting ended, I wondered how many terps would pack up and leave.

On October 6, seven of our 11 remaining translators quit, leaving 3/4 with only four interpreters.

On October 9, our battalion finally boarded airplanes and took off from the Twentynine Palms airstrip, beginning a 10,000 mile journey that would take 3/4 to Germany and then to Manas Air Force Base in the former Soviet Republic of Kyrgyzstan. After a couple days at Manas, we got on military transport planes for a long flight to Bagram—an American air base north of Kabul that had once been the main Soviet air facility during the 1980s.

We donned helmets and flak jackets and put in our ear plugs. As we strapped ourselves into the transport, I looked at the Marines around me. They were poised and confident. I didn't sense a bit of fear. Five hours later, we landed at Bagram—almost a mile above sea level. My pulse quickened as I unbuckled my seat belt and stood to file out of the plane. Moments later, I set foot on the tarmac and looked around. A cool breeze blew as I scanned the great mountains. After an absence of 25 years, I'd finally returned to my native country.

It was a sunny October afternoon. The air facility had three big hangars, a control tower, many support buildings, and even some oversized tents. The mountains were green and snow-free. Old Soviet planes and tanks were still visible around the base periphery—relics of the disastrous war of the 1980s. Even though Bagram was only an hour's drive from Kabul, I'd never visited the place as a youngster. I felt no desire to return to Kabul, despite my proximity. The place conjured up too many bad memories.

We watched aircraft taxi while Marines unloaded wooden pallets with our sea bags from the transport. I scanned the towering peaks where the enemy lurked—along with invisible mines and IEDs. We retrieved our sea bags and gear, got into single file, and moved to assigned billeting space in a large tent where we'd await further transport to Camp Leatherneck.

I felt good—ready to go to work. I chatted up the Marines on either side of my space and then lay on my cot and reviewed some notes. I thought of Germany and Japan. The Americans fought and defeated both countries during World War II but maintained a presence in each nation until both were rebuilt. Now they were both prosperous American allies. Could a similar scenario play out in Afghanistan?

I stowed my paperwork under my cot after most of the lights went out. Before closing my eyes, I regarded the prone Marines racked out on the many military-issue cots squeezed into the big tent. I wondered which ones would not return home with us. Then I closed my eyes and fell asleep in my native land for the first time since 1983.

Chapter 10: Delaram

*"I come in peace. I didn't bring artillery. But I am pleading with you,
with tears in my eyes: If you fuck with me, I'll kill you all."*
- Marine General James Mattis, to Iraqi tribal leaders in 2003

We took another C-130 military transport aircraft from Bagram Air Base to Camp Bastion, the British base in the southern desert west of Kandahar. During the three hour flight, I strained to see out a head-sized window for glimpses of Afghanistan, version 2009. I'd never flown over the country before and imagined seeing little black Taliban figures scurrying around the mountains far below. We flew over greater Kabul, but I wasn't able to see much. I suddenly remembered how Stinger Missiles had taken out those Soviet aircraft. If some former Mujahedeen had any leftovers they were saving for the right moment, we were screwed.

After landing at Bastion we taxied toward a newly-erected hangar building, built mostly of plywood and canvas. A warm breeze blew as we filed off the plane, but it was not as hot as I'd imagined. We organized by company and working parties moved gear and sea bags onto waiting trucks. Transport vehicles drove us the short distance to Camp Leatherneck. The Marines seated around me on the back of our truck wore the required helmets and body armor; everyone but me carried a rifle or pistol. At first glance I didn't fit in with these clean-shaven warriors, with my thick beard and long hair flowing out the back of my helmet. I chatted with the Marines around me while we rolled. My English was now more sophisticated. I spoke more like a Marine, military jargon and acronyms flowing naturally from my lips.

Soon our little convoy passed a sign that read, "Welcome to Camp Leatherneck." This sprawling Marine base had grown from nothing during the previous six months. 3/4 was now part of the Marine Expeditionary Brigade (MEB) headquartered there and commanded by Brigadier General Lawrence Nicholson. We drove to a temporary living area, got off the trucks, married up with our gear, and moved into our assigned spaces in the tents that filled the area. We'd only be at Camp leatherneck a few days to take care of some administrative and logistical issues. Then we'd head to the field and relieve the 2/3 Marines in our assigned AO to the north. While we waited, we learned some Camp Leatherneck history from Nicholson's staff, who told us of the general's first visit to the area the previous February.

Upon seeing the vast empty space west of Camp Bastion, Nicholson had one question for the base's Commanding General. "Can we put a Marine camp in that vacant area out there?"

"Of course," said the British commander. "It's your space if you want it."

The very next day American bulldozers and heavy equipment operators were on the job. Working non-stop for three months, Marine Engineers and Navy Seabees built up an expeditionary outpost sufficient to support regimental-size combat operations. When the MEB headquarters staff arrived in April, Nicholson christened it *Camp Leatherneck*. The term Leatherneck originally referred to a leather stock that 18th century Marines wore around their necks while aboard ships to protect their jugulars from swords brandished by enemies boarding those ships. Camp Leatherneck eventually billeted almost 15,000 people.

On July 2, 2009, *Operation Khanjar* commenced. In Arabic, *Khanjar* means "Strike of the Sword" and the Marines did just that, striking hard with scores of helicopters inserting thousands of Marines into key enclaves along a 50-mile stretch of the Helmand River. American-built irrigation systems from the 1960s had turned this region into fertile farmland—especially for poppies—and the Taliban dominated throughout. Appearing from the air as a giant green snake slithering through a vast brown desert, the Helmand River Valley was home to small cities like Garmsir, Gerishk, Khanashin, and Nawa-I-Barakzayi. The Marines established themselves in these population centers, steadily and inexorably securing surrounding villages—except for Marjah, which planners chose to isolate for the time being. During the following months, the Marines expanded and consolidated their control throughout the region, causing the Taliban to take refuge in Marjah, or move further north—where 3/4 was bound.

Our battalion's Area of Operations included territory in Nimroz and Farah Provinces as well as Helmand, from Bakwa in the west, to the crossroads community of Delaram, to the city of Now Zad in the east—a distance of over 70 miles. Marines from 2/3 were thrilled to see us coming, having been in-country for six months themselves. Like other Marine battalions deployed to that AO, 2/3 had suffered more than its share of casualties, mostly due to the omnipresent IEDs.

Darkside 6, Major Highberger, Operations Officer Major Eric Dougherty, the company commanders, and the rest of the staff coordinated in advance with 2/3 to implement a detailed plan positioning the battalion elements.

In the center of the AO, Darkside 6 set up his battalion command post in the crossroads town of Delaram. Colonel Paul Kennedy, his immediate superior, had his Regimental Headquarters in Delaram as well. Capt Benson and India Company took positions near the battalion headquarters. The battalion mission was two-fold: conduct combat operations as required to increase security and reduce the threat of enemy attack while conducting civil affairs operations to better connect with the locals, develop infrastructure, and earn the trust of the people. This meant we'd dig wells, establish schools, improve roads, provide security and do whatever else we could to show the people that we cared.

Our battalion would be responsible for an area almost the size of the state of Rhode Island. Kilo Company deployed to the west, where Captain Geoffrey Hollopeter's Marines occupied combat outposts that 2/3 had maintained near Bakwa. The Taliban ran major drug operations in Nimroz Province, and Darkside 6 would use Kilo Company to disrupt their criminal drug-running endeavors.

Far to the east, around Now Zad, Captain Andy Tirrell's Lima Company took up positions. Now Zad was a ghost town, abandoned by most of its 100,000 residents, as the Taliban placed IEDs everywhere. The enemy had dug in and created the massive trench complex with built-up defensive positions and bunkers as they prepared for a rare linear-type of confrontation with the over-extended Marines.

The landscape was largely flat, the AO being mostly south of the great mountains, although an India Company platoon under Lt Kelly occupied a mountain redoubt to the north in Golestan.

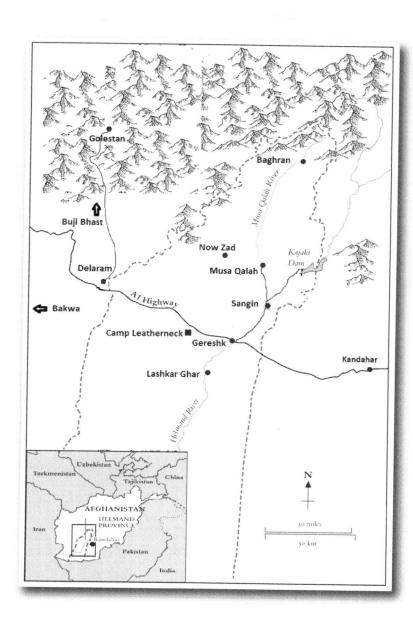

We needed to clear a ground route from Delaram to Kelly's position. The existing road was heavily mined, which isolated several mountain villages. We had to reconnect those communities to each other and to the country's biggest highway, Route 1, which ran through Delaram. Also known as Ring Road, Route 1 was a paved highway that circled Afghanistan. It was vital for the movement of goods, produce, people—everything. The road unified the country. It was so important that even the Taliban didn't mess with it. They placed mines or IEDs on every road but Route 1. The heavily mined secondary road from Delaram to Golestan essentially cut off the northern villages.

To get a sense of the atmospherics in our AO, we needed to walk the ground and talk to the people. The cool climate would make our work tolerable for the bulk of our deployment, from October of 2009 until April of 2010. The cool reception we received from the locals, on the other hand, meant we had work to do if we wanted them to warm up to our presence there.

The tribal make-up in our AO included a preponderance of Pashto-speaking Nourazai, which included my own Barikzoy sub-tribe. When I'd later introduce myself as a Barikzoy, people warmed to me, although villagers and sub-tribes sometimes often bad-mouthed each other. I countered that with "We are all Pashtuns. We are all Durani." It usually worked.

We took our positions, but the natives didn't welcome us with open arms. A deadly riot had taken place when 2/3 was in Delaram; the Taliban were experts at stirring people up against the Americans. Suicide bombers previously tried and failed to get inside the main Delaram battalion compound, so local security remained a priority. There was much to do throughout the AO if we were to both continue and expand upon the civil affairs outreach done by 2/3 and other USMC battalions *and* conduct combat operations.

By late October, Darkside 6 had all the elements of 3/4 thoroughly engaged. The staff planned a variety of missions. Companies conducted patrols in their respective areas to give commanders and troops a feel for the region. Darkside 6 wanted his battalion to take the initiative. The 3/4 Marines were to find and engage their adversaries—and give chase as well, if the enemy tried to disappear.

After arriving in Delaram, I settled into the spartan quarters I shared with Lt Riley, our Company XO, Lt Fafinsky, a platoon commander, and SSgt Cooke, one of India Company's top staff non-commissioned officers. Capt Benson and 1stSgt Haley shared a tent right next to us. We hung ponchos up in our small tents to create private spaces. Our canvas shelters kept out the occasional winter rain and protected us from the constant wind. What more could one ask for in Afghanistan?

Riley was calm, organized, and in control. Fafinksy was a loveable hard-charger who got lots of care packages in the mail, much to our delight. He also had a laptop computer so we could watch some movies, including some that included me, like *Rambo III* and *Ironman*. Like the XO, Cooke was organized and all-business, but unlike Fafinsky, he liked to have it dark in the tent. I soon learned about RHIP—Rank Has Its Privileges—as the light tended to stay on.

The morning after settling in to my new home, I moved around to observe the people in our area. I noticed a group of children hanging out by our compound's gates. They reminded me of myself as a youngster, loitering around the Russian bases. Were the kids spying for the Taliban? I wondered if they hung around to get supplies for the enemy—the way I'd acquired parts of Russian weapons for the Mujahedeen when I was young. I saw Capt Benson at lunch and flagged him down.

"Boss, I'm not sure about all those kids out there," I told him. "When I was their age I hung around the gates of Soviet bases, gathering information, trading for stuff the resistance could use. I stole things. I bet they're doing the same. I don't trust them out there."

"I know," he replied. "They're probably harmless, but we can't take any chances. I'll get with The Old Man and The Two about it." Darkside 6 and the Intelligence Officer would know what to do.

A couple of days later, the kids disappeared.

We'd only been in Delaram for a week when SSgt Cooke asked me to translate for him while he took a motorized security force to meet a 20-vehicle convoy coming from Kandahar. We needed to escort it safely through Taliban country back to Delaram, a 60-mile roundtrip. We moved out in trucks and older hum-vees—instead of the newer MRAP (Mine Resistant Ambush Protected) vehicles, which were designed to help passengers survive IED blasts.

Watching Cooke take charge bolstered my confidence. An Iraq veteran, he could almost smell IEDs. I nicknamed him Sniff Dog. When we came to likely IED locations, Cooke carefully directed the vehicles safely around them. Then, around 20 miles into the trip, we heard a loud explosion.

"All stop," Sniff Dog shouted into the radio, looking at the thick, black smoke billowing in front of us. "I say again, all stop." Then he punched my arm. "Let's go take a look." We climbed out of our truck and moved up the line of vehicles.

"Set up a security perimeter," Cooke yelled to a sergeant in the vehicle behind ours. We walked to the explosion area, and saw that a truck's back wheels were blown off, shreds of rubber strewn all around.

"Damn it, Corporal!" Cooke yelled at the driver. "This is what we don't want. Are you OK?"

Afghan roads are perilous

"I'm good," said the driver. "Should have missed that spot. Sorry."

Fortunately, nobody was seriously injured. It was a relatively small IED, though skillfully placed. The truck looked like it could continue the mission. We changed the blown tires and cleaned up the mess. Small buildings near the road provided cover for the enemy, and I felt eyes on my back while we worked.

"See anything suspicious?" Cooke asked, noticing me scanning the buildings.

"Faces in windows," I replied. "Not sure if they're friendly."

"We can't sit here too long," Cooke said urgently. "We don't want to give a sniper time to draw a bead on a driver, or have a mortar team to drop a few rounds on us. Keep looking around. Tell me if you see anything that looks weird."

While Cooke and company labored over the truck, I continued to watch for movement. Fearing a sniper might draw a bead on me, I grew increasingly nervous. I maintained a 360 degree surveillance around our stalled convoy, moving constantly. A moving target was harder for a sniper to hit, and I wanted to survive my first mission.

It took over an hour to fix the truck and get rolling again. We moved ahead cautiously, but thankfully there were no more explosions. We reached the link-up point and met the inbound convoy from Kandahar. Now we had to turn around and escort all these vehicles and their crucial supplies back along the same route through Indian Country to Delaram. Sniff Dog worried that the Taliban would anticipate us returning the same way and lay in more IEDs. The bad guys could dig a hole and place a mine in less than five minutes and we'd just spent a couple hours linking up and organizing the convoy. So engineers went ahead to secure over 20 miles of road.

We moved along slowly. Our driver was tense and nervous as he tried to keep our wheels following the tracks of the vehicle in front of us. *The lead driver must really be nervous*, I thought, since his vehicle was the one most likely to hit something. We were well on our way back to Delaram when SSgt Cooke called for the convoy to stop. He had a bad feeling about IEDs and wanted more engineer support in front of us. One of the vehicles also needed to reposition its load. Soon afterwards, we heard the loud *thunk* of the first mortar round as it hit.

It landed 100 yards away, but we felt the concussion from its blast. I looked at Cooke, who was on the radio immediately to alert Delaram.

"We've got to get that truck moving!" he exclaimed, jumping out of our vehicle, with me right on his heels. More impacts followed, each one closer than the last. I recalled the words of the fat interpreter at

Twentynine Palms. *Why do you want to go get blown up in Helmand Province?*

Sniff Dog was everywhere—directing people, working his radio, reporting the situation, and keeping other vehicles rolling through the impact area. Less than five minutes later, the stricken truck was moving again.

"Go baby!" I yelled, as I saw it take off. Then another mortar round hit, less than 50 yards away. Cooke saw me standing behind him and screamed "Fazli! Get down or back in the vehicle. This isn't Hollywood!"

Another convoy truck rolled past us and a Marine standing in the back yelled down to Cooke: "I think they're shooting from behind those buildings over there," pointing to a cluster of mud huts less than a mile away. I stared at the buildings, straining to see signs of life, before Sniff Dog grabbed me and pulled me towards our vehicle. We jumped in, much to the relief of the driver who was now behind the wheel of the only truck not moving, as the explosions came closer.

"We need to move!" shouted Cooke.

"No shit!" yelled the driver, jamming it into gear.

"Are you going to shoot back?" I asked, gesturing toward the village.

"Nah," said Cooke. "That's what they want us to do. They want us to hurt some civilians. We won't do that. But don't worry. We're moving and help is on the way."

I felt alive and alert. I looked out the window at the distant buildings now receding behind us and thought, *Screw you, Taliban!* I felt the same elation that I'd experienced when the Soviets fired at me in Kabul, almost 30 years earlier.

There is nothing more exhilarating than to be shot at without result.

If the Soviets had been ambushed like us, they'd have obliterated every building, house, and structure within range. The Russians had raked my steep hill with automatic weapons fire after I'd fired a single stone from my slingshot down at their convoy. I wondered if younger Afghans understood or appreciated American restraint. The Marine discipline impressed me. Sniff Dog knew what he was doing. We accomplished the mission. The vehicles and supplies got through. No Marines or civilians were injured. Marines like Cooke knew how to take control under fire and also understood the Code of Pashtunwali.

During my first two weeks in Delaram I didn't do much interpreting, but when we captured a Taliban fighter hurrying away from an IED emplacement, we needed to find out what he knew. While preparing for my first prisoner interrogation, I imagined the scenario, my thoughts colored by war movies I'd seen in America. I relived the tension and stress I'd felt watching the classic interrogation scene at the beginning of Quentin Tarantino's *Inglourious Basterds,* which came out earlier in 2009. Should I gently prod the prisoner at first, and then kick, punch, and beat him if he didn't talk? What if the prisoner became violent? I shook myself out of my fevered fantasy. Our questioning would be conducted by American professionals, not German Nazis. I walked over to the interrogation building.

I'd interpret for an intelligence officer during the session, in a small, windowless room with three chairs, a small table, and the stereotypical single light bulb hanging from the ceiling. A voice recorder sat on the table. The young Taliban prisoner looked at me with wide eyes when I walked in—the big bad cop with the full-faced beard. The prisoner had a slight adolescent beard and couldn't have been over 18. He wore dirty clothes and worn-out sandals. I was a bit surprised he wasn't handcuffed.

The American interrogator, a lieutenant, sat at the table scribbling in a notebook. The lieutenant was unarmed, although two Marine military policemen stood just outside the poncho liner-covered doorway. I sat on the side of the table away from the wall, in between the lieutenant and the prisoner, who faced each other. The lieutenant was very patient and measured as he asked me to interpret his words. He started simply. "What is your name?"

"Staa saa noom saa sheey dee?" I asked.

No answer.

"Ask him where he's from," said the lieutenant.

"Chera showendey kawee?" I asked.

The prisoner remained silent.

The Talib wouldn't talk. The officer scribbled more notes and then stared at the prisoner, whose earlier wide-eyed look gave way to a defiant stare. The lieutenant looked at me.

"Ask him his name, again," he said.

"Staa saa noom saa sheey dee?"

The prisoner looked at me, then the lieutenant, and then leaned back in his chair and silently stared at the ceiling. Frustration grew inside me. We were getting nowhere, but if the lieutenant was exasperated, he didn't show it. He wrote more into his green, military issue notebook. Eventually, the officer told me to warn the prisoner that if he didn't talk to us we'd turn him over to the ANP—the Afghan National Police.

I looked at the officer and smiled, and then employed a bit of theater. I paused for effect and stood up and walked to the door. I pushed aside the poncho liner and saw the two MP's standing on either side. They looked at me. I winked at them and then backed back into the interrogation room. Remaining on my feet, I faced the lieutenant. I asked him to repeat what he wanted me to ask, which he did.

"Are you sure?" I asked, winking at him.

"Yes, quite sure," said the officer.

I whirled and faced the prisoner, showing him my fiercest face. He looked back at me, his defiant demeanor melting away. I stared back and said nothing, letting the tension build. Now the prisoner looked down at the floor, instead of the ceiling.

I turned back to the officer. "Are you sure?" I asked again, loudly.

"Yes," said the officer, his eyes sparkling a bit, as he picked up on my cues.

I faced the prisoner again, this time with a pained expression. "I have some very bad news for you," I said softly in Pashto.

The prisoner looked up from the floor, but said nothing.

I looked at the officer again. "ANP?"

"ANP," he responded.

I changed my tone from soft to matter-of-fact. "The ANP wants you," I explained. "We wanted you to talk and help us so we could help you. But you have nothing to say so there's nothing we can do. We're turning you over to the ANP."

The prisoner looked at me, then the officer, then me again, tears welling up in his eyes. "I beg you," he finally said in Pashto. "Don't give me to the ANP. They'll torture me and kill me!"

"Then you need to answer some questions," I said. "You need to help us. And you need to tell the truth. I am of the Barikzoy Tribe and I can easily tell if you are lying."

The silence continued, but was then broken by the sound of an older Marine loudly chewing out a junior Marine for something, maybe 20 yards away from the interrogation room. The harsh words further unnerved the prisoner.

"What do you wish to know?" asked the Talib.

"Staa saa noom saa sheey dee?" *What is your name?*

The Talib started talking. He told us who he was, where he was from, and what he did for the Taliban. He also gave us the names of some local Taliban leaders. He tried to answer every question. Finally, the interrogator had nothing else to ask.

The military policemen came in to escort the Talib away. As he went out the door between the two burley Marines, he turned back to look at me.

"Daer manana," he whispered—Pashto for *thank you.*

The interrogation session motivated me and buoyed my confidence. The intelligence officer complimented me on my style and our results. I appreciated his words, although I knew my Pashto was still rusty. We got the job done, but I knew I'd get better at it. I reviewed the interrogation in my mind when I hit the rack that night. I thought about ways to improve my translations, using words that conveyed a truer sense of meaning. I also thought about the prisoner. Would he or his family face gruesome reprisals if the Taliban found out he'd cooperated with the Americans?

The earlier convoy ambush was what Marines called a kinetic event— meaning shots were fired. There would be more such events. However, much of what we did was non-kinetic. Getting to know the people. Meeting and greeting. Starting Civil Affairs projects. Repairing streets. Fixing roofs. Digging wells.

At first, the villagers were wary when we patrolled through their areas. They held back from greeting us and often seemed nervous. When we approached, they wouldn't maintain eye contact. Reluctant to talk, they offered us neither water nor food, which conflicted with the Afghan tradition of hospitality to visitors and travelers. Some were actual Taliban members or sympathizers; others feared them.

When Capt Benson and I first visited District Governor Asadullah Haqdost in Delaram, I introduced myself as Fahim, an interpreter from the Barikzoy tribe, and Asadullah responded warmly. My tribal affiliation was a big plus, and I talked it up whenever I could.

Most Afghans are illiterate, but they are skilled at sizing up people and reading them, compensating with attention to the subtlest of physical cues, facial tics, eye movements, posture, attire, and voice inflections to improve communication. Pro-Taliban Afghans looked harsh and I couldn't get them to smile. They'd stare at me and know that I knew who they were. We then chose our words carefully. It was a mental chess game. We couldn't detain people just because of how they looked. When we found someone suspicious, however, we took their names and made notes about where they lived, what they did, who they knew, and with whom they were aligned. This growing database proved invaluable to our intelligence people, who worked 24/7 to identify bad guys and their sympathizers.

I like people and am naturally outgoing. As my Pashto sharpened, I increasingly enjoyed my work. I taught more Pashto to India Company Marines. I made sure all our Marines knew how to say "Hello" and "How are you?" and "Thank You" and "Goodbye." They took pride in developing linguistic skills—which also made me proud of them. The locals also appreciated the Marines talking to them in Pashto, and learning their cultural and religious traditions. Small things mattered. For example, Marines learned not to be seen eating or chewing gum during religious times, like before, during, or after Ramadan or Eid. Respect for Islam was crucial to mission success.

People in our AO grew used to seeing our 3/4 Marines moving around them. Many locals were curious about me. Was I Afghan or was I American? Of course, I was both, and it was gratifying to be a bridge between the two worlds. I was assertive and emphatic as a terp, but tried to have fun and maintain a sense of humor as well. I liked to engage youngsters as we patrolled villages. When I got kids to smile and laugh, their parents warmed to us. When we returned to a village, the people remembered us and showed more hospitality.

Mingling with the locals

After meeting and greeting the locals for several weeks, Darkside 6 decided it was time to host a *Shura*—a gathering of influential elders from the communities around Delaram. He wanted to create an opportunity for his boss, Col Kennedy, to connect with the people. Kennedy commanded Regimental Combat Team 2 (RCT-2), which included 3/4.

On the day of the Shura, people just kept coming. More than 700 locals showed up. For security purposes, we hosted the event in the battalion compound. Delaram Sub-Governor Asadullah spoke at length, as did Kennedy. They told the Afghans that we wanted to help them. The locals responded by describing some areas where they could use help— such as with road improvements. They wanted to secure Buji Bhast pass and the road north to Golestan in the mountains, where we'd placed Lt. Kelly's platoon. We said we'd help clear it out. Our plans to secure the road pleased the elders, and the Shura ended on a high note.

A couple of days later, I was with Capt Benson and some other Marines on a security patrol. People recognized us from the Shura and approached us with useful information. We got some tips about who was planting IEDs, and where. A merchant called us inside his humble, one-room store and said there were two IEDs short distance away near a little bridge. We thanked him and Explosive Ordnance Detail (EOD) quickly took care of it.

Later, after one young Afghan man ran a mile just to give me a tip, Capt Benson said "Fahim, I've got to get you your own cell phone." And he did.

I gave that phone number to everyone I could. It was a great idea. Most Afghans hated the Taliban, but many didn't dare be seen giving me information. But they could call—and they did. Within two weeks, my phone was constantly ringing with information about IED emplacements—at least during the day. The Taliban wouldn't allow cell phone towers to operate at night. Usually, the IEDs involved homemade explosives (HME) using fertilizer. The enemy could put them in place fairly quickly. Containers with HME pressure plate detonators were buried in highly trafficked areas throughout the region. Still, with the *Call Fahim* cell-phone program, we'd sometimes know about an IED even before the Taliban had finished putting it in.

Most of the phone calls provided actionable intelligence. The tips gave us names and solid locations for Taliban fighters. Once, we received a warning of an impending rocket attack. Another time, we learned of a plan to shake-down a passenger bus. Occasionally, we'd get a message that turned out to be someone trying to get even with a neighbor. That score-settling was rare, however.

This new influx of intelligence didn't necessarily mean that locals were suddenly pro-American, but the IEDs were as much a threat to them as they were to us. They'd call us and we'd take care of things. They liked that we weren't corrupt and didn't need bribes to provide a service.

We could quantify the number of wells we dug or the number of schools we started. It was harder to measure attitudes or gauge the effect of the example we set. When Marines finally leave Delaram, corruption will remain. However, people will remember how we did business. They'll know that things can get done without bribes—that there are better ways to live. Capt Benson's emphasis on Afghans doing real work for real pay also changed the status quo mindset. Paying Afghan workers a set wage for cleaning the streets sent a message. If they showed up and did the work on time, they got paid. No bribery. No shakedowns. No intimidation. The first step in changing their culture of corruption was to let them experience a better way.

Not everything that happened after the Shura was good. It was very quiet the next day, which worried me. During the afternoon we heard some AK-47 fire and when we investigated, we found out the mayor of Delaram had been shot to death, his car driven away by his assassins. The mayor had spoken well of the Americans at the Shura, so the message from the Taliban was clear: "If you cooperate with the Marines, be prepared to die." The locals were fairly quiet for a few days after the assassination.

Interpreters could do great good in Afghanistan—or bad. For example, a miscommunication with Sub-Governor Asadullah threatened weeks of hard work at establishing a positive relationship between his office and 3/4.

A sub-governor, or district governor, was a government official who ranked below the provincial governor in the Afghan hierarchy. Most sub-governors in southern Afghanistan had either been killed or compromised in recent years, but with an increasing American presence, some government officials took the chance of working with us. They typically came from large families from traditionally powerful clans, or tribes. They could access funding from official sources for mosque construction, road repair, local police, and modest municipal projects. They also adjudicated local disputes and oversaw sanctioned taxation. Their power threatened Taliban dominance, and they needed special security support—unless they paid off the Taliban for protection. We wondered what shade of grey most officials were. Asadullah was the senior government official in greater Delaram. He had little staff beyond two trusted friends, a son, and some policemen he'd brought with him from his home area in southern Nimruz Province. Of the Nourazai tribe himself, his job was difficult and dangerous, since so many tribal villages were in serious conflict with each other. It would be a victory for the Taliban if they could assassinate him.

India Company had set up a living area in a compound adjacent to Asadullah's quarters to emphasize our support and solidarity. As time passed, we became friendlier with his people. Then one day, a British intelligence officer arrived with information that someone in the sub-governor's entourage was a potential suicide bomber. The Brit and his terp met with the sub-governor, explained the situation, and asked if they could search the area and personnel working there.

Asadullah later claimed to have responded, "OK. But be careful when searching some of my guards, because they are unsophisticated and un-educated and could over-react to being touched."

However, the Brit's interpreter claimed that Asadullah said, "If you touch my people they'll start shooting."

That was an unacceptable answer to the officer, whom I'd heard lacked patience and finesse. So he reported a dangerous situation to Capt Benson and recommended an immediate search of all personnel.

The Boss was not in a position to take any chances regarding the safety of his troops, so he pressed forward and arranged for a search/shakedown. This understandably offended Asadullah and he threatened to kick us out of his area. We lost all the trust we'd built up.

Capt Benson wanted to mollify Asadullah, but the sub-governor refused to meet with him. There was too much local pride to overcome. The Boss turned to me for help, and I went to work.

When the sub-governor finally agreed to see me, I was properly contrite. It took days, but we eventually set up a larger meeting which included Asadullah, Capt Benson, the British officer, his terp, Lt Gent, and me. There was some spirited debate about who said what to whom and how and when.

"From now on, I only talk to Fahim Fazli," insisted Asadullah. Darkside 6 eventually got involved to help smooth things over. The problem was that the terp working with the British officer was a translator of Tajik background with limited Pashto capabilities, so it was also a tribal thing. Locals regarded him—a northerner—with suspicion.

We eventually worked things out with the sub-governor and re-established our relationships. We thoroughly searched the official compound and confirmed that Asadullah's people were all loyal. Sadly, a rocket-propelled grenade later killed the Brit. We never found out who fired it, but we suspected it was a consequence of the British officer alienating the locals. His interpreter was wounded and evacuated. Given the Pashtunwali Code, it was all too easy to create conflict between tribes. Reconciliation took time, patience, and hard work. Still, we kept at it.

One day, Capt Benson called me on the radio in my quarters. "Hey, Hollywood. TV reporters are here and they want a tour of Delaram. Can you help us out?"

"Sure, Boss," I replied. "You know I'm not camera-shy."

I linked up with the Boss and an ABC-TV news team and we walked around the bazaar, talking to locals. I noticed the cameraman getting a lot of video of me along the way. When we got back to the compound the reporter, Miguel Marquez, interviewed me for a special segment.

ABC-TV ran the piece on World News Tonight. It was a human interest feature that showed clips of me playing a terrorist, whacking around Robert Downey, Jr. and Kiefer Sutherland. They interspersed shots of me in Afghanistan engaging the locals as an interpreter. They called me a hero and a goodwill ambassador. Capt. Benson said some flattering things.

"People flock to him," said the Boss. "He doesn't have to talk to anyone for more than thirty seconds before they're best friends or brothers."

The point of the piece was that I'd left a comfortable situation in Hollywood to serve my country in a dangerous place with the Marines. I soon received hundreds of messages from all over America, among them one from Amy saying I looked good in my uniform on TV—despite my ever-growing beard.

Some Delaram missions didn't directly involve India Company. One such operation involved higher level intelligence officers searching for a local Taliban leader run by using special personnel dedicated to that mission. The MEB had a secret special operations section which worked with reconnaissance Marines, Army Special Forces, Navy SEALS, and even CIA assets to target Taliban leaders. I was resting in my quarters during that search when my cell phone rang, and a voice speaking Pashto said, "I know who you're looking for and where he's hiding."

I told the caller I'd get back to him. I was excited—I needed to tell the Boss.

Capt Benson brought me to an operations center equipped with monitor screens that provided views of Delaram from specially placed cameras we called GBOSS (Ground Based Operational Security System). I got the informer back on the phone and when he described some buildings, we zoomed the camera on those spots. We saw Marines moving into view. As my contact talked to me, I interpreted for Capt Benson, who conferred with intelligence personnel controlling their own people's movements. Eventually, for simplicity's sake, he got me directly involved in the operation and out into the streets so the informer could personally guide me and three Special Ops Marines to the hiding spot. I imagined finding a rat-hole like the one from which Iraqi dictator Saddam Hussein emerged in 2003.

My contact guided us down a narrow street to an old dwelling. A large figure in a blue burqa emerged from the building as we approached, but we didn't try to question her. We needed a female terp for that. The contact talked us up onto the roof where we were sky-lined for all to see. Suddenly, the Boss called on the radio and said to watch out for a trap. He was afraid the caller was setting me up to be shot. The word on the street was that the Taliban had put a price on my head. My contact guided us down a ladder into a room with a rug covering a trap door. I stepped away from the rug, wondering if the trapped rat would come out shooting, or blow himself up. Two Marines pointed rifles at the rug while the third Marine, Sergeant Johnson, pulled it away to reveal the trap door. He pounded on the door but received no response.

"We're going to open this door!" I yelled in Pashto. "We'll shoot if we have to."

Then Johnson pulled open the door and we looked down into a dark, empty rat-hole. I thought back to the "woman" who'd rushed out in the burqua.

"That person in the burqua was probably the Taliban leader!" I exclaimed. "She seemed too big to be a woman."

We rushed outside the building but the burqua-clad figure was long-gone—disappeared into a maze of residential dwellings.

I thanked my contact and told him to call back anytime. The Fahim-phone accepted calls 24/7. Capt. Benson later told me the Special Ops guys were impressed with how we almost nailed the Taliban leader. They'd been tracking him for weeks.

As I didn't have a security clearance I wasn't privy to all the secret missions our Special Operations people conducted. However, later on the Boss told me that they finally nailed that Taliban target, and that the intelligence I helped India Company gather over time had made a big difference in that case, and others as well. He couldn't tell me specifics, but it meant a lot to know that my work had helped the cause.

The weeks passed and the 3/4 Marines became part of the landscape around Delaram, as they continued patrolling and engaging the locals in preparation for future operations. The strategic importance of the crossroads town was underscored by the high-level visitors who regularly stopped by.

One day, Major General Richard Mills came to Delaram as part of a pre-deployment visit to the Marine Corps AO. He traveled with BGen Nicholson to tour the areas of operations; he'd later replace Nicholson as the Marine Commander in southern Afghanistan. The generals met with regimental and battalion commanders, as well as other staff members and Afghan officials. Before concluding the visit, they decided to take a brief, unscheduled trip to the local bazaar.

Capt Benson worried about bad guys, of course. He asked me to accompany the flag officers on their tour, to help with security by eyeballing the crowd for Taliban types. At first only a few people were out on the street, but more quickly gathered when word spread that VIPs were in the area.

I felt like I was reprising my part as a bodyguard in *Homeland Security*. Some of the locals seemed excited, while others skulked, looking suspicious or annoyed. The malcontents typically stood scowling—arms folded, projecting menace. One such man stood watching us with a particularly hateful stare. I could tell he despised Mills and all he represented. I moved toward the man and our eyes met. He hated me, too. He no doubt considered me a traitor. I looked for a weapon, but none was obvious.

I went up to him and said, "Hey! How are you?" in Pashto. Our eyes locked and he maintained an icy stare. I stayed between him and the General until Mills moved past. The man turned his glare from me to the General and walked away, though I continued to keep an eye on him.

The man hadn't given us cause to detain him, but we had to be vigilant. We couldn't hold people based on their looks, however much I might sense that they were dangerous. They had to make a hostile move first. Months later, Col Kennedy tried to meet and greet some locals near a similar bazaar and was hit in the face by a rock. The Marines providing his security immediately killed the rock-thrower, which nearly started a riot. It's better to engage potential rock throwers *before* they did anything.

When we weren't out on patrols, I came to enjoy my humble quarters with Lt Fafinsky, Lt Riley, and SSgt Cooke. I got to know these Marines well as the weeks went by. We talked about all kinds of things—the war, music, families, women, sports. They were particularly interested in my journey, my Afghan roots, and the Hollywood stuff. And I enjoyed hearing stories of their home states. We were often joined by other India Marines. A Louisiana Marine talked about Cajun food. A Texas Marine talked about how everything was better in Texas. A Massachusetts Marine talked about the Red Sox. Politics occasionally came up, more often with officers and older non-commissioned officers than with younger troops. The Marines trended conservative, but still provided a whole spectrum of views.

Before becoming an American citizen, I'd studied U.S. History and learned that our national motto, *E Pluribus Unum*, is Latin for "Out of many, one." To me, that meant coming together, despite ethnicity, geography, race, or religion. I marveled at how most American tribes got along and wondered if we could similarly bring the Afghans tribes together.

Anyone walking around Los Angeles can see people from a hundred different countries speaking a hundred different languages, and generally getting along. That's unimaginable in most other parts of the world. *If so many tribes could come together in California to cooperate and flourish, why couldn't the tribes in Afghanistan do likewise?* I wondered. The Sunni Muslim traditions of most Afghan tribes could unite them, but those ties are overshadowed by tribal loyalties. Wahabbi-inspired intolerance sets Afghanistan back. The culture can be mean, full of angry men cruelly abusing women or hurting animals for no reason.

My tent-mates and I discussed the situation concerning an Afghan man who'd wanted to become a Christian. President Karzai interceded when mullahs sentenced him to death for his so-called apostasy, because if the death sentence had been carried out it would have threatened our allied coalition. How could Western countries fight for a regime that allowed people to be executed simply because they chose to be Christians?

We hoped we were fighting for a Western sense of cultural fairness. Many of the local injustices stood in the way of our mission, including how females were treated.

"I feel bad for the women here," said Cooke. "They seem to get married off when they're fourteen or so and then they get stuck inside a mud hut the rest of their lives. Will that ever change?"

"Things will get better when more people can access the internet and watch satellite television and get outside news and information," I said. "Of course, it would help if they could read. Education would broaden everyone's perspectives—except the mullahs. We need to show better ways."

"How can we show them better ways?" asked Cooke.

"Just let Afghans see Americans being Americans," I said. "Afghans read people well and copy behaviors that work."

I explained that the Taliban shut down all the television channels when they took power in 1996. They'd used their morality police to completely censor remaining media sources. People caught with televisions were imprisoned or flogged. But things changed after the Taliban overthrow in 2001. Along with the influx of forces from our 40-nation coalition came an information flow that could not be staunched.

"Under the Taliban there was only one radio station," I said. "And it only aired religious propaganda. Most of the people listened to it though, because there was nothing else. So not only do we need to teach people to read, we need to give them more options so they can compare viewpoints and think more critically. More radio stations and more newspapers. But until that happens, Afghans need to see us acting honorably. They may not be able to read books, but they can read us!"

There is nothing the Taliban hate more than the imagery of American women Marines and women soldiers carrying weapons and sometimes ordering men around. It drives them crazy. Female assertiveness challenges the very foundations of the Taliban belief system. Elevating the status of women could temper the violent strains throughout Afghanistan's warrior culture, but Afghan females need good role models. Then brave Afghan women need to assert themselves and start the changes incrementally—women like Dr. Sima Samar of the Shuhada Organization, which ran a hospital in one of Kabul's most desperately poor neighborhoods. It will take time, but honoring and appreciating women is crucial for a better Afghan society to evolve.

"When American forces phase out of Afghanistan, the images of assertive, confident women will remain," I said. "Memories that could forever change things for the better. It will take time, though."

"Well, I guess Fahim's figured out how to save Afghanistan," said Fafinsky before he finally turned the tent light out. "Give women more power. We just have to get his plan up the chain-of-command to General McChrystal."

After a month of adapting to the Afghan desert and getting a feel for the people and the dynamics of our AO, we received word from RCT-2 to proceed with a major mission planned for December. *Cobra's Anger* would be one of the largest combat operations of the war. It was time to kick the Taliban out of their stronghold in Now Zad, and 3/4 would be right in the middle of it all.

Chapter 11: Combat and Comfort

"The Marines I've seen around the world have the cleanest bodies, the filthiest minds, the highest morale, and the lowest morals of any group of animals I have ever seen. Thank God for the United States Marine Corps!"
- Eleanor Roosevelt, First Lady of the United States, 1945

As November turned into December, 3/4 solidified its presence throughout the Area of Operations. Around Delaram, Capt Benson and India Company continued the outreach to the locals and developed closer relationships with elders in a dozen villages within a ten-mile radius. In the west, Capt Hollopeter and Kilo Company brought a bazaar back to life near Bakwa and put constant pressure on illicit narcotic operations. Kilo Marines worked with DEA agents and the Marine Air Group to identify, isolate, and assault opium processing labs and drug transport hubs.

A major development in the east, with Capt Tirrell and Lima Company, was *Operation Cobra's Anger*, designed to push the enemy out of its stronghold in Now Zad. Formerly the most populous city in the region, Now Zad once even had electricity, which was rare for Afghanistan. Unfortunately, in 2006 the Taliban gained control, and the lights flickered and went out. Now Zad lost its glow and became like most communities dominated by the Taliban—dark and foreboding.

As the city lay strategically between Kandahar and northern Helmand Province, the Taliban knew that coalition forces would seek to recover the ancient metropolis—a community which had guarded the foothills to the great mountains since antiquity. The Taliban spent months placing mines and IEDs in and around buildings throughout the city. As a result, daily explosions killed scores of noncombatants and maimed hundreds more. Eventually, most civilians fled and Now Zad turned into a near ghost town. The way the Taliban audaciously flaunted their local power invited attack. In addition to mines, the enemy built up a network of trenches and bunkers. It was unusual for the Taliban to dig in and fight that way. Instead of mingling with civilians or melting away into the night, the enemy brazenly stood behind their built-up areas around Now Zad, in effect saying "Bring it on!" This set the stage for a rare linear confrontation, rather than the standard guerilla warfare.

British and U.S. forces viewed these enemy positions through binoculars from outside the danger areas. When they occasionally tested the Taliban defenses, the probing patrols suffered dozens killed and disfigured by IEDs and mines. It was an awful place.

After BGen Nicholson and the MEB had established bases and outposts throughout the lower Helmand River Valley during *Operation Khanjar* in the summer of 2009, operations officers turned their attention to Now Zad. This fight would largely fall to 3/4. LtCol Wetterauer and his staff threw themselves into detailed planning for *Operation Cobra's Anger*: evaluating terrain, weather, enemy situations, alternate courses of action, available personnel, potential logistics support, and intelligence assessments.

Although India Company was itching to get into the coming fight, Darkside 6 needed us to maintain our positions around Delaram. So he flew in most of Kilo Company from Bakwa to support Lima Company. The 3/4 battalion commander utilized other attachments attached other units as well, as he implemented the final attack plan. Recon Marines, British troops, and indigenous Afghan National Army (ANA) forces would also be employed. Engineers would play important roles, since new minefield-breaching technology would be used for the first time.

Darkside 6 had wanted to use tanks as part of the assault, but unfortunately, the Americans had no tanks at hand. The previous February, Nicholson had asked top Army General David McKiernan for permission to bring Marine tanks to Afghanistan, but McKiernan refused the request. The Army General was concerned that heavy armor might evoke bad memories of the heavy-handed Soviet occupation in the 1980s, and he feared American tanks would alienate Afghan civilians. The senior NATO officer in Afghanistan, McKiernan pointed out that he wasn't singling out the Marines by withholding equipment; the *Army* didn't have tanks, either.

This lack of armor was unfortunate for Nicholson—and for Darkside 6—given that the Marine AO was excellent tank country. Most

Afghans still referred to any large American vehicle as a tank anyway, so the use of tanks likely wouldn't have alienated them further, especially with the right outreach between Marines and civilians. Luckily, Danish forces had tanks at Camp Bastion, so Nicholson followed the Marine philosophy of *innovate, adapt, and overcome.* He borrowed the Danish tanks for 3/4 to use in the attack.

During the early hours of December 3, CH-53E helicopters and V-22 Ospreys dropped Kilo Company and Reconnaissance Marines behind Taliban positions to unnerve the enemy. Then, Darkside 6 unleashed the M1 Assault Breacher Vehicle (ABV) for its first-ever combat action. Nicknamed *The Shredder*, the 72-ton, 40-foot long ABV had a 1,500 horsepower engine, a 50-caliber machine gun, and a front-mounted 15-foot wide plow that carved its way through danger areas. The ABV was also equipped with M58 MICLIC Mine Clearing Line Charges, rockets essentially, that carried high-grade C-4 explosives up to 150 yards forward, detonating hidden bombs at a safe distance.

The ABV accomplished its mission, clearing a safe swath through the Taliban minefields. The Marines then closed in on the enemy from the front as well as the rear. Moving quickly and violently, and utilizing combined arms—direct fire, indirect fire, tanks, air support, and eventually Hellfire missiles—the Marines quickly overwhelmed the enemy defenses, routing the Taliban. When the 3/4 Marines warily entered and liberated Now Zad, they discovered fighters had taken refuge in the ghost town, where they stashed their weapons and maddeningly posed as civilians. Since the Taliban didn't wear uniforms they were indistinguishable from the few noncombatants who'd remained the city. While most of the bad guys slipped away, the good guys now controlled Now Zad. We'd later figure out how to put the squeeze on these Taliban fighters who'd eluded us. There were no reported coalition or civilian fatalities in the operation, and Taliban loses were reported as 16 killed and five captured.

Although India Company wasn't slated to play a major role in the operation, I was supposed to travel with Capt Benson and the company headquarters element to Now Zad to support the effort. Unfortunately, a sandstorm kept us from flying out of Delaram, so Darkside 6 told us to stay put. We later heard accounts of how successful *Operation Cobra's Anger* had been, thanks to 3/4 leading the way.

In January, *Operation Cobra's Anger II* further consolidated our gains to the north of Now Zad into the Hindu Kush. Marine engineers worked with specially-trained locals to clear thousands of IEDs and mines throughout the area, with Lima Company establishing crucial security around the city, clearing pathways and roads so people could return home. Afghan nationals did much of the work, with top-level funding and personnel support from the International Security Assistance Force (ISAF) in Kabul. Over 30,000 civilians who were forced to leave Now Zad after 2006 gratefully returned to their earlier neighborhoods. People brought life and light back to their old homes. Bazaars reopened. Locals mingled on the streets. Calls to prayer brought the Muslim faithful back to the mosques. The District Governor's office reopened. Capt Jason Brezler's Civil Affairs (CA) Marines won the trust and affection of these former refugees who were so happy to return to Now Zad. The CA detachment identified neighborhood leaders and engaged key elders. They ingratiated themselves to the population by learning what the people needed—building materials, health care support, sanitation equipment, tools—and then providing it. The noteworthy work by Brezler and company provided lessons and models which Marines later copied throughout the AO. People at MEB headquarters called Now Zad a "catastrophic success," meaning that we did so well so fast in Now Zad that the regional development people were hard-pressed to follow-up with resources for infrastructure improvements. So Marines went ahead and cleared streets, rebuilt houses, dug wells, and provided food and medicine on their own. The Jarheads even started some schools—including one for girls. Brezler sometimes dressed up in mufti when engaging the locals, like Lawrence of Arabia. Some called him "Brezler of Now Zad." This outreach endeared us to the Afghans.

During the following months, Nicholson continually pointed to Now Zad as an example of a successful model for Helmand Province. The kudos made all of us in 3/4 proud, but there was still much to be done.

Back in Delaram, India Company helped the crossroads town become a safe enclave. The earlier anti-American riots there were now just memories. Local security patrols did their jobs, taking the initiative away from bad guys, who no longer moved about with impunity. Still, the India Marines were ready to do more. The Boss wanted his guys to show their stuff in a big operation, like Kilo and Lima Companies did during *Cobra's Anger*. I wanted to show my stuff, as well. I was sure I could bridge the cultural gaps between the Marines and the Afghans, given the opportunity. I'd never been in a fire fight, though. How would I react when bullets flew? I didn't regret my decision to return to Afghanistan, but I did want to survive, help India Company succeed, and go home to America.

With Delaram's security stabilizing, it was time for India Company and other 3/4 elements to make good on the promise made at the Shura to open the road up from Delaram into the mountains. Maj Dougherty planned an operation to the north called *Swift Change* to secure the crucial gateway of Buji Bhast Pass. This would open up a ground route to our outpost in Golestan, where Lt Kelly and his detachment continued to receive supplies by air.

This mountain territory was important ground. Unlike most of our AO, it was steep, hilly terrain. Tribal rivalries meant villages were often in conflict with each other, although they seemed united in their hostility toward the Marines. Earlier, coalition forces moved in and out of Buji Bhast, and in the process broke down lots of doors and damaged many farmers' fields. They'd also angered people by mixing flour, tea, and sugar into villagers' fertilizer, making it harder to convert to HME for IEDs. Territorial and vicious dogs attacked coalition intruders, and consequently many canines were shot dead, further alienating the locals. As we got closer to Buji Bhast with our patrols and visits to villages, we became quite aware of the dog problem.

"Boss, we just can't be shooting these peoples' dogs," I said to Capt Benson. "It only makes them hate us."

"Our guys can't stand there and get bitten by vicious animals," he responded. "They didn't join the Marines for that."

"Instead of shooting them, we could offer them food, even stuff from MREs," I suggested.

"Do you think dogs would actually eat some of the stuff in our MRE's?" responded the Boss with a laugh, referring the "Meals-Ready-to-Eat," the self-contained, individual field rations that sustained Marines at remote combat outposts.

"Well, maybe not the tuna fish, but I know there's other stuff they'd like," I said. "Maybe we could requisition some emergency dog biscuits from the States. How would you and Susan like it if someone came to your house and shot your dog?"

"You're just an animal lover, Hollywood," said Capt Benson. "But you're right. How is it Gunny seemed to like you so much when you came to our house? He never likes new people at first."

"Dogs sense fear," I explained. "But they also respond to affection, if people get close enough. I can help with that. And if some dogs are really vicious, we just need to respond with sticks and stones instead of bullets."

The Boss was right about me being an animal lover. Some family members once had a pet duck at their place in California, and the duck was unhappy. I snatched that bird in the middle of the night, put it in the back of my car, and took it to a duck pond where I released it. Another time my mother rescued a homeless dog with a broken jaw in Orange County. I spent hundreds of dollars fixing that dog's teeth so he could be adopted. Yet another time my friend Ryan bought a dog for his girlfriend Gina. When things didn't work out between Ryan and Gina, Tazi ended up staying with me for several months until a suitable home with a big yard could be found.

To the Marines, the native dogs were vicious, threatening animals. However, these large hounds were also beloved family members at countless Afghan homes. Killing them not only broke people's hearts, but also challenged the Code of Pashtunwali and threatened our mission to develop relationships with the locals.

I needed Capt Benson's sympathy to promote humane treatment of these animals. "What if someone hurt Palang?" I asked him. Palang was a typical Afghan dog, a big Shepherd stray that Indian Company had adopted. Palang loved to run around the compound, tail wagging, looking at his Marines with trusting, big brown eyes. The India Marines loved and protected Palang; invoking his name brought the Boss around.

"OK, OK," said Capt Benson. "I get it."

Now, when we came to a new village, the Boss put me out in front, not only to talk to the locals, but also to talk to the dogs. I was a bearded

Afghan who spoke the native language, and the dogs responded to me. I became adept at calming down agitated dogs as well as Afghan locals.

Capt Benson thought it ironic—me as dog's best friend, as opposed to dog being man's best friend. The ill-will brought on by the earlier dog-killing was incompatible with our mission, so it was important to find ways to coexist with the animals. I taught Marines Pashto dog commands and explained that dogs didn't like being pelted with things—and that sticks and stones were better weapons against them than bullets. Cheaper, too.

As we pushed north, we found that while locals were suspicious and unwelcoming, they were also curious about us. Villagers around Buji Bhast generally hated the dictatorial Taliban, who didn't hesitate to cut off hands—or other things—of those who offended them. Locals just wanted to be left alone. They also hated the ANP so much that when houses needed to be searched, the villagers asked that it be done by Marines, rather than by the corrupt indigenous forces.

Operation Swift Change took us north, higher and deeper into the mountains. My role mattered, as we sought to connect with a suspicious population that saw Marines as gun-toting aliens. However, as word spread north through Buji Bhast that we were OK to deal with—and that we were going to stick around—we soon received red carpet treatment which meant we no longer needed to break down doors. People brought us tea. They ate goat with us. They kissed us.

"I've never been kissed so much in my life," said Capt Benson.

"It's too bad that it's only men who kiss you," I replied.

As for the use of fertilizer in explosives, we took a firm stance but showed patience. We explained our concerns and eventually walked the fields with farmers so they could show us where they used fertilizer and why it was important, and by so doing we got a better sense of which farmers might use fertilizer to make explosives. We were always in the intelligence business.

We still lacked female interpreters, and the quickest way to alienate the populace was to mess with their women, so we had to be careful. Memories and stories of Soviet gang-rapes still influenced local thinking.

When we came to a dwelling we needed to secure, I'd go in first and calm the people.

"Greetings," I'd say in Pashto, smiling my biggest smile. "I am Fahim of the Barikzoy Tribe. We are very happy to visit your town. We want to get to know you so we can work together to make things better here." Patience, grins, and friendly banter usually turned apprehension into anticipation.

Connecting with elders was always a priority

"This is a nice house," I'd go on. "It reminds me of my cousin's place in Kabul. Except he was a pig and didn't keep his home nice like you do here."

I'd explain what we needed to do and politely ask for their help. "We want to make sure every place is safe," I added. "Could you please help us?"

Elders assisted us by segregating the women, putting them into rooms which we'd previously cleared. Then we'd use an elder, a father, or a little boy to communicate with the women as required. Segregating the females created challenges when searching buildings with only one or two rooms, but we worked out a system where the women stayed in one area while other family members alerted us as to the locations of Qurans, other religious items, and valuables. We treated the locals with respect and they responded well.

"Will you be back again to visit?" was a question we'd often hear after we finished searching, chatting, and exchanging things.

"I hope so," I'd reply. "Here's my phone number. Let's stay in touch."

The Soviets' hostility to religion was a big mistake. They purposely destroyed or desecrated religious items as part of a strategy to turn devout people into refugees who'd flee to Pakistan. The less-religious people left behind were more vulnerable to Communist influences. So we made it a point to protect holy relics. Religious artwork or any reference to Allah or to Mohammed was treated similarly to the Quran—with deference and respect. Many homes had holy verses elegantly printed on special fabric which people framed and then positioned to cover holes in walls—where stuff might be hidden. We'd remove the framed material with great care and put it back with equal gentleness.

Capt Benson also controlled a pot of Afghani money from the Commander's Emergency Relief Program (CERP). The MEB channeled considerable CERP funds to him through Darkside 6, and the Boss had the authority to allocate it to locals who'd seen their property damaged due to coalition activities. Capt Benson subsequently heard many claims about broken doors, run-down fields, and dead dogs. The Boss distributed money to compensate accordingly—although it soon seemed as if every Afghan had had a dog killed during earlier actions.

Follow-on missions to *Operation Swift Change* continued through the Afghan winter. Advance patrols secured objectives around population centers. Then larger elements entered villages and inquired about IED locations. We'd always find people who'd point us to mines. Most people hated IEDs, which killed more Afghans than Americans. Wherever we went, we'd try to connect and communicate with the people. A common question was, "Are you going to destroy our poppy?"

Capt Benson had a stock answer for that: "We don't seek to ruin your current crops, but we hope you can someday transition away from poppies and drugs to food crops."

There is much opium and heroin money to be made from poppies in this desperately poor country. According to the United Nations Office on

Drugs and Crime, 92% of the opiates on the world market originate in Afghanistan. This amounts to an export value of about $4 billion, with a quarter being earned by opium farmers and the rest going to district officials, insurgents, warlords, and drug traffickers. The soil and climate in our AO were ideal for poppy growing. Farmers feared we'd destroy these lucrative crops—and their livelihoods. We reassured them that poppy field eradication was not our primary mission, but we continued to press them about raising other crops. They always replied that nothing brought in the money that poppy did, and the crop issue remained a losing battle.

Otherwise, things went well. After Marine patrols cleared a village, Capt Benson and I made concerted efforts to connect with the locals. We found that villagers always knew we were coming. Our command element sometimes drove into a village, but we often walked—Capt Benson, two radio operators, a corpsman, a squad of trigger-pullers, and me. As we approached the mud-hut dwellings, we'd see kids darting around, telling people we were coming.

"OK, Boss, do you think they'll welcome us here?" I'd ask, as we walked up the narrow dirt road to the next village, always watching for the disturbed earth that might mean an IED.

"Hollywood, that all depends on whether or not they heard you were coming."

"I think they like that you give out money," I'd respond. "You're a combination of Santa Claus, the Easter Bunny, and the Candy Man!"

A smiling elder would usually appear. "Khomandan Sahib Benson and Barikoy Sahib Fahim!"

We've been waiting for you.

When we got to the tiny village of Dukta, I greeted the first person I saw on the dusty, main street. "Salam alikam, Haji Sahib," I said as I kissed his hand. "Who is a senior elder here?"

"Greetings," the man responded, appreciative of my deference. "That would be Haji Kareem. I can take you to him."

Our entourage spread out, Marines taking low profile positions on either side of the street as Capt Benson followed me and the villager to the elder's house. After I was introduced to Haji Kareem, I kissed his hand and introduced him to the Boss. They shook hands.

"I heard you were coming," said Haji Kareem. "Welcome. Come and sit. We'll have tea."

We tried to create a relaxed, informal atmosphere. We removed our boots and sat cross-legged on the floor in the first room we entered. A young man served us tea. We heard female voices in another room, presumably a kitchen, and soon the smell of roast goat permeated the air.

Patience was a virtue. If we'd blown in with an agenda which called for fast action, it would have turned people off. We projected humility and tried to get Haji Kareem to talk, which he soon did. I interpreted for the Boss, who asked the elder about his family and his village. We listened attentively, but eventually I gently steered conversation to issues we needed to address. We had to search buildings, starting with Haji Kareem's house.

"We have a problem you may be able to help us with," said Capt Benson.

"What is that?" said Haji Kareem.

"There are a couple houses we need to search," explained the Boss. "But if we only search two houses, the Taliban might be able to figure out who is helping us. What should we do?"

"Maybe you should search every house," said Haji Kareem. "Then they can't point fingers."

"What would be a good house to start with, so that we can set a good example?" asked Capt Benson.

"Why not start with this house?" said Haji Kareem. "My wife will take the girls into her room while you search here and in the kitchen, and then they can go into the kitchen when you search their room."

After the search became Haji Kareem's idea, it ran smoothly. When other villagers saw the elder working with us, they also cooperated, as long as we remained patient and careful. Our skills improved with every village we encountered.

People brought us blankets, candy, and bread. They sometimes offered shawls and hats as gifts—non-perishables which we couldn't accept. We couldn't carry around extra weight, and if we accepted gifts from one place, we'd have to accept them everywhere, or else run the risk of offending people. However, most villagers happily accepted gifts from us—like radios, which we showed them how to use, as well as how to access some of the new radio programming the MEB sponsored as part of its Information Operations campaign. People loved the programming we provided through our "Radio-in-a-Box" program, so we set up a transmitter in Delaram. The MEB cultivated and trained several local radio personalities, who enjoyed doing broadcasts in Pashto and playing Afghan and Indian music. As an actor, I could relate to these budding media celebrities. Listening to them reminded me of how much I enjoyed performing in front of an audience.

My favorite was Vijay the Deejay, a real ham who played taped music and loved to talk. A radio show was perfect for him. The Taliban banned music wherever they could, so anyone who listened to Vijay the Deejay made a risky political statement that benefitted us—or maybe they just liked the music he played.

Eventually, we convened a big *Shura* for the villages around Buji Bhast Pass. We set up a speaking area in a flat location next to the road in a relatively neutral area, so no tribe would have a home-field advantage. We provided tea and bread. Dozens of men came to the gathering, sitting on the ground in tribal groups.

As different leaders spoke, we identified some deep-seated tribal rivalries that we'd need to address. The first elder spoke Pashto with a unique accent and a deep, loud voice. "We are happy to have the American Marines as our guests," said the portly Haji Jamil, of the Popalzai tribe. "Thank you for fixing our road. Now we need you to help us move some people from the Mohammedzai tribe who have been on our land improperly."

After Haji Jamil finished speaking, he went back and sat with his group. A hush came over everyone as the next elder approached the speaking area. A tall man, made taller by a large white turban, slowly made his way forward. This elder from the offending tribe, Haji Abdul, had a long white beard, a grey robe, and black sandals. He used a walking stick and moved slowly, but purposefully. The sudden silence created uncomfortable tension. The elder fixed his gaze on Capt Benson. "What you just heard is not true," he said. "The land is rightfully ours."

I again interpreted for the Boss as Haji Abdul made a case that his people were victims. He cited his ancestors' movements and claims, but given the lack of formal record-keeping, it would be difficult to prove who had the better claim. I anticipated applause from his tribe or catcalls from the other tribe when he finished his response to Haji Jamil, but everyone was respectfully silent. Other speakers followed without incident.

We listened to everyone and the lieutenants took notes. When the elders were finished, I interpreted Capt Benson's remarks for the crowd. The Boss thanked everyone for being there and promised to do what he could to improve communication and infrastructure. After the crowd dispersed, he gathered the company leaders and we discussed how to resolve the local disputes. We'd become diplomats as well as warriors.

"Jamil will never talk to Abdul," said Lt Fafinsky. "So how can they fix the boundary thing?"

"They'll both talk to us," I replied. "We just have to listen. And then pass on their sentiments the right way, so no one is offended. Eventually we'll find grounds for compromise and then we can suggest some solutions."

Eventually, Haji Jamil did meet directly with Haji Abdul. While they didn't resolve the boundary problems at their first meeting, just getting them together was a success story. They developed a personal relationship, which was a foundation for further tribal reconciliation.

The villages needed to come together, but there was no unifying force, in the sense that hatred of the Soviets had unified much of the country in the 1980s, at least for a while. Could we somehow bring the tribes together against the Taliban, despite the fact that the Taliban drew adherents from among the disaffected of *all* tribes? There were also subtribes with varying degrees of ethnic and religious differences, and political issues, too. Some areas had cooperated more with the Communists than others, and some were friendlier to the Taliban than others. We saw civil wars within civil wars, and as we know from American history, civil conflicts become very personal—fighting takes place on disputed homeland territory, cousin often fighting cousin. I wasn't sure we could overcome the long history of bad blood in an area so immersed in Pashtunwali. The legacy of mistrust and injury along our road to Golestan hung like a cloud over the many tribal areas. Still, the elders knew that it was in their villages' best interest to have movement and commerce taking place on the road, so we played on that. We focused on connecting with key elders from each village. While they wouldn't talk to elders from other villages, they would talk to us. We slowly brought them together.

These civil affairs success stories weren't as sensational as Now Zad-style combat victories, but they were crucial if we were to prevail in our overall mission.

It took time, but we made progress. One elder at a time. One village at a time.

After several days in the mountains, we needed re-supply and radioed Delaram to send us some food. The battalion took our coordinates and sent a transport plane to drop some supplies to us by parachute. The drop occurred after midnight, as such planes didn't fly unescorted during the daylight hours. Unfortunately, due to windy conditions or faulty grid coordinates, the supplies landed well away from our position—in the Taliban zone. We were forced to go on reduced rations for two days until the supplies made it through.

Avoiding CH-53E rotor-wash

"Military precision" is an expression I've heard used many times. While such precision may be commonplace on parade grounds, I learned that in warfare, precision is not the norm. The India Marines often had to adapt to evolving circumstances, unexpected developments, and changes in plans.

I wondered if the enemy liked our MREs.

During a visit to a Buji Bhast village in late January, I discovered I was a wanted man.

"The Talibs are very strong in the village to our north," said a friendly elder named Naseem. "Let me tell you where they like to put road mines. And I will give you names of some of their leaders."

We carefully noted his information to pass on to our battalion intelligence section. Then Naseem chuckled and told us that the Taliban knew who the terps were, and that they especially hated them. An effective interpreter was seen as the worst type of traitor—a *jawsoos*.

"The Talibs know about the translator called 'Hollywood,'" Naseem said in measured Pashto. "They know he makes people laugh. They know that when you move on from a village that the people you leave behind are happy with Americans. They really hate Hollywood. They want him dead. They've offered money to whoever kills him."

"How much money is he worth?" asked the Boss, after I translated the elder's comments.

"Three hundred thousand Afghanis," said Naseem.

"I need to see what that means in dollars," Capt Benson said to me. "But tell him the Taliban greatly overstate Hollywood's value." The Boss knew I'd laugh as I translated that.

Three hundred thousand Afghanis! I made a mental note to tell Amy about this—but not until I returned home safely. I wanted her to know that her husband was worth a lot of money in the old country.

That evening Capt Benson told me that 300,000 Afghanis was only worth around 6,000 American dollars. I was disappointed.

"That's not so much," I said to the Boss. "Especially considering you said the Taliban overstated my value!"

A couple of miles north of Dukta was an even smaller collection of adobe mud huts, maybe a dozen buildings. As was standard procedure, I walked ahead of our little column as we approached the dwellings. A dog started barking, which led to more barking and soon there was a cacophony of howling. I offered some dried meat to the first loose dog that approached me and it quieted. Two other dogs were similarly charmed and I moved to the center of the little cluster of buildings. The only human about was an old one-legged man sitting on a stool in front of the largest house. He'd watched me calm the dogs with amusement.

I approached his stool and smiled, saying in Pashto, "Salam alikam, Haji Sahib. I am Fahim of the Barikzoy Tribe." I bowed slightly.

"Salam alikam," he responded. "I am Hamid."

"Where is everyone?" I asked.

"In the fields," he said.

By this time, the Boss had caught up and I introduced him to Hamid, while the Marines behind us set up the usual perimeter and pulled out their canteens. I interpreted some pleasantries and then Hamid asked an interesting question.

"Do you hate Russians?"

"No," said the Boss. "I only hate dogs that don't shut up." One dog wouldn't stop yelping, but barking was constant background noise in any Afghan village. "Why do you ask about the Russians?"

"They took my leg," said Hamid.

"I am so sorry," replied Capt Benson

"The Russians claim there is no God," said Hamid. "Do you believe in God?"

"Yes," said the Boss. Then he reached inside his shirt and pulled out a crucifix.

"This image shows Jesus Christ on the cross," he said. "I am a Christian. You know Jesus is in the Quran, yes?"

"Yes," said Hamid. "This is good."

Even though Capt Benson was not a Muslim, it seemed important to Hamid that the Boss trusted in some sort of higher power. It was a good impulse on his part to show the crucifix, which affirmed that the captain believed in an important prophet in Muslim scripture.

"Please come inside my house," said Hamid as he used his crutch to stand up. "Let's have tea." The Afghan man was not offended by Capt Benson's Christianity. His hospitable response showed an encouraging level of tolerance. The notion that most Muslims want to kill all infidel non-believers is a false one. The Boss showed his crucifix again and again in the weeks ahead. After straining to see Jesus' image, Afghans often warmed to us. They'd hurry to get us things and offer gifts. We were infidels no more.

The 3/4 senior enlisted Marines were a lot like the Afghan elders. Gunnery Sergeants and First Sergeants had the wisdom that Afghans valued and didn't sense in our younger Marines. Officers had their roles, as did the junior enlisted and the non-commissioned officers. However, older Marines like Master Gunnery Sergeant Warren Coughlin, a reserve Marine from Hanover, New Hampshire, exemplified the civil affairs component of our mission. He helped get a school built in Delaram with minimal support from higher-ups outside our AO. He worked on projects all around Delaram—along with his capable interpreter, Amanullah Afzal, who, like me, was a transplanted Afghan from Kabul who later called California home.

Dick Cavagnol, a civil affairs specialist assigned to Delaram, acquired funding from USAID sources to rebuild portions of the Delaram High School behind the police station. Coughlin went over to the developing school site regularly to disburse supplies donated by the "Spirit of America" aid organization. He often distributed the materials directly to the children so as not to compromise the Headmaster, whom the Taliban watched closely.

Coughlin was generous, kind, and patient. He loved kids and often grabbed me to interpret so he could better connect with them. He gave them candy, clothes, and even radios. He taught them how to do high fives, and how to speak some English words.

"These kids are so sweet and innocent," he said to me. "Just look at them. Have them tell me what they need."

Coughlin became a Pied Piper. Afghan youngsters followed him everywhere. He often took their pictures and then showed them their images on his digital camera, which they loved. He constantly advocated for the kids and their families. He pressed the Boss or the Gunny for tools and supplies to give to the locals.

Coughlin also emplaced a water well system around the Delaram Bazaar—a major civil affairs success story. It cost over $130,000 and consisted of four 120-meter-deep wells, 2.5 kilometers of water distribution lines, and numerous spigots along with four pumps and pump houses. This project brought water to the hundreds of shopkeepers and people of the eastern half of the bazaar along Route 1—Ring Road—the most important highway in the country.

The work of Marines like Coughlin showed the people that Americans actually built infrastructure that helped them every day—unlike the Taliban, who destroyed their homes and livelihoods.

While we made great strides in building relationships with locals, we didn't always get through to our Afghan National Police (ANP) and Afghan National Army (ANA) indigenous partners. One morning, Capt. Benson and I were meeting with a visiting Marine Corps lieutenant colonel in our Delaram Compound courtyard when a sweaty, disheveled ANP guy ran in through the gate yelling in Pashto that someone with a fake ANP uniform and an AK-47 had just ridden his bicycle into our area and it looked like trouble.

Capt Benson was exasperated. He hoped to see the ANP deal with the more routine situations. "Isn't this something you all can handle?" I interpreted his message to the Afghan policeman.

"He's an imposter," the ANP messenger explained. "He killed four policemen in a village twenty miles from here. Then he stole a bike and took off."

Then we heard gunfire. AK-47 fire.

The Boss and the lieutenant colonel ran back inside for their weapons and body armor. I ran to the compound wall to see what was going on. I didn't have a weapon and seldom wore my flak jacket in garrison.

I found a place to stand on a box so I could look over the compound wall. A bicycle lay in the street and the fake cop with the rifle was running towards a store, away from the police station. I looked to the right and saw six ANA troops hurrying up the street, past the police station, and towards the store. The shooter darted into the doorway, took a knee, took aim at the ANA soldiers and fired a burst from his AK-47. An Afghan soldier dropped in the street and the other five took cover. Marines behind me in the compound were yelling and running to firing positions around the compound and up in a tower. The shooter picked up on the noise from our compound and fired towards the tower. I heard the "snap" of bullets passing over my head. I ducked for a few moments, and then cautiously peeked over the wall. I saw the shooter on both knees in the doorway, working with his rifle's magazine, possibly reloading. Then, to my horror, I saw two youngsters in a dead-end alley adjacent to the store. They'd ducked in there when the shooting started, trying to be inconspicuous as they huddled in a corner of the alley.

I looked back and saw Marines taking firing positions. Had they seen those kids around the corner from the shooter?

"Hold your fire!" I screamed back to the Marines. "There are kids out there!"

I looked out to the street. The shooter peered around the doorway corner towards the five remaining ANA troops who had taken cover. They were ready for him and when they saw him, they fired a volley. The shooter went down, falling back into the doorway. Then silence.

I yelled in Pashto towards the ANA. "Hold your fire! He's down." Then I yelled the same thing in Dari, as many ANA were from the north and didn't speak Pashto.

I hoped the ANA wouldn't keep blasting away. Their mentality boiled down to shooting, killing, and destroying. Fear, payback, and revenge overwhelmed their more humane instincts. It was impossible to get intelligence information from prisoners if the ANA shot first and asked questions later. It also made it harder for the enemy to surrender if they thought they'd be killed or tortured.

In the doorway, the shooter moved slightly, but his weapon lay in front of him on the street. The ANA troops emerged from their concealed positions. Four of them hurried to their prostrate comrade, while the fifth cautiously moved towards the store. Blood surrounded the fallen Afghan soldier, who'd taken several rounds in the chest.

"He's gone," yelled an ANA trooper in Dari, as he knelt over the soldier's body. That was a cue for the fifth soldier to run toward the shooter, who was still alive. The ANA soldier raised his weapon and fired a burst into the rogue's head, finishing him off.

Capt Benson and a team of Marines headed out the gate towards the store. The Boss yelled to me to come with them. "Where's your damn Kevlar?" the Boss screamed at me. "What the hell's wrong with you?"

Unlike everyone else, I had no weapon, helmet, or flak jacket. Pumped up by adrenaline, I'd positioned myself to see the action rather than running for my gear. My response showed a lack of discipline, but I'd controlled some Marine fire while communicating with the ANA. The kids may have been hit in some crossfire if I hadn't seen them in the corner of the alley.

"Let's get over there," said Capt Benson, and we moved toward the store. The youngsters who'd been hiding came out and stood over the rogue's body, along with the store owner and the ANA soldiers. The Boss told me to ask the store owner what he'd seen. I glanced at what was left of the shooter's head, and before I could speak I started gagging. The man's brains were spilling out of his bloody head. The ANA guys laughed at my discomfort.

Capt Benson just softly said, "Whenever you're ready, Fahim. Whenever you're ready." Some images get burned into your mind, never to go away. That dead shooter will always be with me.

We assessed what we knew about the incident at a company meeting that evening. One of the ANA soldiers attended. The Boss was pissed. "It's too bad we didn't take the shooter alive. Our intel people would have loved to interrogate him."

I interpreted for the ANA soldier, who had a ready response in Dari: "Our soldier, who was killed today, was getting ready to return to his home in Jalalabad. He was getting married next week. The scum got what he deserved."

The room was very quiet after I interpreted. Everyone there understood the value of capturing prisoners. Everyone there also understood how hard it can be to be humane when confronting an enemy who had just blown away your buddy.

A couple of weeks later, two trucks pulled into our compound with five civilians who been hurt when an IED blew up their vehicle. I watched an injured man carry a young girl to our Aid Station, while a bloodied woman carried a smaller girl. A young boy limped behind them as well. A sixth passenger, a grandfather, was already dead, killed at the scene of the explosion. Marines and corpsmen hurried to assist the family, who were covered with blood. After placing the girls on operating tables, the medical staff sat the father down to treat his injuries, and then a corpsman called me over to interpret. "Can you help them?" the father wailed, more concerned with his daughters than with his own injuries. "Will they live?"

Only after the corpsman reassured the father that they would get the best of care could he close his eyes and let us clean his wounds. Tears flowed out of his closed eyes, his own pain mingling with his grief for his daughters. Both badly injured, one girl was awake and crying, the other unconscious and still.

I moved from patient to patient, translating as I went. The Marines and corpsmen tried so hard to help these poor injured civilians, scrambling to stop bleeding, treat wounds, and hook up intravenous devices. As I looked at the little girls, I thought of my Sophia and tears came to my eyes. The injured woman resisted being treated, but I calmed her in her own language and then she let us touch her. Eventually, we evacuated the victims to the Battalion Aid Station.

They all survived, although one of the little girls was paralyzed. The notion of that little girl never walking again tore at my heart. She was the one who'd been conscious earlier, and I thought she was so beautiful and brave. I tried not to think of Sophia being hurt like that. Questions raced through my mind. Why did children have to get hurt in a war? Why did there have to be a war at all? How could the Taliban do this to innocents? Was there an IED out there waiting for me? Some locals directed their anger over such things at the Taliban. However, others felt that there'd be no IEDs at all if not for the American presence in their land. The Taliban encouraged this thinking whenever civilians got blown up.

In late March, Capt Benson and I were patrolling between villages with some Marines from 3rd Battalion, 7th Marine Regiment (3/7), the battalion coming in to replace 3/4, when we got a call about a skirmish between the Taliban and the ANP. The Boss got on the radio and redirected a 3/4 patrol to the site. We found that the Marines had trapped the enemy in a house, and at least one Taliban combatant was still alive. Through another terp, the Marines convinced the Talib to quit firing, drop his weapon, and come out. Unfortunately, when the fighter emerged, an ANP guy shot him in the head.

This shoot-first mentality on the part of indigenous forces was something we sought to overcome with better training. In fact, BGen Nicholson had created an academy near Camp Leatherneck where Americans taught Afghan army and police trainees. Of course, that didn't help the Talib who'd just surrendered.

The Marines stopped the ANP shooter from putting more bullets into the Talib, who had survived the first head shot, and they got the wounded fighter onto a vehicle and drove him back to the Marine Compound. Only one corpsman was in the compound, so I offered to assist with emergency medical treatment. I applied some basic First Aid, carefully applying gauze over his bleeding head wound. Like most Taliban fighters, he was young, perhaps in his mid-twenties, with a short, black beard. His green eyes fluttered occasionally as he moaned. I didn't see an enemy as I treated him, but rather a fellow human, dying before my eyes. Our goal now was to save the life of a luckless Afghan man.

We carried the Talib into the Aid Station on a stretcher. The corpsman hooked him up to an IV and we worked on his grievous wound, which wouldn't stop bleeding. We hoped to interrogate him so I tried to talk to the dying fighter, giving him water, and holding his hand.

I asked him his name and his home village, but all he did was mutter. I tried to get him to repeat a verse of the Quran, but he didn't understand me.

"Allah Akbar," he whispered. "Allah Akbar."

Comforting the dying Taliban fighter

Gore was everywhere and the fighter's brain gave off a horrible smell. His blood covered my hands. I felt the bullet hole in his head and tried to stop the bleeding, but it gushed out of his mouth. I cleared his mouth so he could breathe better and gave him a sip of water. He seemed to rally.

"Help me! Please help me," he pleaded in Pashto. "I don't want to die! Why did they shoot me?"

I thought of my mother, the mid-wife, and tried to comfort the Talib. He talked a little more and then lost consciousness. I performed CPR, utilizing some of the training I'd received at Fort Benning and Twentynine Palms. The corpsman and I worked on him for at least 20 minutes before he was evacuated.

I asked the corpsman how he felt about trying to help an enemy. "Fahim, you already know the answer," he said softly. "It's our job to save lives." He thanked me for my help.

The Talib died the next day.

The death of the Taliban fighter haunted me. He'd surrendered and shouldn't have been shot. I had to stop dwelling on the gruesome memory. The dead Talib wasn't coming back. I needed to help the Marines teach the ANA and ANP to act like professionals instead of undisciplined gang members, to avoid such incidents in the future.

The arrival of the official advance party from 3/7 was a sign that 3/4's days in Afghanistan were numbered. We happily showed them around our AO. They were gung-ho about taking our place and we were thrilled they were coming. At one meeting, a 3/7 captain asked for an example of civilian outreach that he could use to inspire the incoming 3/7 Marines. I told him the story of Lance Corporal Acevido, who was with a battalion down in the Helmand River Valley.

"Lance Corporal Acevido is a hard-charging Marine from East L.A.," I explained. "He and his squad were on a patrol when a camel herder approached them for help. The herder had a pregnant camel in great distress, unable to give birth. He was afraid his camel would die. So Acevido got a rubber glove from the corpsman and just reached up into the camel and pulled out the baby. The mother made some weird noises but seemed to be fine. She started licking the newborn. The camel herder did a dance and kissed Acevido on each cheek. That's the type of outreach that can help win this war."

We shared other stories, some poignant, some humorous—like the one about the patrol that found an unmanned aerial vehicle in the desert lashed to a small tree.

"Did they think it would fly away again if they didn't tie it down?" asked a 3/7 Marine. "Were they holding it hostage? Did they want ransom? Was it ambush bait?"

"You're over-thinking," I replied. "You give the Taliban too much credit. Many are illiterate fools. They blow themselves up putting in IEDs. We end up treating them. How crazy is that?"

Later, I escorted the 3/7 captain to the company headquarters to visit Capt Benson. We passed some Marines who were wearing utility trousers and t-shirts while holding sledgehammers. They were breaking big rocks into smaller rocks, sweating heavily.

"Why are they breaking rocks?" asked the captain.

"Punishment for unauthorized alcohol possession and for mishandling of weapons," I explained, and then I feigned an Italian accent. "You breaka the Boss's rules, then you breaka the Boss's rocks! Justice is swift and harsh here in Delaram!"

March turned into April, which meant it was time for 3/4 to prepare to return to the U.S. I enjoyed my job during our final weeks, as we moved around the AO getting friendly receptions—although some fanatics still wanted to kill us. I could pick them out. I'd occasionally lock eyes with bearded, turbaned men who would glower at me and mutter "Jawsoos" as I passed them on a street or in a bazaar.

Traitor.

Most Afghans, however, were pragmatic survivors, not Taliban fighters. They did what they had to do. Some who hugged us also planted explosives to hurt us.

Still, some Taliban-types only worked with the enemy out of coercion, or economic necessity. *Ten-dollar Taliban,* we called them. They needed money and were not committed fanatics. The percentage of Afghans in our area who were hard-core Taliban was small—and getting smaller, despite Pashtunwali. Only one civilian was seriously injured as a result of 3/4 actions during our seven-month deployment

One April day, a couple of weeks before pulling out of our AO, I received an interesting call on my cell phone.

"Is this the one called Hollywood?" asked a man, speaking softly in Pashto.

"Yes, of course," I replied. "Who are you?"

"You don't need to know my name," he said. "I am with the Taliban."

"What can I do for you?" I asked, cautiously.

"We have watched you for a long time, and yes, many wanted to kill you," he replied. "But many others tell us how you and the Americans help our people. They see what you've built and know there are times when you could shoot or drop bombs, but do not. You create laughter. People like you. Many have asked that we not kill you or other Americans, like Sahib Benson or Sahib Coughlin. The Taliban around Delaram argue about you. Do we keep trying to kill you, or do we listen to all the people who say to stop trying to kill you? There was a vote among our fighters yesterday. I must now tell you that we will no longer try to kill you, Benson, or Coughlin."

"Thank you," I said. "That is wonderful news. Can we meet directly and talk more, face-to-face?"

"Someday, perhaps," he said, before hanging up.

I was alone in our tent, sitting on my cot. I rose and walked outside. It was mid-day, bright, sunny, and warm. I looked to the north, to the great Afghan mountains, beautifully silhouetted against a bright blue, cloudless Afghan sky. A sense of wonder came over me. For some reason, the caller needed to share what had happened at the meeting where the fighters had that vote. The Taliban hadn't given up, but according to some warrior code the caller needed to acknowledge the impact the Marines and I had had on people around Delaram. A feeling of triumph came over me, and I didn't resist it. The phone call was a wonderful reward for our efforts, to be shared and savored. On this day, in this place, the enemy had sent an unsolicited message that we'd prevailed, in a fashion. I couldn't wait to tell Capt. Benson about the call when I saw him later in the day.

"Hey Boss!" I said. "Great news! The Taliban called and said they're not going to try to kill you and me anymore. I guess we've won!" I laughed.

Capt Benson smiled his biggest smile. And he can correct me if I'm wrong, but I think his eyes may have watered a little.

Chapter 12: Full Circle—Back to America

"Love your country. Your country is the land where your parents sleep,
where is spoken that language in which the chosen of
your heart, blushing, whispered the first word of love. It is
the home that God has given you, that by striving to perfect
yourselves therein, you may prepare to ascend to him."
-Giuseppe Mazzini, Italian Journalist and Nationalist

In mid-April, 3/4 finished its turnover with 3/7 and that battalion took over our AO. As we packed up our gear and prepared to leave, people of all ages and backgrounds approached us and asked us to stay. From Now Zad to Delaram, from Golestan to Bakwa, Afghans bid us farewell—sometimes tearfully.

During my last walk through the Delaram Bazaar, I said goodbye to a merchant I'd gotten to know well. "Will we ever see you again?" Abdul Khalid asked. "We want you to stay!"

"I'd like to bring my wife Amy back here," I replied. "She's a shopper, and you have such great bargains."

Abdul Khalid laughed, and his eyes danced. A seller of goods, he was by necessity a talker. Prices in Afghanistan were always negotiable. We'd always enjoyed bantering.

"I'm sure you understand that I miss my family, my friends, and my old job. And I even miss the ocean."

It occurred to me that Afghans see plenty of sand, but never a seashore. They didn't know what they were missing, but I couldn't wait to feel cool sea breezes again and look at the vast Pacific from the heights of Dana Point.

"I understand," said Abdul Khalid. "We trust you. I'm not so sure about the other Americans."

"You can trust the Marines who are replacing us," I reassured him. "They're good men who will help you, just like we did."

Leaving the bazaar, I ran into Qudos Khan, the Chief of Police, also of the Barikzoy Tribe—another local that I'd gotten to know well. "The crime rate has gone down since you've been here," said Khan. "No one throws rocks at the Marines anymore. We'll miss you."

"The Marines coming in will keep doing what we've been doing," I replied. "You just have to get to know them."

I went to say goodbye to District Governor Asadullah, who embraced me. He'd recovered from his earlier pique, as evidenced by an award he presented Darkside 6 at a dinner in the battalion compound. He also asked about the new Marines coming in.

I explained that the 3/7 Marines were of the same tribe as 3/4 and that they'd continue where 3/4 left off. Though we'd miss and worry about our Afghan friends, we all wanted to go home.

We soon took the first step back to America—flying in CH-53 helicopters and V-22 Ospreys from Delaram to Golestan, where we helped orient our incoming 3/7 relief. Finally, we loaded onto helicopters to leave Golestan for good. As we lifted off from that remote mountain base, I looked out a window and saw a 3/7 Marine with a rifle waving to us. It reminded me of that scene near the end of *Platoon* where Sgt O'Neill (John C. McGinley) waves to the helicopter that was finally taking the young soldier Chris Taylor (Charlie Sheen) out of a combat zone to start his journey home. We then flew through south through the mountain passes to close things out at Buji Bhast. Three days later, we flew over the Afghan desert to Camp Bastion. From there, trucks took us next door to Camp Leatherneck, which had grown and expanded since we'd passed through it the previous October. Crowded with around 15,000 people, it had become one of the largest communities in Helmand. Excited to be headed back to the U.S., young Marines counted down the final days of 3/4's deployment. Our battalion spent over a week organizing for the return and then, in increments, companies got on vehicles to return to the Camp Bastion airfield to board air transports and continue the 10,000 mile-long journey back to America.

I was pleased that my work with 3/4 had not gone unnoticed with the headquarters staff at Camp Leatherneck. MajGen Mills presented me with one of his special flag officer coins in a special ceremony where LtCol Matthew Seipt, a logistics officer with 3/7, also presented me with a flag which had flown over Camp Leatherneck. My eyes filled with tears as I listened to the wonderful remarks these Marines made about me and my contributions to the cause.

My MEP contract called for me to stay in Afghanistan another six weeks. So I said goodbye, temporarily, to India Company and the 3/4 Marines. I'd catch up to them at Twentynine Palms later in the summer. A lonely, empty feeling washed over me as I watched the final transport vehicle pull away from a Camp Leatherneck staging area with the last of the 3/4 Marines aboard.

After 3/4 left, I moved into a tent with some other interpreters and tackled a variety of routine tasks at Camp Leatherneck, but didn't return to the field as a full-time terp with a ground unit. I thought about visiting Kabul—but making internal travel arrangements was complicated, and I wasn't that anxious to return there anyway. So I stayed at Camp Leatherneck and counted down the days until it was my turn to journey back to California.

Something extraordinary occurred while I marked time in Camp Leatherneck's 100 degree heat. Amy's sister Heather had a son Matthew whose father James had remained out-of-touch with them for 20 years. Finally, Amy located him through Facebook and arranged a reunion between Heather, Matthew, and James. They sent me a photo of the three of them, along with a message that James' brother was a Marine officer somewhere in Afghanistan.

Soon afterwards, I was in line at a Camp Leatherneck D-FAC (Dining Facility—what Marines used to call a Chow Hall) and saw a Marine captain who looked like James. I have a good memory for faces and thought I'd go talk to him.

"Hey Skipper," I said. "I'm Fahim Fazli. I was an interpreter with 3/4."

"Howdy," he replied, and he introduced himself and explained that he was a Civil Affairs Officer working with 3/7.

"You don't happen to have a brother in California, do you?" I asked.

He did, and we figured out we were both uncles to the same young man. Who knew? I made friends easily with the Marines, but this new friend was also a long-lost relative of sorts. More than ever, I now felt like a member of the Marine Tribe. Perhaps this unlikely Camp Leatherneck friendship could also somehow strengthen Heather's new relationship with James. This providential meeting was another confirmation that I'd made the right decision to go with the Marines.

On another night in early June, I lay on my cot in the terp tent contemplating all the times I'd almost been killed. By the Russians when they'd fired up on that steep Afghan hillside where I hid as a teenager with my slingshot. By the Communist pamphleteers who stabbed me and tried to arrest me in my own Kabul neighborhood. By the Soviet mines during my 1983 escape through the mountains. By the Taliban IEDs, which blew up adjacent vehicles but not mine when we convoyed near Delaram in 2009. By that rogue shooter across from the India Company Compound in Delaram in 2010. And by other enemies who knew there was a price on my head as I moved around the 3/4 AO throughout our deployment.

I was still around, against some pretty strong odds, so I thought God must have a plan for me. I still wanted to do a book and I kept notes and photos from throughout the deployment. Not being a trained writer, I described my experiences on a voice recorder. I had Marines sign waivers to allow me to use their photos and words if the book project ever moved forward. Despite my fluency in several languages, my English writing skills weren't sufficient to author a book by myself. I did have the business card of a Marine Corps historian, Lieutenant Colonel Michael Moffett. I'd met him at an event with Darkside 6 and the sub-governor at 3/4's headquarters at the Delaram base in March. A reserve infantry officer and a college professor, LtCol Moffett was traveling around Afghanistan visiting USMC Forward Operating Bases and Combat Outposts conducting interviews and recording Marines' stories for Marine Corps University's History Division. He was interested in my story, too.

Although I felt very much a part of the Marine culture and believed in the mission of *Operation Enduring Freedom*, I also wondered about the long-term prospects for our cause. Some said it was a lost cause, or an unworthy cause—that supporting President Karzai's regime wasn't worth all the blood and treasure. Many Hollywood people spoke out against our Afghanistan mission. Woody Harrelson's comments were typical. He said that "The war against terrorism is terrorism. The whole thing is just bullshit."

My terp tent-mates and I sometimes talked about whether Afghans themselves could ever maintain a viable central government without extraordinary coalition support. One evening, after enjoying a fabulous meal at the D-FAC, I sat with several other terps on benches outside our tent, watching a beautiful sunset turn from orange to crimson to purple to black as day slowly turned to night and the temperature became bearable.

"Steak and lobster again," said Lufti, who was preparing to go to the field with a battalion which had just arrived. "I'm going to miss the food here."

"I'll miss the people," I said. "But I'm ready to leave."

"When all the Americans leave, things will fall apart," said a terp named Tarik, who like me, had recently returned from the field.

"Maybe," said Lufti, "But the Taliban will never regain power in Kabul. The coalition has invested too much to let that happen. Every province will just keep having its own little civil wars, like always."

"I'm afraid this country is still cursed," I said.

"Don't you think the Taliban will just take over again when the Marines go home?" asked Tarik.

"I don't know about that," I replied. "We really made progress where 3/4 was."

"The locals need to figure out how to take care of themselves," said Lufti. "They can't depend on the ANA."

We concluded that the means that people in the provinces might use to counter the Taliban might not find favor with NATO officials or President Karzai—who doesn't want to see regional warlords return. However, local militias with ties to the ANA could do the trick. Their rules of engagement would likely differ from those governing the Marines. The Taliban doesn't fight fairly and the people who must live with them need to do what they have to do to counter them.

"I wonder if anyone ever sees which Taliban fighters leave the night letters," said Lufti, referring to anonymous messages put on house doors in the dark, warning residents that they'd be killed if they cooperated with the Americans.

"We need to deliver night letters to the Taliban themselves," said Tarik. "Fight fire with fire. See how they like their own medicine."

Our coalition rules of engagement would never allow for such things, although there were rumors that Special Forces sometimes used unorthodox techniques. I smiled at the notion of a Taliban fighter getting a night letter.

As my departure date drew near, I thought a lot about my parents. Had it not been for the Communist take-over, we'd likely have all lived out our lives in Kabul. Tragic and traumatic events brought us to America and our desperate journeys tested our relationships. I longed to be closer to my folks. I wanted the strong emotional connections that I saw others have with their parents, but those bonds never really developed for me. The drama surrounding my marriages led to appreciation and understanding with my mother, but my relationship with my father remained prickly and unsatisfying. I yearned for something better but there was so much stubborn pride to overcome. I resented earlier abuses and he resented losing the authority he'd exercised when we lived in Kabul.

My return to Afghanistan did help me to understand my father. I saw how much my old country had changed in 30 years and realized what a shaky social foundation held it up. My father was a product of the culture that spawned the Taliban. He didn't have the luxury of growing up in America and being exposed to all the diverse influences that might have shaped him into something softer and more compassionate. During my time in Helmand Province, I often saw men acting cruelly and realized they knew no other way. I could now sympathize with my father, and I wanted him to know that. I decided to call home.

Due to the time difference between Afghanistan and California, I got up in the middle of the night and walked to a communications tent that was filled with computers and telephones. Usually, there was quite a line for a turn at the telephones, but when I got there, no one was waiting. There was only a sign that said "River City." This expression was code meaning that a Marine had been killed and that no one could call home until the next of kin was notified. It was frustrating, but I understood the policy.

The River City condition was lifted a couple of nights later, and I returned and stood in the normal long line outside the communications tent. With any luck, I'd get through to California. An Indian technician sat by the doorway, handing out small pieces of wood with numbers that matched up with telephones inside. Once we got into the tent, we had 20 minutes to talk on a phone. I finally got my number—eight—and hurried to a spot on a bench in front of that telephone. I dialed up my parents' number and waited. The Marine seated right next to me—seven—spoke loudly into his phone. He was obviously frustrated.

"Damn it, honey, I only have one more minute," he said loudly. "I know it's not convenient for you back there, but this is when I can call. It's not easy to get on a phone. I don't want to fight with you."

"Numba Seven, Numba Seven!" yelled the Indian. "Time's up! Time's up!"

"I know, I know," he said on the phone. "We'll fix things. Please don't be angry! I gotta go."

"Numba Seven, Numba Seven!" yelled the Indian. "Time's up! Time's up!"

The Marine on the phone—Numba Seven—was anguished. His time was up and instead of a nice conversation back home, he'd gotten into a fight with his woman and now had to leave the tent, angry and worse off emotionally than when he arrived. I vowed that wouldn't happen to me; I'd leave the tent happy.

I finally heard the phone ring at my parents' California home. "Hello." I recognized my father's voice.

"Dad, it's me, Fahim! Can you hear me!"

"Fahim!" he replied. "Yes, I can hear you. Where are you now?"

"I'm at Camp Leatherneck, getting ready to come home. I can't wait to see everyone."

"We want to see you too," he said.

My mom got on an extension. "Fahim! Is this really you?"

"Yes, Mother," I responded. "I can't wait to see you all. Is everyone OK?"

My mother launched into a detailed report on what everyone was up to, and I soon anxiously looked at my watch. I heard the Indian guy yelling at other people that their time was up, to get off their phones, and leave the tent. I finally interrupted my mother. I didn't have much time.

"Hey, I have to get off the phone soon, but I really need to tell you something."

"Oh no, what's wrong?" asked my mother. "Are you hurt?"

"No, no," I said. "I'm fine. I'm great. I just need to tell you some things. I've learned so much from coming back here. I understand you better. I see some things that I didn't see before, about our family. I can now tell my right from my left."

I thanked them for bringing me to America. Though speaking to both parents, my words were meant for my father. I needed them to understand the appreciation and gratitude which now filled my heart.

"Coming back here and seeing this country reminded me how hard life is in Afghanistan," I said. "When I look at the mountains, I think of how Father somehow got Hares and me through so we could find Mother again."

"Numba Eight! Numba Eight!" yelled the Indian. "Time's up! Time's up!"

"I have to go now," I said. "I just need to say 'Thank you' and 'I love you.'"

"I love you, too," said my mother. I held the receiver to my ear, waiting for words from my father. None came.

"Numba Eight! Numba Eight!" yelled the Indian. "Time's up! Time's up!"

"Good bye," I said. "Talk again soon!"

I hung the phone up and headed back to the tent entrance, giving the numbered piece of wood back to the Indian.

Mission accomplished. My parents—especially my father—heard the words I'd wanted to say for a long time. I didn't expect my father to tell me he loved me. He never did. But now he knew I loved *him*. I had to say things for him, things that he couldn't say. He'd earlier acted out of a combination of fear and love to do the best he could for his family under extreme circumstances, when we escaped from Communist Afghanistan in 1983. While that journey was a search for my mother, it was also a search for my father—even though he'd made the escape with me. Ironically, it took a 10,000 mile trip back to Afghanistan 26 years later for me to truly understand his journey. I'd finally found my father.

The day I was finally to begin my journey home, I said goodbye to my friends in the terp tent and stuffed my gear into my sea bags. Then I happily boarded a truck at the Camp Leatherneck staging area for the short ride to the airfield at Camp Bastion.

C-130 transport planes brought me from the Camp Bastion airfield to Kandahar, and then back up to Bagram Air Base—where I'd first returned to Afghanistan the previous October. After a brief delay there, I flew on to Qatar where I boarded a chartered civilian plane for the trip back to the United States. It was a long flight, but I was ecstatic about returning home and reuniting with Amy and Sophia.

Looking out at the cloud formations through the aircraft window, I thought of the flight I'd made through similar skies in 1985, which took me to America for the first time. Now the flight to the United States represented a return home—not a journey to a new world. I was flying from the land of my birth to the land of my rebirth.

I slept fitfully on the plane and reflected on the previous 15 months. My time with the Marines had made me stronger and more confident. I felt complete and whole—like a perfect ring or a full circle. I felt sorry for the terps who'd quit the previous summer, before 3/4 deployed. I wished that they could know how rewarding it was to put everything on the line with a warrior tribe for a good cause.

Before deploying, I hadn't realized that so many from my old tribe lived in greater Helmand Province. When I went there with my new tribe—the Marines—most of the Barikzoy tribe still welcomed me when I introduced myself as one of them. Of course, there were also Taliban fighters from my old tribe as well. They called me *jawsoos*. Who's right and who's wrong? My Marine experiences with 3/4 around Delaram convinced me that I was on the right side.

Our plane stopped in Bangor, Maine, where the locals welcomed us back during a short airport layover. Those wonderful Mainers, mostly older people, just wanted us to know they appreciated our service. Then it was on to Atlanta, where I had to check out from the Mission Essential Personnel offices.

A van took me from the airport to the company building and I reconnected with SFC Roberto Chavez, who embraced me and told me he'd seen stories of me in the news. The people at MEP treated me like a hero. Instructors and administrative personnel made it a point to introduce themselves and shake my hand. One secretary hugged me and cried.

I wondered how many people—besides Amy and Sophia—would greet me when I finally reached California. My parents, brothers, and sisters knew of my pending return. So did others I knew in Hollywood, as well as some friends from the Afghan community. The warm receptions in Bangor and Atlanta buoyed my hopes for a special California homecoming. I didn't necessarily expect a parade with marching bands, cheerleaders, floats and speeches, but like most people who've deployed, I imagined a wonderful "Welcome Home," with lots of people, hugs, kisses, and emotion.

After we completed some paperwork in Atlanta, Chavez drove me to Fort Benning, where I returned some gear. Then it was on to Atlanta's Hartsfield-Jackson International Airport and a flight to Orange County.

It was July 2, 2010. Just before we landed at John Wayne Airport, ahead of schedule, I had a bit of reunion anxiety. We'd been briefed about that feeling at a special class at Camp Leatherneck. Counselors explained that our loved ones had necessarily grown more independent in our absences, and they'd inevitably developed new routines. I understood that, but wondered how reuniting with my girls could be anything but wonderful. I walked into the terminal, and soon saw little Sophia with a sign that said "Fazli." It reminded me of coming to America for the first time in 1985 and seeing the man from Christian Aid Mission holding the Fazli sign as we entered the terminal at JFK. She looked like a chauffeur! So cute. I took a picture of her and Amy with the sign. We hugged and cried and just enjoyed the moment.

At first, I was surprised and disappointed that no other family members or friends showed up and I tried not to dwell on that. I just appreciated my girls. They were what really mattered. Still, I wished that more people from the Afghan community could have embraced our efforts—my efforts—in the old country. I'd received mixed messages from them about serving with the USMC, even from my old friends in Orange County. It hurt that some people considered me a traitor or a spy because I helped the Marines.

After my sea bags finally arrived at baggage claim, we packed everything into the car and drove back home to Dana Point. Our seaside community looked so inviting, as did the big Welcome Home banner the girls hung in front of our house. I spent two days adapting to the new time zone and walking around with Amy and Sophia, telling them certain stories of my adventure—that there'd been a price on my head was something that could wait for later. I happily listened to stories of their adventures. A mouse loose in the house wasn't as scary to me as incoming mortar rounds, but in their world, it was traumatic.

Then I called Capt Benson at Twentynine Palms and told him I was back in the U.S. and was ready to return the last of my USMC gear. He told me to bring my wife and daughter with me when I came over to the base. So Amy and Sophia made one final trip with me to The Stumps.

We continued to swap stories as we drove past the now-familiar landmarks on the way to the Marine Base. I described some of the characters that I hoped they'd meet: The Boss, the First Sergeant, the Gunny, my three tent-mates, and others. Once I turned my gear in, I might never see any of these men again. Returning my equipment would mark a rite of passage—my last day with the Marines. I wanted to savor the moments, knowing that the next day I'd channel my energy into my return to Hollywood.

When we got to the India Company area, I was delighted to see the India Marines waiting there for me. A formation was called, and Capt Benson spoke to the unit, recognizing my contributions to 3/4 and the India team. He presented me with a plaque and a special I/3/4 coin. These were treasures I'd always savor. The Boss called me a real warrior and a true American.

Could there be higher praise than that? Everyone cheered and I posed for photos with my Marine buddies. I'd finally received that long-anticipated and joyous "Welcome Home" from a big, happy crowd. It just happened at Twentynine Palms instead of the airport. I thought back to what SFC Chavez had told me at Fort Benning in 2009, when he'd heard I'd be working with the Marines: *If you become part of their family, they'll always be there for you. You can count on that.*

With the Boss, Captain Benson, at Twentynine Palms

The old Army NCO was right again.

Then it was time to leave Twentynine Palms for the last time. It was time to return to Dana Point for good. I drove Amy and Sophia out the main gate, off the base, and made the right turn onto Route 62, towards Joshua Tree.

"That was very special," said Amy. "They like you!"

"Yes," I replied. "They're my brothers."

"You'll miss them, won't you Daddy?" said Sophia.

"Yes, Sweetie, I sure will." I said. "But no one wears a uniform forever."

I wanted to maintain the rhythms and patterns I'd established with the Marines and apply them to the life I was returning to in California. I'd be early for every appointment. I'd be proactive and take the initiative. I'd approach every challenge with a sense of urgency. And I'd do it with a smile, with an appreciation for the opportunities that awaited me as a civilian. The Marines accepted missions with relish and figured out ways to accomplish them. My new mission was to succeed in Hollywood. I'd figure out a way.

We turned off Route 62 and onto Interstate 10 West. I thought of my first visit to The Stumps and of my uncertainty a year earlier as I prepared to return to Afghanistan. I thought of the interpreter revolt. I'd said then that when I came back from deploying, I'd be able to sleep well and live with myself. What I'd visualized had come true.

"I feel so good" I said to Amy. "I've finally paid my dues to my country."

"*Both* your countries," Amy responded. "I'm so proud of you!"

I smiled. At that moment, I felt totally free of any uncertainties, doubts, questions, or regrets. I was whole. I'd completed my Full Circle.

Mokamala dayra.

موکمله دایره

From Formal Evaluation of Fahim Fazli
by Captain Ryan Benson, USMC

Subj: Letter of Recommendation in the case of Fahim Fazli:

Fahim Fazli is currently employed as my cultural advisor and linguistic professional. My role as a company commander in Afghanistan has been to build close relationships with Afghan government officials, to mentor and train elements of the Afghan National Security Forces, to re-establish Afghan infrastructure at the local level, and to establish a mutual level of respect and understanding with the local population. Fahim's cultural and linguistic expertise has been critical in my ability to immediately establish a rapport with every Afghan I meet. Fahim's cultural background and ability to utilize Pashto, Dari, Farsi, and Urdu have made me successful as a battle-space owner.

As my personal linguist Fahim has gone everywhere in India Company's battle-space that I have gone. He has accompanied me on every patrol and every movement. His level of motivation and personal drive have been constant throughout the deployment, whether patrolling in temperatures of more than 100 degrees or going firm for the evening in 40 degree rain. During *Operation Swift Change*, a heli-borne operation to clear the Buji Bhast Pass, Fahim operated along side the Marines of India Company facing the same dangers and hardships they faced. His linguistic and cultural skills were crucial in the clearing of over 12 villages, covering more than 17 kilometers, over a three-day period.

As a United States citizen Fahim Fazli is a patriot. He put aside a successful career as an actor in Hollywood and left his wife and daughter at home in order to give back to the country that has given him so many opportunities. Moreover, he asked to be placed with Infantry Marines in order to help Afghanistan; the country where his life began. Fahim saw this as an opportunity to serve his country while trying to help his former home.

Spending the last 10 months with Fahim has been an absolute pleasure. He has proved to be a compassionate man who is honorable, faithful, and completely trustworthy. He has become a brother not just to me, but to each of the Marines under my charge. He has been a tremendous asset to both myself and to India Company as a whole. Fahim Fazli is enthusiastically recommended for duties of increased authority and responsibility.

R. P. BENSON

Acknowledgements

It would be impossible for me to list and thank all the kind people whose paths I've crossed during my tumultuous life's journey. I do want to recognize all our United States Marines, particularly those of the Third Battalion of the Fourth Marine Regiment (3/4) and especially India Company. I love them all and I am so proud to be of their tribe.

I need to acknowledge Lieutenant Colonel Michael I. Moffett of the United States Marine Corps Reserve, now retired. I believe it was more than fate that caused our paths to cross in Delaram in 2010. Not only do we share the same birthday, but we share the same values, including faith, hope, and trust. He believed that my story was one that should be told, and he worked at staying in touch with me after we both returned to America, and he made several trips from New Hampshire to California to move our project forward. We never talked about money or contracts. We just shook hands and worked together on my story.

LtCol Moffett introduced me to two wonderful people in Los Angeles— Captain Dale Dye, USMC (retired) and his wife, Dr. Julia Dye. They saw potential in my story and their Warriors Publishing Group would eventually make *Fahim Speaks* a reality. Their vision and understanding of the Marine and Hollywood Tribes made Warriors Publishing Group a perfect match for my story.

Thank you, Dr. Kathy Smith of the New Hampshire Humanities Council, and Julianna Danson of Dana Point, for spending so much time reviewing drafts of my narrative.

I am grateful to Sam Sako of Middle East in Hollywood for his encouragement regarding not only this book project, but also my acting career. The same goes for my manager, Tulci Ram.

Special appreciation also goes out to the Shah Durrani family, now living in Holland: Wali, Farzana, Edris, Minne, and Morsel, and Georgetown University Professor Dr. Jonathan Wiggins.

There are so many other family members and Hollywood friends who have been helpful and encouraging over the years. I can't begin to list them all, but I want to collectively thank all of them for their special support and encouragement.

And of course, I thank God for Amy and Sophia. I can't imagine a life without their priceless love.

Mom, I wish you were alive to see my book.

Michael Moffett

MICHAEL MOFFETT is a professor, writer, and reserve Marine Corps infantry officer who served in *Operation Desert Storm* before returning to active duty with United States Central Command after the 9/11 attacks for the beginning of *Operation Enduring Freedom* in 2001. LtCol Moffett again returned to active duty with the Marines in 2010 as a field historian for Marine Corps University to document USMC efforts in Afghanistan, again, as part of *Operation Enduring Freedom*. A native Granite Stater, Professor Moffett teaches at New Hampshire Technical Institute and writes a column for the *Weirs Times*.

Fahim Fazli

FAHIM FAZLI was born and raised in Kabul, Afghanistan. He fled the chaos of his homeland in 1983 and eventually came to the United States as a refugee. After moving to California, he worked in a variety of occupations before becoming a member of the Screen Actors Guild in 2003. He left his acting work from 2009-10 to return to Afghanistan as a linguist with the

United States Marines. Now residing in California, he and his wife Amy have one daughter, Sophia.

Learn more at www.fahimspeaks.com

Gunner Shake Davis, U.S. Marine Corps, might be out of the active ranks but he's anything but retired. His adventures continue in bestselling author Dale Dye's exciting File Series of scintillating novels.

Laos File

Searching for long overdue answers to what might have happened to American POWs listed as Missing In Action in Southeast Asia, Shake Davis uncovers a conspiracy and some very painful memories from his days as a combat infantryman in Vietnam.

Peleliu File

When a cabal of dedicated anti-western power-players develops a conspiracy to unleash biological warfare on America, Shake Davis is called on to use his career contacts, historical acumen and military skills to help U.S. special operators in a breath-taking chase through infamous World War II battle sites.

And, coming later in 2012:

Chosin File

In the midst of a clandestine mission to rescue his best buddy lost on a covert reconnaissance mission in North Korea, Shake Davis re-visits the infamous Chosin Reservoir and helps discover a plan to hit the worldwide power grid with a devastating EMP generator. Things get double-dicey when the former North Korean dictator dies and Marines must take down a merchant ship in the storm-tossed China Sea.

For these and other quality military fiction and nonfiction, visit
www.warriorspublishing.com

14299670R00125

Made in the USA
Lexington, KY
20 March 2012